LITERACY FOR LIFE
THE DEMAND FOR READING AND WRITING

edited by
Richard W. Bailey and Robin Melanie Fosheim

NEW YORK
THE MODERN LANGUAGE ASSOCIATION
OF AMERICA
1983

Library of Congress Cataloging in Publication Data
Main entry under title:

Literacy for life.

Includes bibliographies.
1. Literacy—Addresses, essays, lectures. I. Bailey,
Richard W. II. Fosheim, Robin Melanie, 1956-
LC149.L4985   1983   302.2   83-8265
ISBN 0-87352-130-7
ISBN 0-87352-131-5 (pbk.)

Portions of Arthur M. Cohen and Florence B. Brawer,
"Functional Literacy
for Community College Students,"
are adapted from a chapter of their forthcoming book,
The American Community College: An Interpretive Analysis,
to be published by Jossey-Bass, Inc.

Published by The Modern Language Association of America
62 Fifth Avenue, New York, New York 10011

Contents

iii

Literacy in the Marketplace

Literacy and Education

Appendix

Literacy is for the most part an enabling rather than a causal factor, making possible the development of complex political structures, syllogistic reasoning, scientific enquiry, linear conceptions of reality, scholarly specialization, artistic elaboration, and perhaps certain kinds of individualism and alienation.

—Kathleen Gough

Preface

Learning and using the skills of literacy have engaged a major share of human attention in Western societies since ancient times: reading has been valued because it gives access to other minds; writing, because it helps us to know ourselves and to articulate our inchoate thoughts and emotions for our own benefit and for the scrutiny of others. So certain have we been that literacy is an unqualified good that our schools have made it the foundation of all other learning, and literacy programs around the world have consumed a major share of investment in modernization and development. Literacy—as Kathleen Gough writes in the passage we have chosen as the epigraph for this volume—is "an enabling . . . factor" upon which societies base both their social organization and the scope they afford to individual creativity and ambition.

Plans for this volume emerged from an interest among faculty at the University of Michigan in developing new strategies to improve the teaching and learning of literacy. A variety of programs at Michigan foster research and training in the effective transmission of literacy from teachers to students, among students through peer teaching, and through community programs designed to reach parents, workers, and citizens. Throughout these efforts, we and our colleagues have continually questioned the assumptions that inform our endeavors, not because we doubt the importance of literacy, but because we are convinced that a continual reexamination of basic principles will help us escape the limits of traditional practices, meet the challenges of new circumstances, and accommodate the changes consequent on the technology of information that is now extending and even transforming the historic place of reading and writing.

The essays that constitute this book offer a diversity of perspectives on literacy—viewpoints informed by reexamination of the past, by successful innovation in teaching, and by speculations of persons who see the demands for literacy in law, government, science, and the mass media. Each author was invited to consider the future agenda for literacy with only one constraint: predictions were to be short-term, extending only to the end of the decade in which we now live. Imagining a more remote future, we believe, leads to apocalyptic visions, ones that stimulate the imagination by their very novelty but give little guidance for immediate action. Printed paper may eventually be replaced by digital storage, but not in our decade. Instantaneous communication may supplant the delays of the postal and publication systems, but not for most of the world's population in our times. New modes of perceiving and transmitting ideas may at some point transform the way we come to know things, but reading and writing will remain essential to the articulation of knowledge for many years to come. In accepting our invitation to write for this volume, those who have contributed their views have accepted the constraint we placed upon them. Their essays clarify the present roles of literacy and the forces that shape the immediate future; their suggestions offer a sound basis for planning and for action.

In this brief preface, we will not survey the variety of conflicting and complementary views expressed by our authors. (In his introductory essay, Jay L. Robinson provides an encompassing overview of the volume and draws from it conclusions that will be of particular interest to persons in higher education and in policy-shaping roles in government and the foundations.) What we can emphasize here, however, is that all the contributors recognize that the notion of literacy is complex and that no sharp boundary can be drawn between those who are literate and those who are illiterate.

Definitions of literacy differ, but the best ones, we believe, avoid absolutes and take into account varying circumstances. One such definition was formulated in 1962 by UNESCO, the international agency that has assisted many nations in assessing the literacy of their populations and in providing guidance for effective literacy programs:

> A person is literate when he has acquired the essential knowledge and skills which enable him to engage in all those activities in which literacy is required for effective functioning in his group and community, and whose attainments in reading, writing, and arithmetic make it possible for him to continue to use these skills toward his own and the community's development. (Hunter and Harman 14)

Such a definition recognizes that the same absolute command of reading and writing may make a person effective in one community and inept in another. In the same society, an individual may be literate in one domain and yet effectively illiterate in another. As changing technology makes some skills obsolete, so changes in the demands for literacy can render useless some forms of reading and writing while placing high values on others.

Once literacy is defined in terms of a context and a community, it needs to be viewed as part of a complex set of social factors. Though literacy is enabling, individuals who command its skills may lack opportunities or the desire to exercise them. Others, whose skills are insufficient to meet the demands of the community, may find ingenious and adroit ways to function effectively, perhaps by engaging the assistance of more skilled helpers or by evading the kind of literacy that daunts them. Such complicating circumstances make it enormously difficult to estimate the level of literacy present in a society and even harder to guess what the future will demand. The contributors to this volume offer several estimates of the number of "functional illiterates" in the United States. Some mention the 23 million believed to "lack the competencies necessary to function in society"; others, the estimate that 57 million adults "do not have skills adequate to perform basic tasks" (Hunter and Harman 27). Whatever the number cited, it is inevitably large, and most observers believe that as many as a third of our citizens do not meet present-day demands for literacy. From a global perspective, as Sarah Goddard Power shows in "The Politics of Literacy," the number of functional illiterates constitutes an even greater share of the world population.

Two responses to the current state of affairs are possible: one is to make the teaching of literacy more effective and more available; the other, to organize reading and writing to accommodate rather than to exclude persons whose literacy is below the level demanded by society. Both efforts are, of course, going forward simultaneously: the first in a myriad of conventional and unconventional educational settings; the second in increasing attention to readability, clarity, and document design. (In this volume, the first effort is given particular attention by Daniel Fader, Janet K. Carsetti, Arthur M. Cohen, and Florence B. Brawer; the second is discussed by Paul B. Weisz, Janice C. Redish, and Lee Odell.) Both need to be considered in planning for the immediate future.

While our contributors presume the skills of literacy to be essential for rewarding employment, they also recognize that the habit of reading and writing enriches one's entire life. (That aspect of literacy is given special attention by William E. Coles, Jr., Edwin J. Delattre, and Frank J. D'Angelo.) Quantitatively, at least, reading and writing for recreation are now more common than at any time in the past. More abundant leisure time has brought with it increasing uses of literacy for personal pleasures, some immediate and intrinsic, and some a consequence of hobbies and avocations. As Paul A. Strassmann estimates, half of the American work force is engaged in the information industry; an even greater share of the population enjoys reading and writing for their own sakes.

No single volume can encompass the entire range of social issues, educational reforms, and cultural trends that bear upon the present and future of literacy. All that we can claim for this book is a breadth of views that emerges from the careful reflection of its authors. Now that it is completed, we are delighted to see that there is unity in its variety, and if not all the possible questions that might have been raised are answered, there is at least a common recognition of the issues that need to be addressed in planning and in action. The essays here assembled were first prepared for a conference held in June 1981 in Ann Arbor, and they have been revised (sometimes drastically) in light of conversations among the authors made possible on that occasion. The conference was sponsored by the English Composition Board at the University of Michigan; a grant from the Andrew W. Mellon Foundation supported the conference; preparation of this volume was supported in part by a grant from the Ford Foundation.

Presentations by the contributors to this volume were discussed and amplified by persons who served as panelists and moderators at the conference. These included the Hon. Charles W. Joiner, federal district court judge, Eastern District of Michigan; Layman E. Allen, professor of law and research scientist, University of Michigan; Tom Downs, attorney, Lansing, Michigan, and member,

National Conference of Commissioners on Uniform State Laws; Irwin Alterman, attorney, Southfield, Michigan, and chair, Committee on Plain English, State Bar of Michigan; John C. Shafer, assistant professor of English, Humboldt State University; Gunder A. Myran, president, Washtenaw Community College; Peter Clarke, dean, Annenberg School of Communications, University of Southern California; Robert G. Diforio, president and publisher, New American Library; Jack Caldwell, president, Channel 56, Detroit; Neal Shine, managing editor, *Detroit Free Press;* Alfred H. Slote, executive producer, Michigan Media, University of Michigan; Thomas M. Dunn, chair, Department of Chemistry, University of Michigan; Elizabeth Douvan, Catherine Neafie Kellogg Professor of Psychology, University of Michigan; Wilbert J. McKeachie, professor of psychology and director, Center for Research on Learning and Teaching, University of Michigan. We are especially grateful to these persons for their contribution to enlarging the scope of our understanding of contemporary literacy.

As we prepared this collection for publication, we were given useful advice by Richard M. Ohmann, Wesleyan University, and Walker Gibson, University of Massachusetts, Amherst. The Committee on Teaching and Related Professional Activities of the Modern Language Association recommended publication of the volume; we are glad to acknowledge their counsel and that of Walter S. Achtert, director of book publications and research programs for the association.

Richard W. Bailey
Robin Melanie Fosheim

Works Cited

Gough, Kathleen. "Literacy in Kerala." In *Literacy in Traditional Societies.* Ed. Jack Goody. Cambridge: Cambridge Univ. Press, 1968, 133-60.
Hunter, Carman St. John, and David Harman. *Adult Illiteracy in the United States: A Report to the Ford Foundation.* New York: McGraw-Hill, 1979.

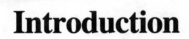

Introduction

The Users and Uses of Literacy

Jay L. Robinson

The scope of this volume is broad, but so too is its subject. Literacy is variously defined, variably embodied in its possessors. Seventy percent of the world's citizens are literate, but with skills ranging from the ability to read simple signs or instructions to the ability to read and comprehend—even to conceive and write—works of explanatory power and aesthetic beauty. Literacy has been studied by historians, by psychologists and physiologists, by sociologists and linguists, by rhetoricians and literary critics. Given its complexity of manifestation in human activity, it is a thing usually approached only from some particular perspective. Yet to understand literacy and its uses requires that one see more than a narrow view allows; hence we offer a sampling of views, both from practitioners and from those who study practice, as an attempt to enlarge understanding about literacy. In most of the essays in this volume, writing is emphasized, although reading is not ignored.

The collection addresses three audiences: those who teach writing and reading; those who make policy influencing what is to be taught, how, and to whom; and those citizens who would influence the influential. Problems with the literacy of American students, and of American workers and professionals as well, have been widely reported and look to be real. To solve existing problems and, at the same time, to anticipate new needs growing out of rapid social change will require of teachers and policymakers a firm grasp of both the conditions that impose new demands and those that impede the acquisition of literacy; hence this volume treats the uses of writing and reading in the world of work as well as in the classroom.

The articles are grouped into four sections. The first, "Literacy, Politics, and Policies," explores the social contexts for literacy. Sarah Goddard Power writes about world literacy, showing "how the notion of literacy can be used as an analytic tool to examine the international distribution of power—the core subject of politics" (21). Her concern is "not only with *who* can read but also [with] what is available to be read," the latter a direct function of power and influence. Her discussion of the third-world demand for a New World Information Order and its conflict with Western notions of press freedom exemplifies the interrelations of literacy and politics. Richard Bailey notes similar interconnections in his description of the historical spread of English as a world language and in his speculations about the future of literacy in English. Both these articles remind policymakers that questions of literacy cannot be divorced from questions of political and economic power. If, for example, the international use of English does in fact decline because of political and economic change, as Bailey projects that it will, so too will the power and influence of English-speaking nations.

Alton Becker and Edwin Delattre write about cultural conflicts and the personal consequences of literacy—Becker by describing his own attempts to become literate in an alien system; Delattre by describing the plight of being an "outsider," an illiterate or marginally literate person in a culture requiring advanced literacy. Both articles remind us that questions of literacy cannot be divorced from questions of personal and cultural values. As Becker notes, "going from one literacy to another, like going from orality to literacy, is . . . a major break in the pattern that connects the items of learning" (48). To encourage such movement is to introduce something alien and to challenge deeply felt values and understandings: an important lesson for teachers of cultural and political minorities.

The five articles in "Forms of Literacy" explore the relations of print and print literacy to other media and to their associated "noetic" systems: systems for shaping, storing, retrieving, and communicating knowledge (the term is Walter Ong's). Robben Fleming worries about the fate of millions of functional illiterates when most jobs require literacy, while suggesting that telecommunications media, with their ever-broadening reach, might be employed to teach print literacy. A similar suggestion is implicit in Gavriel Salomon's essay, but his primary focus is these prior questions: Is there such a thing as "television literacy"? If so, what is it and what is its relation to print literacy? He also asks whether the influence of television has inhibited or enhanced the capacity of students to acquire print literacy (a question raised by other essays in this volume). Salomon's tentative answers are important, based as they are on research into a topic that has invited much speculation.

Deborah Tannen writes about the relations of spoken and written discourse, as does Frank D'Angelo. Tannen asks these questions: "What is it about reading and writing that makes them so difficult to master? Why is it that every child learns to talk fluently, while many never learn to write with anything near fluency?" (79). Tannen argues that the strategies of oral and written discourse connect in a continuum and that student competencies in the former can be used to develop competencies in the latter. D'Angelo, however, stressing differences between the two modes, speculates that a major cause of students' deficiencies in writing may be their reliance on oral modes of thinking, on noetic systems developed in essentially oral subcultures. He argues that modes of thinking characteristic of print literacy must be taught overtly if students are to learn to write competently.

In the final essay in this section, Paul Strassmann suggests that the spreading use of the interactive computer "may change some of our traditional concepts of literacy" (115). Strassmann's is the most radical view of the future and of demands that students and their teachers may have to confront: "The young people now in schools will have to operate in a work environment dominated by electronics. Will they be adequately equipped to perform well in this environment?" (117). Strassmann's position is that computer literacy will supplement rather than replace traditional print literacy, with the latter continuing to function in various uses. But if communication by computer becomes as dominant in the workplace as Strassmann's vision suggests, not to provide computer literacy for our students will be to disadvantage them economically and socially. Crucial questions for educational policymakers will be these: Who should teach computer literacy in our schools? Math teachers? English teachers? How will the money be found to reequip American classrooms—and equip enough of them to ensure access for more than a small (and perhaps elite) number of students?

Section three, "Literacy in the Marketplace," is a sampling of statements on the uses of literacy in various professions and occupations. Paul Weisz argues the need for intelligible literate expression in science to serve these purposes: as a tool in interdisciplinary research, as a means of overcoming the intellectually and socially harmful effects of overspecialization, as a medium for communicating the humanly and socially relevant findings of scientific inquiry. For Weisz, the search for such a medium of expression is no trivial matter: "We need to engage language and communication . . . for the maintenance and survival of our society" (136). James White sees a similarly humane purpose in making ordinary citizens conversant with the language of law, conceiving of that language not as a collection of technical terms and usages but as a body of constitutive social practices governing the ways we organize ourselves and regulate our interactions. For White, "literacy is not merely the capacity to understand the conceptual content of writings and utterances but the ability to participate fully in a set of social and intellectual practices" (147). Janice Redish, describing the language customarily found in bureaucratic documents, chronicles recent attempts to reform it. She too finds the usages of bureaucratic language deeply rooted in social practices and in a particular conception of government as "impersonal guardian of the public welfare" (162); hence the attempt to change bureaucratic language is at base an attempt to change the way government functions in relation to its citizens.

Lee Odell, Dixie Goswami, and Doris Quick, in the final article of this section, report on a study of writing in another nonacademic setting—writing done by legislative aides. Their purpose is to find out whether such a study "might give us a useful perspective on writing that goes on in colleges and universities" (176). The four articles in this section convey these messages: literacy *is* important in the world of work—so important in the professions as to be constitutive of their purposes and procedures; workaday literacy is much more than a matter of mechanics and might well reward the attention of a humanist. Perhaps when academics realize this opportunity, we might begin to move toward an alignment of our classroom practices with the real needs of our students.

Classroom practice is the focus of the final section in the volume, "Literacy and Education." Ralph Tyler argues that tests of student writing are commonly designed for sorting students rather than for assessing their learning. He views such a purpose as inconsistent with the aim of educating all students, and he offers criteria for more appropriate tests. Arthur Cohen and Florence Brawer survey attempts in community colleges to meet the needs of ill-prepared students for instruction in reading and writing; Janet Carsetti describes similar needs of troubled youth in various alternative educational settings and the attempts of Project READ to meet them. Daniel Fader and William Coles speak even more directly to teachers of writing. Fader urges the adjustment of teaching practices to compensate for loss in American homes (because of television) of those conditions that promote personal literacy. Coles argues for writing as an antidote to powerlessness. For both Fader and Coles the ultimate value of writing for students is a deeply personal one: an activity leading to self-identification and a sense of control.

Although the perspectives in this volume are diverse, and positions and claims either contrasting or sometimes in conflict, dominant themes and common concerns run through the essays. Most of the authors address one or more of these five clusters of questions:

1) What are the needs for literacy in our time? Are any of these new or special—particularly as we take a prospective view of social and political change?
2) What is "literacy" anyway? How can we construct useful definitions in response to social needs, educational possibility, and the characteristics of our students?
3) What are the salient characteristics of our students as we assess their potential for achieving literacy and their disposition toward doing so? Are students of the eighties in some ways different from those of decades past?
4) How can we ensure access to literacy for all students—especially for those with needs divergent from the norm?
5) How can we best foster literacy in schools and colleges? Must they change, and if so, how?

What Are the Needs for Literacy?

Although we may well be over the threshold of the change from an industrial to an information society, the printed word has not lost its place in high-tech-nological, electronic America, nor is it likely to. Neither has it lost its place in international communication, at least in most domains. Certainly, television occupies leisure time once given (perhaps) to literate pursuits; certainly, television and radio are becoming primary sources of news and information for increasing numbers of people; and as certainly, telephone and interactive computer communication are taking the place of letters and written memoranda in private and public affairs. But writing and printing and reading are still pervasive activities, as we would expect them to be from this brief characterization of media change by Walter Ong:

> the media in their succession [from talk to script to print to electronic images and impulses] do not cancel out one another but build on one another. When man began to write, he did not cease talking. Very likely, he talked more than ever; the most literate persons are often enough extraordinarily fluent oral verbalizers as well, although they speak somewhat differently from the way purely oral man does or did. When print was developed, man did not stop writing. Quite the contrary: only with print did it become imperative that everybody learn to write—universal literacy, knowledge of reading and writing, has never been the objective of manuscript cultures but only of print cultures. Now that we have electronic communication, we shall not cease to write and print. Technological society in the electronic stage cannot exist without vast quantities of writing and print. Despite its activation of sound, it prints more than ever before. (*Presence of the Word* 88-89)

The essays in this volume make clear that the uses of print are at least as diverse as they were before the advent of electronic media and that the ability to read and write may, without exaggeration, be called a survival skill. These are the pertinent facts and assertions:

> in 1800, the unskilled in all categories [of employment] constituted more than eighty percent of the labor force; in 1900 they made up sixty percent; and in 1980, about six percent. . . . Now jobs requiring no schooling are few in number, while tasks requiring at least a high school education make up nearly two thirds of employment opportunities. (Tyler 198)
>
> Since the 1950s our country has become predominantly occupied with the creation, distribution, and administration of information. By 1990 about fifty percent of the work force will be manufacturing objects and producing food. The rest will occupy most of the time just communicating. (Strassmann 116)
>
> Literacy is certainly related to success in nearly all community college programs: transfer courses demand proficiency in reading, writing, and mathematics, and licensure examinations admitting students to practice after completing technological programs typically demand the same. Many community college programs are closed to students who cannot pass an entrance examination that is based on literacy. (Cohen and Brawer 210)

. . . Americans spend 785 million hours each year filling out 4,987 different federal forms. (Redish 167)

. . . in our increasingly bureaucratic and legalistic world . . . frustrated citizens are likely to feel that their lives are governed by language that they cannot understand—in leases, in form contracts, or in federal or state regulations. (White 138)

Meanwhile, it is estimated that there may be as many as 57 million adult illiterates in the United States. (Fleming 64)

In this country and globally, the correlation between illiteracy and poverty is virtually absolute: to be without letters is to do without adequate food. The correlation between advanced literacy and economic sufficiency is, although not absolute, nonetheless high: to restrict literacy is almost inevitably to impede economic advancement.

But there are ways other than economic in which literacy may be a survival skill. Sarah Power writes:

If there is a clear relation between level of literacy and quality of life, there is an equally clear connection between the distribution of literacy and the possession of power. From the earliest times, literate members of society have had disproportionate power: priests, oracles, poets, and medicine men have all shared as the source of their power a certain literacy, and their modern counterparts—professors, lawyers, engineers, and doctors—continue to exercise power, in part because of their control of language. (24)

As she and Richard Bailey note, the powerful are not always willing to share and thus dilute their power. Throughout history, deliberate attempts to restrict literacy have ranged from the suppression of native languages and literate traditions to the segregation of the powerless into separate and inferior schools or, through tracking, into inferior classrooms. Attempts to exploit the results of restricted literacy have become prevalent in our own time and have ranged from inappropriate literacy testing (for suffrage, for entrance to educational programs, for job certification) to the studied nurturing of professional jargons. Paul Weisz's call for an accessible language of science, James White's for a literacy of law, Janice Redish's for a plain language of bureaucratic management—each is a call for an open, democratic society. If it is important that students acquire literacy for purposes of economic advancement, it is imperative to their roles as responsible citizens that they understand the functions of literacy and its relations to power. Bailey says this about the double consequences of becoming literate:

While basic literacy may well be essential for political consciousness, increasing dispersion and sophistication of literacy are not necessarily accompanied by greater freedom and more participation in governmental affairs. Though literacy may create the potential for political transformation, the institutions through which it is transmitted—the schools—promote the traditional values of a society, foster obedience to authority, and socialize the young to accept roles within the established order. (39)

Our century offers all too many examples of the consequences of uncritical and unquestioned socialization. Schools must teach students how literacy can be used responsibly to advance human freedom.

There is a potential nightmare embedded in Paul Strassmann's vision of an information society dominated by interactive computers. Inevitably and inexorably, because of their cost and because of their sophistication, the media will become ever more centralized; fewer and fewer people will control the broad flow of information. Centralized media invite and make possible the imposition of centralized political power. If such a conjunction should occur between centralized media and centralized power, where would revolutionary ideas come from if not from experience of the past as recorded in books? How would such ideas circulate, if not through the printed word? Reading is a private, even a secret, act, yet it intimately connects one mind with others. Books and pamphlets are relatively easy to smuggle across closed borders; paper and ink are relatively cheap.

Literacy is a survival skill—in economic terms, in social terms, and in political terms. It can become a profession for an increasing number of our students as we move into the age of information. If we train such students well, especially those who will put words into the media, we can help avoid the nightmare of a closed and controlled society. As Janice Redish tells us, making government documents clear is more than a matter of making government run better; doing so can make government more open to scrutiny, more accessible to its citizens, and more humane in its relations with them.

What Is Literacy?

Literacy is more than a survival skill, of course, as many of the authors of these essays emphasize. Yet as long as there are millions of functional illiterates in our country and as long as most of them are poor, we cannot forget that basic literacy is essential to economic and social well-being. Teachers and policymakers are Edwin Delattre's "insiders": they are literate, educated members of the middle or upper-middle class. As insiders, we are attracted to definitions of literacy expressed in terms of cultural value: literacy as humane education, for example, or as the exercise of critical intelligence. But because we are teachers and policymakers and have accepted public responsibility, we must not rest content with definitions of literacy that make us, as insiders, easily comfortable, simply because they describe what we are—our needs, our biases, our preferences and predilections. The inside is not worth occupying if it is walled with neglect of pragmatic human needs.

If we think of literacy not as an end but as a means, we can see that basic skills offering access to jobs can also serve as the basis for a more expansive literacy. Consider these three definitions:

> Whether defined in terms of oration or script, literacy requires the ability to extract information from coded messages and to express ideas, feelings, and thoughts through such messages. Broadly defined, then, literacy is the mastery of specific mental skills that are cultivated in response to the specific demands of coded messages. (Salomon 68)
>
> . . . I start with the idea that literacy is not merely the capacity to understand the conceptual content of writings and utterances but the ability to participate fully in a set of social and intellectual practices. (White 147)
>
> [Literacy] gives access; . . . it lets us inside, where we have an opportunity to see and appreciate what is possible for us. It lets us reach each other. It makes us the heirs and beneficiaries of civilization. (Delattre 53)

Literacy gives access to genuine education: the sort that would allow one to refound one's own civilization. "To be unable to read is to be farthest away from this ideal, to be cut off throughout life from a basic understanding of civilization" (Delattre 52).

Now consider a list of survival skills provided by Janet Carsetti:

> In order to survive in a literate society, people need the skills of literacy— skills that allow one to complete a job application, use a telephone book, read newspapers, leases, road signs, labels on prescription medicine, directions on food packages, and more. (223)

Such skills clearly require an "ability to extract information from coded messages": to read a label is to understand its conceptual content; to read a lease with comprehension is to understand its functions in a set of social practices; reading a newspaper prepares one to read a text on modern European or African history. We can meet the needs of our students for survival skills even as we introduce them to a broader range of social and intellectual practices and lead them toward "genuine" education.

William Coles reminds us that teachers need definitions of literacy that justify its uses and persuade students to learn to read and write. How do we construct definitions of literacy that inform and enable effective program development?

We begin, I believe, by thinking of literacy as functional in particular contexts for particular purposes and by recognizing that functional literacy is relative, not absolute. Arthur Cohen and Florence Brawer cite a useful definition of functional literacy:

> . . . functional literacy is related to the milieu in which people find themselves. A functionally literate person in some school settings may be functionally illiterate in certain jobs. And a person who is quite able to communicate within the confines of certain jobs may be functionally il-

literate for purposes of a college transfer program no matter how that program is defined. (215)

We need to define the various milieus—the various occupational, social, and intellectual settings—in which our students will be expected or may wish to function; then define the skills that they will need. What kinds of skills give access to school learning? to learning in the humanities? in the natural sciences? What kinds give access to effective interaction with governing bureaucracies? to participation in mainstream social activity? Which skills provide access to a richer personal and cultural life? Which protect against the abuse of literacy? Only when we have asked ourselves and our students what they will need reading and writing for—only when we have defined literacy in terms of real purposes in real settings—will we be able to justify our teaching and make it effective. Only when we have surveyed real uses in real settings will we be able to define skills common to them all—to identify and itemize global skills that might in fact serve as basics.

Have Students Changed in Their Disposition toward Literacy? If So, How Can We Best Provide Access to Literacy?

Those who have argued that the literacy of contemporary students differs from that of their predecessors point to many possible causes for the change. These three, however, are most often cited: the influence of television, the persistence of orality as a dominant mode of communication (and its enhancement through television and the telephone), the appearance in classrooms—especially those of colleges—of students who were once denied entry.

Has television changed our students? Daniel Fader believes it has, and so profoundly that "children must now be regarded by their teachers as a species different in kind from the species that inhabited North American classrooms in the first half of the twentieth century" (240). In most homes, he suggests, the switched-on set has displaced reading for information and pleasure and has silenced conversation—familial discourse in which a child might find his or her own voice. As a result, students lack "preparation for and predisposition toward acts of literacy" (241). Gavriel Salomon finds a similar effect, caused not by a change in basic capacity but by a change of habit: watching television, he suggests, does not demand the exercise of higher mental processes, although it could. "It is not impossible," he says, "that children acquire the expectation [from watching television] that pleasurable information can be obtained effortlessly, an expectation they then carry over to written material" (75).

If we wish to assess the capacities and habits of our current students, it is important that we understand the influences of television. Television is a powerful and all-pervasive medium. But to formulate the issue as "tv v. literacy" invites oversimplification, as does the related formulation "orality v. literacy" (a point Deborah Tannen makes).

Alton Becker uses the term "graphocentrism" to name our society's fixation on print: an addiction most severe perhaps among teachers of literacy and literature. Those of us who teach such things acquired our educations through contact with the printed word, and we are tied, more than we sometimes realize, to a single literate tradition and its particular biases. We have failed to pay sufficient attention to the complexities in our own society's means for "shaping, storing, retrieving, and communicating knowledge." We know that our students use more numerous and varied means than print alone; yet as teachers we have not brought that knowledge to conscious awareness, nor have we put it into practice. Our own bias toward print has led some of us to equate literacy—the possession of letters—with learning itself, instead of seeing written language as "a specialized tool of a literate, schooled culture" (Olson 10). The same bias has caused us, in some of our testing, even to equate literacy with intelligence. I quote David R. Olson:

> . . . it [is] clear that what we call "intelligence" in our culture is little more than a mastery of the forms of literate uses of language. What is called abstraction, for example, reflects largely the mastery of the genus/species structures implicit in all language but made explicit by the literate Greeks. Take as a simple example the I.Q. test question: "How are an apple and a peach alike?" If a child responds in terms of the universal and oral coding of experience by saying "They are both to eat," he gets only one point; if, on the other hand, he gives the literate genus/species answer, namely, "They are both fruit," he gets 2 points by the test norms. A high I.Q. then reflects, I suggest, a high literate orientation. . . . Competence with oral uses of language, that aspect of language that is universal, is not only not measured but reliance upon it would often tend to put one at a severe disadvantage in some tests. (23)

Frank D'Angelo agrees with Olson, Ong, Jack Goody, and others who have argued that certain modes of thinking could not come into being without the development of writing, print, and print literacy; that such modes—abstract, analytic, deductive, inferential—cannot be practiced without access to writing or to print:

> The thinking of literate people tends to be more abstract, discrete, definite, and articulated, consisting of generalizations, deductions, and inferences. Without writing, according to some scholars, the mind cannot participate in the kinds of analytical, sequential thinking necessary to develop even a single magazine article. (104)

The study of the relations of writing to thinking and learning is exceedingly important, but the results of such study are still highly tentative. Two cautions seem appropriate.

Sylvia Scribner and Michael Cole say this about the arguments of Ong, Goody, Goody and Watt, and Havelock:

> Intriguing as these speculations are, their significance for a theory of psychological consequences for *individuals* in *our* society is problematic on two counts. These scholars derive evidence for cognitive effects of literacy from historical studies of cultural and social changes associated with the advent of widespread literacy. Inferences about cognitive changes in *individuals* are shaky if they rest only on the analysis of *cultural* phenomena. . . . Secondly we need to distinguish between historical and contemporaneous causation (see Lewin, 1935). The development of writing systems and the production of particular kinds of text may, indeed, have laid the basis *historically* for the emergence of new modes of intellectual operation, but these over time, may have lost their connection with the written word. There is no necessary connection between the modality in which new operations come into being and the modality in which they are perpetuated and transmitted in later historical epochs. Forms of discourse initially confined to written text may subsequently come to be transmitted orally through teacher-pupil dialogue, for example, or through particular kinds of "talk" produced on television shows. One cannot leap to the conclusion that what was necessary historically is necessary in contemporaneous society. There is no basis for assuming, without further evidence, that the individual child, born into a society in which uses of literacy have been highly elaborated, must personally engage in writing operations in order to develop "literate modes of thought." That *may* be the case, but it requires proof, not simply extrapolation from cultural-historical studies. (73)

Gaining more "conscious control of certain kinds of mental activities" may well help students to improve their writing, as D'Angelo argues (111). But we should not assume—yet—that certain mental activities are peculiar to literacy or even that learning to write better necessarily ensures learning to think better.

We should also recognize that the kind of thinking D'Angelo refers to is most characteristic of certain branches of science and philosophy. Though highly favored in our culture, it is not the only mode of thinking human beings engage in, nor is it the only kind that gets expressed in writing. We do, after all, have stories and poems and drama; reminiscences and reflections and animadversions—modes that may well be closer to everyday talk (as Tannen shows) and to a commonsense perception of reality. In short, the noetic processes reflected in writing and print are manifold, not uniform. There are many kinds of writing, many ways of shaping and communicating meaning through written words.

It is proper to be skeptical of neat oppositions, such as tv versus literacy, orality versus literacy. We should be even more skeptical when these are taken to imply dichotomous mental capacities. Because writing and thinking are so obviously complementary, we leap to apply the findings of cognitive scientists.

But we should not base the teaching of writing on abstract schemes of cognitive development when these schemes fail to account for the complexity we find in the uses of written language, of spoken language, and of nonverbal systems. The noetic world our students occupy is a rich one. It does not divide simply— as Ong himself says—into a neat separation of what is oral from what is literate. After all, students who are predominantly oral are merely students who have had little experience with the written word. Without such experience, without instruction, students will have limited access to the products of abstract thinking. But if properly motivated, students can be helped to use their common sense. They can learn to employ oral strategies in writing or, when it is appropriate, to move toward writing that is more like writing. They will control more abstract modes of thinking and writing as they come to a broadened education in disciplines that employ such thinking essentially.

We do not need to ignore—certainly we cannot afford to diminish or denigrate—our students' oral skills, especially if we wish to keep newly opened doors open. In arguing for a cognitive approach to writing, D'Angelo calls attention to changes in school and college student populations ("more disadvantaged students," "more high-risk students," more "students who in past years may have dropped out before graduating from high school"):

> What we do know for certain [about causes of "the literacy crisis"] is that the student population has changed. Many students come from what Walter Ong would call a "residually oral" culture, a strata within the mainstream of society where oral modes of expression permeate thinking. They come from homes where speech is more widespread than reading or writing. (104)

Citing her own research, Tannen demonstrates that "residual orality" is not limited to groups of the sort D'Angelo refers to but is also a characteristic of certain groups whose members are highly educated. The groups whose residual orality is likely to be seen as a problem, however, are those groups who either have been systematically denied access to education or have consistently refused it—perhaps because its promise has not seemed real. These residually oral students *are* outsiders, in more ways than Delattre's term implies. Their language is often an expression of rebellion, always a means to convey group identity and loyalty—a way of asserting that they are *inside* on the outside. A language of identity and loyalty, a language of rebellion, is not readily abandoned or easily supplanted. The best pedagogy ever devised will not work with students who rebel against learning.

Bailey alludes to the very serious problem of resource allocation for literacy programs in third-world countries:

> . . . most third-world countries will not be in a position to develop simultaneously both universal and selective educational systems. Universal education enhances general literacy but at a level too low for citizens to

function in roles that lead to increased national wealth; selective education yields economic benefits but at the expense of the egalitarian ideals that are espoused by many third-world nations. (39)

The United States faces similar problems—especially in the face of growing public resistance to high expenditures for education. How to provide access for all and whether to provide access for all will become the difficult questions. There are too many functional illiterates, too many high school graduates who do not meet the expectations of employers or of college faculties, too many college graduates who fail similarly when entering the workplace or graduate school. Rapid technological changes complicate our problems: there are too few people adequately trained for the kinds of jobs described by Redish and Strassmann. We will need knowledge and wisdom: knowledge about the functions of literacy and the processes by which it is acquired, wisdom in deciding whom to help and how much. The needs of the powerless and unlettered are too easily lost when needs exist among the powerful and lettered.

What Must Schools and Colleges Do?

The schools cannot be blamed exclusively—as Paul Copperman insists they must—for the rate of functional illiteracy in the United States. The vastness of the estimated numbers—25 to 57 million—indicates the working of social and economic forces too powerful for their effects to be countered completely, even by good programs in excellent schools. Yet schools have been slow—some of them recalcitrant—in instituting programs of proven value, especially when such programs are aimed primarily at the poor and the ignorant, who constitute the main body of functional illiterates. Project READ, as Carsetti documents, is successful with just such a clientele; many aspects of her program should be adapted and used in more conventional educational settings. Cohen and Brawer point to several highly successful compensatory and remedial programs in community colleges; but at the same time, they identify three factors that may hinder the adoption of workable programs: teacher attitudes, administrative timidity, and public niggardliness.

> Veteran faculty remember when they had well-prepared students in the 1950s and early 1960s. They may feel nostalgic, perhaps even betrayed, because the conditions under which they entered the colleges have changed so. (214)

> Nothing—not even education in the higher technologies—is more expensive than the varied media and close monitoring demanded by slow learners. Many college leaders fear publicizing the extent of their compensatory education programs lest their funding be threatened by legislators and members of the public who raise embarrassing questions about paying

several times over for the education that was supposed to be provided in the lower schools. (218)

Most of us do become impatient with teaching the rudiments to the same students year after year, and in our impatience we may conjure up a golden past when students were both prepared and polite. Perhaps we can't be blamed for the number of functional illiterates, but we *are* culpable for attitudes that defeat the attempt to meet their needs. We are blamable as well if we do not use our voices—in our unions and in other professional organizations—to make public these assertions: all education is in some sense compensatory or remedial; all good education is costly; educational costs, unlike many others our society incurs, lead to profits—in the social calm and cohesion that allow for productive work.

Some problems in student literacy can be blamed on English departments and English teachers for letting themselves be persuaded to bear sole responsibility for the teaching of reading and writing. In part, the history of our profession and the public's perception of our role imposed the responsibility on us: historically and in the public mind, the English teacher is *the* teacher of reading and writing. But in larger part, our venality has made us easy to persuade. We have enjoyed economic advantage in accepting the responsibility: doing so makes it easier for us to justify required English courses, even those exclusively in literature; doing so has made it possible for many university English departments to fund large graduate programs, even in the face of declining enrollments and diminished professional opportunities. Inertia and venality do not result in well-planned programs sensitive to present needs.

Good programs will result only when English teachers recognize and persuade their non-English department colleagues that reading and writing must be taught—and can only be taught effectively—by all faculty in all disciplines. Such an approach is essential in the schools, if for no other reason than numbers: the average student load of the average high school English teacher does not permit the kind of attention to reading and writing that average students need. Moreover, the kind of functional literacy now demanded of high school and college graduates cannot be taught by one kind of teacher.

As the authors of this volume have defined it, literacy is:

1) the ability to crack a code: to make sense of marks on paper;
2) the ability to derive information from that code;
3) the ability to derive personal, social, cognitive meaning from the information derived;
4) the ability to act on such meanings;
5) the ability to make inferential and other cognitive structures from the meanings acquired in order to find new meanings.

As we move up this hierarchy of mental operations, we move into the realms of our separate academic disciplines: the inferential structures of the scientist are not the same as those of the poet. When students need to learn the inferential structures of chemistry or sociology or literary interpretation, they can learn them best from practitioners in those disciplines. Similarly, when students need to communicate what they have learned—to fellow scientists, to colleagues in business, to policymakers who will read their research reports—they can best learn the communicative strategies and special languages used in such communications from those who know and employ them. "Reading and Writing across the Curriculum" is not a trendy term for a modish practice: it is an educational imperative in the complicated world we and our students inhabit.

Raymond Williams, in a challenging critique of dominant trends in literary study, reminds us that the term "literature" once applied more broadly than to imaginative works of a certain kind and quality. In one of its earlier usages "it was often close to the sense of modern *literacy*"; its reference was to "a condition of reading: of being able to read and of having read" (46). Histories, biographies, works of philosophy, and political and scientific treatises were all works of literature. Williams traces the specialization of the term to the domain of "creative" or "imaginative" works, and the development of literature departments in academies as units concerned exclusively with this narrowed domain and with the practice of criticism. It is interesting to remember that many university English departments developed from and replaced earlier departments of rhetoric.

The question I want to raise as a final one is whether or not English departments can serve as units around which effective programs in literacy can be organized. Is their concern with literature, in its modern sense, too narrow to serve public and social demands for a fully functional literacy? The question derives in part from several statements in the recent report of the Commission on the Humanities, which argues persistently for the importance of literacy in contemporary intellectual life and for the special responsibility of humanists in fostering it. But the report defines literacy more broadly than most English departments would:

> Our citizens need to become literate in a multiple sense. We all need to understand the characteristics of scientific inquiry and the repercussions of scientific research. We must all learn something about the use of the media and of new technologies for storing, transmitting, and expanding knowledge. Without this sort of literacy, our society as a whole will be less able to apply science and technology to humanistic needs, less able to measure the human effects of scientific achievements, less able to judge the information we produce and receive. (18-19)

Perhaps the time has come for the establishment of another kind of department or, at the very least, a new kind of interdisciplinary program. The functions of such a unit would be to conduct research into the nature and functions of literacy in developing and fully developed societies, to communicate the results of that research to students training for professional roles in contemporary society—roles that many of the contributors to this volume have described, to encourage and coordinate the absolutely essential development of a cross-disciplinary concern for literacy, and to work with schools to foster similar concerns and to develop sequenced programs from grade one through grade sixteen.

Research on the nature and acquisition of literacy is now being done in many disciplines: anthropology, linguistics, psychology and psychiatry, history, philosophy, literary theory, social and cultural history, and sociology. Few English faculty conduct or read broadly in such research; even fewer English composition programs are informed by it. Given their specialization, which is as narrow as that of any other discipline, I do not believe that English departments, as presently constituted or as likely to be constituted, will accommodate the research and training so obviously necessary to meet the needs of our students and our society.

Works Cited

Commission on the Humanities. *The Humanities in American Life*. Berkeley: Univ. of California Press, 1980.

Copperman, Paul. *The Literacy Hoax*. New York: Morrow, 1978.

Goody, Jack. *The Domestication of the Savage Mind*. Cambridge: Cambridge Univ. Press, 1977.

————, and Ian Watt. "The Consequences of Literacy." *Comparative Studies in Society and History* 5(1963):304-45. Rpt. in *Literacy in Traditional Societies*. Ed. Jack Goody. Cambridge: Cambridge Univ. Press, 1968, 27-68.

Havelock, Eric A. *Preface to Plato*. Cambridge: Harvard Univ. Press, 1963.

Lewin, Kurt. *A Dynamic Theory of Personality*. New York: McGraw-Hill, 1935.

Olson, David R. "Oral and Written Language and the Cognitive Processes of Children." *Journal of Communication* 27(Summer 1977):10-26.

Ong, Walter J. *Interfaces of the Word: Studies in the Evolution of Consciousness and Culture*. Ithaca, N.Y.: Cornell Univ. Press, 1977.

————. *The Presence of the Word: Some Prolegomena for Cultural and Religious History*. 1967; rpt. Minneapolis: Univ. of Minnesota Press, 1981.

Scribner, Sylvia, and Michael Cole. "Unpackaging Literacy." In *Variation in Writing: Functional and Linguistic-Cultural Differences*. Ed. Marcia Farr Whiteman. Hillsdale, N.J.: Lawrence Erlbaum Assocs., 1981, 71-87.

Williams, Raymond. *Marxism and Literature*. Oxford: Oxford Univ. Press, 1971.

Literacy, Politics, and Policies

The Politics of Literacy

Sarah Goddard Power

The first part of this paper is devoted to discussing some definitions and descriptions of literacy around the world. With these definitions in mind, I show how the notion of literacy can be used as an analytic tool to examine the international distribution of power—the core subject of politics. Finally, I show how implications arising from the distribution of literacy provide a framework for understanding an issue currently under intense discussion: international press freedom and the demand for a New World Information Order. Press freedom shapes the gathering and dissemination of information and is thus a subject that links literacy with access to information and power. From this perspective, we are concerned not only with who can read but also with what is available to be read.

What Is Literacy?

Most commonly we understand literacy to mean the ability to read and write, but we can also define literacy in terms of a person's culture. In 1964, UNESCO initiated an Experimental World Literacy Program based on a newly developed concept of "functional literacy," defined in the following terms at a world congress of ministers of education held in Tehran in 1965:

> Rather than an end in itself, literacy should be regarded as a way of preparing man for a social, civic and economic role that goes far beyond the limits of rudimentary literacy training consisting merely in the teaching of reading and writing. ("Literacy" 6)

During the 1970s the notion of functional literacy was gradually extended. Realizing that an absolute definition of literacy is neither appropriate nor applicable to all areas of the world, officials came to see literacy as part of a culture-specific educational process. In 1975 the UNESCO International Symposium at Persepolis adopted a declaration that stated, "Literacy creates the conditions for the acquisition of a critical consciousness of the contradictions of society in which

21

man lives and of its aims" ("Literacy" 6). Similarly, Aklilu Habte, director of
education at the World Bank, noted:

> It is quite interesting to talk about illiteracy in a country like the United
> States, and to talk about illiteracy in some of the developing societies—
> Africa, Southeast Asia, some of Latin America. The difference is fantastic.
> We are not talking about situations where schools exist, where everyone
> has a chance to go to school but somehow doesn't learn. We are not talking
> about situations where teachers are available. We are not talking about
> situations where the increase in population is somehow under control. We
> are talking about two different areas. And yet in the end both produce
> individuals who are not functional within their societies, or who could be
> made more functional. (48)

Habte's observation recognizes the premise of functional literacy: within
the context of a given culture, a literate person is one who can gain access to
information and transmit it to others. In contrast to more conventional definitions
of literacy, the notion of functional literacy does not necessarily entail the ability
to read and write. In parts of Nigeria, for example, a system of drummed
communication known as the "bush telegraph" is still used. According to the
definition of functional literacy, Nigerians who understand the meaning of distant
drum beats and pass along their own information by means of a drum are perfectly
literate in that context, even though they may lack the ability to read and write.
The same is true of the shamans of the Arctic, who use memory devices and an
oral tradition to acquire and pass on a vast range of information. Though they
do not read and write, they are literate in the Inuit tradition and use their knowledge
in the same way that literate persons do in a society employing reading and
writing.

A functional definition of literacy not only makes possible comparisons
across very different societies and cultures; it also makes transparent a devastating
truth about illiteracy: regardless of the nature of society, an illiterate cannot
function successfully within it.

I will discuss one more notion of literacy because it has direct bearing on
the international political issue of literacy and news flow. I call it "global literacy":
the ability to acquire information and communicate across national and cultural
barriers. In an increasingly interdependent world, this ability is becoming more
and more important. The notion of global literacy, of course, is closer to conventional definitions, since communication across different cultures and languages usually requires the ability to read and write. Without this ability, the
bush telegrapher, for example, will be unable to communicate with others except
in face-to-face settings, since drum beats cannot conveniently be stored for future
reference or sent to faraway places. Similarly, for the North American shaman's
knowledge of medicine to come into the world's storehouse of understanding,
the shaman must go outside the oral tradition and find a vehicle to record and
transmit his knowledge beyond his immediate surroundings.

The Distribution of Literacy

The world literacy problem in the past twenty-five years can be summed up in one simple observation: although many countries have succeeded in substantially reducing the percentage of illiterates in their populations, the absolute number of illiterates is constantly rising because of soaring population growth. The distribution of literacy around the world varies considerably: women are less literate than men; countries in the Southern Hemisphere are less literate than those in the North; the rich are more literate than the poor; white races are more literate than black, brown, yellow, or red; urban populations are more literate than rural ones.

The following facts elaborate one of these generalizations and show the close connections between literacy among women and national development: In 1960, fifty-eight percent of all illiterates worldwide were women; today, that percentage has increased to sixty percent since women have not shared equally in the literacy programs of the past twenty years. "Out of every 100 women over 15 in Africa and Asia, 84 and 57 respectively [in 1970] are illiterate, as against only 2 illiterate women for every 100 in North America and 5 in Europe and the USSR" ("Women and Illiteracy"). In many places, the situation is even worse than the statistics imply, because women are not encouraged to pursue education beyond a rudimentary level that counts as "literacy" but does not provide access to significant information and hence to power.

Better nutrition, family planning, and domestic hygiene are closely correlated with literacy. Studies in Bangladesh, Kenya, and Colombia show that rates of infant mortality decline as mothers gain more education. A survey of households in São Paulo, Brazil, revealed that for any given income level, families were better fed the higher the level of the mother's education. Education tends to delay marriage for women and to increase their chances of employment. Educated women are more likely to know about and use contraceptives to limit family size and help families escape the cycle of poverty.

Nick Eberstadt speculates that educating girls may be one of the best investments a country can make in future economic growth and welfare. Since the great expansion in educational opportunities worldwide over the last thirty years,

> a change in the rhythm of life has occurred: instead of being married off, increasing numbers of women either stay at home and find work, or go off to work in their early 20s and late teens. With greater education, job skills, experience outside the family and a smaller age differential between herself and her husband (age at marriage has *not* been rising for the men), young brides are in a better position to bargain over family size. (52-53)

When women can negotiate a "bargain" that reduces population growth, nations can escape from the cycle of poverty.

If there is a clear relation between level of literacy and quality of life, there is an equally clear connection between the distribution of literacy and the possession of power. From the earliest times, literate members of society have had disproportionate power: priests, oracles, poets, and medicine men have all shared as the source of their power a certain literacy, and their modern counterparts—professors, lawyers, engineers, and doctors—continue to exercise power, in part because of their control of language.

The connection between literacy and power is two-way: just as literacy often gives people access to power, power generally gives people access to literacy. People who are male or rich or urban or white-skinned or from the Northern Hemisphere are more powerful, and, because more powerful, they are more literate. If control of language constitutes control of scarce and prized goods, powerful people will make sure they possess disproportionate amounts of that precious stuff called literacy. Until very recently, one mechanism used by most elites to maintain their power was to restrict literacy by restricting access to education. The idea of mass public education is recent and revolutionary.

Western colonialists of the nineteenth century recognized that they needed to create a cadre of native teachers and clerks in order to exercise authority in Africa and Asia. Viewing India in 1834, Charles Trevelyan saw that a few English rulers could govern only by creating an Indian elite imbued with the literacy and values of Britain:

> Educated in the same way, interested in the same objects, engaged in the same pursuits with ourselves, they became more English than Hindus, just as the Roman provincials became more Roman than Gauls or Italians. (quoted in McCully 72)

Trevelyan did not, perhaps, foresee that this Indian elite would come to be leaders in the anticolonialist movement, just as the Roman Gauls eventually emerged as independent French people. Whatever he may have thought, we now recognize that people usually gain political power and independence by becoming literate. As political independence became imminent in India, Gandhi and Nehru recognized that literacy was as important for all citizens of a democractic state as it had been for the servants of empire, and they fostered mass literacy campaigns—not to make citizens "more English" but to make them more "Indian" in the exercise of power and authority.

These examples suggest that the relation between political power and literacy is complicated. It becomes even more complicated when one considers the distribution of political power among nations. In what Daniel Bell has labeled the "postindustrial age," a nation's power must be measured not simply by millions of tons of steel produced or automobiles assembled but also by the quality and quantity of the information it can summon up on short notice and use to effect significant control and change (see Power and Abel 117). Powerful nations are literate. The United States possesses great wealth and power, much of which has been reinvested to make its citizens even more literate. Literacy and the information industry can themselves be sources of national wealth and prestige. Yugoslavia has not been regarded as a powerful nation during the past thirty years, despite its break with the USSR and its experiments with worker self-management. But recently, Tanyug, the Yugoslav news agency, has played a leading role in setting up a news pool for third-world nations. Each member sends to Tanyug headquarters in Belgrade its press releases, texts of speeches, and direct news reportage. The Third World News Pool editors translate and distribute this information around the world. In the world news community, Yugoslavia has risen to a nation of first rank because of its activity in promoting global literacy.

Press Freedom and the New World Information Order

The relation between national power and global literacy has been explored over the past seven years, primarily within UNESCO. A furious and, until recently, largely unrecognized argument has raged about the confusing and complex issue of freedom versus government control of the world's news and information. Developing countries have expressed a sense of desperation, frustration, and anger as they have faced the power of Western reporters and news agencies in a world fast becoming a global village populated by "global illiterates" dependent on a small minority of "global literates."

The issues that animate this argument become apparent with examples. Nearly ninety percent of the international news stories printed on a given day in an Indian newspaper are reported, edited, and moved (3.4 million words per day!) by one of the four great international wire services—Associated Press, United Press International, Reuters, Agence France Presse. One can easily see why the editors of such newspapers might conclude that their view of the world— and that of their readers—is highly colored by assumptions and attitudes that are almost entirely non-Indian. Similarly, Smith reports the following incident (121). A high-ranking American arrived at the Cairo airport on a U.S. military plane and tried to telephone President Sadat. His call soon became hopelessly snarled in the overloaded domestic telephone system. In frustration, he placed a call that moved through a U.S. satellite to Washington and then back to Cairo, quickly reaching President Sadat. Such an experience is not uncommon and clearly exemplifies a new imperialism of communication.

Various attempts have been made to create a new supply of information designed to force Western editors to see national and international events from a third-world perspective. In creating the Third World News Pool, eighty-five nations were motivated by a need "to re-guarantee a threatened political independence rather than [by] a deeply felt desire to partake in the indigenous culture" (Smith 38; see also Pinch). In a declaration adopted by the General Conference in 1976, UNESCO agreed that their contribution to this effort was in "liberating the developing countries from the state of dependence resulting from specific historical circumstances which still characterize their communication and information systems" (Najar 22).

Western control of information goes far beyond the collection and dissemination of news. American exports of feature films account for more than half of all films shown in Chile, Colombia, Uruguay, Bolivia, Brazil, Ecuador, Paraguay, Peru, and Venezuela. Similar figures for television programs reveal the dominance of Western media in virtually all the emerging nations of Asia, Africa, and the Middle East.

In *The Geopolitics of Information,* Anthony Smith points out:

> The mere recital of figures does little to illustrate the true implications of media dependence. The presence of overseas owners of indigenous newspapers, the flow of advertising controlled by foreign agencies, the dependence upon foreign equipment to supply the whole of a radio or television system and the importation of foreign mass entertainment material in cities which have sprung up only in the post-colonial era all mean that the whole outlook of a nation's media . . . takes place in the context of a foreign culture. (46)

The third world's charge is simple: *"Unfair!"* But it goes further than that. Third-world leaders recently articulated a far-reaching and hostile critique of the world news and information system dominated by the independent capitalist press. Their claims, as described by Philip Power, include the following:

> Western wire services reporting about third-world countries are uninformed and concentrate on the negative or sensational. What requires a press that is free of government control to be accurate or responsible?
>
> The great bulk of the international news used by third-world newspapers, radio, and television is produced and controlled by Western news agencies; very little news produced by third-world journalists flows to the West. If this imbalance in flow is an inevitable consequence of "press freedom," why should the third world accept a situation so contrary to its own interests?
>
> The flow of news, ideas, and information from the West has overwhelmed local attempts at information independence and has resulted in a new kind of imperialism of the mind. Is not the West's attachment to the idea of the free flow of information nothing more than an excuse for a new kind of imperialist exploitation?

It is easy enough to understand what has provoked the demand for a New World Information Order. But what makes that demand so difficult for the West to meet is that it consists of two separate issues: first, the demand for fairness in news and information, based essentially on ideas of distributive justice; and second, the underlying analysis which claims that the root cause of an unjust world information system is the very fact that it is free of government control.

It is this last point that makes defenders of press freedom widen their eyes in alarm. They argue, writes Power:

> If developing countries want a better deal in news and information, we can help by more sensitive reporting and by offering training and technical help to third-world media. But if the third world argues that the root cause of the imbalance in flow is a world news and information system free of governmental control and if it insists that the only remedy is imposition of control by governments or by UNESCO, then it is asking us to betray our most deeply held principles, which we cannot do.

It is the two-sided, ends-means nature of the argument over world news and information—the agreed end being fairness, but only one of the possible means to that end being government control—that makes it so important to sort out exactly what a New World Information Order would involve.

A moderate version of a new world information system, generally supported by the West, focuses on improving and expanding the news and information capacity of the third world without necessarily reducing or circumscribing the existing news systems of the developed world. It would concentrate on upgrading the technical means by which news is reported and distributed and avoid prescribing the content of the news. In general, it would express the difference between improving the plumbing pipes in a house (the means of distribution) and requiring the inhabitants to use water of only one temperature (controlling the content delivered).

In practice, the moderate approach would involve research sponsored by UNESCO, governments, and the private sector into the communications needs of developing countries; technical help for them to improve their newspapers, radio, television, telephone, and telegraph systems; setting up regional nonaligned news pools or even a worldwide North-South cooperative news agency operating somewhat like Western wire services, but without supplanting them.

A radical version of the New World Information Order offered in 1978 by the Tunisian ambassador to UNESCO, Mustapha Masmoudi, depended much more heavily on active intervention against Western news media by governments and by UNESCO. It would define responsibilities and duties of the news media; require the news media to give governments the right of reply when allegedly inaccurate stories are published; define cases in which governments may deny journalists access to news sources; give individual governments the right to censor, restrict, or tax the flow of news and information across their borders; and set up a supranational tribunal to check media performance and provide remedies for complaints about false or biased news stories.

If adopted, the radical version of the New World Information Order would have serious consequences for the United States. It would mean accepting the idea of state control over all news and information coming into or leaving any nation, and it could result in censorship of news stories. If implemented, the proposals would greatly reduce the amount of information about the world available to Americans and their government and would eliminate or drastically curtail the activities of Radio Free Europe, Radio Liberty, and the Voice of America. The most extreme consequence could be the nationalization of information throughout the world.

There is a solid argument for press freedom that we in the West, with our rich and developed societies, have forgotten how to make with force and skill, namely "that a press free of state control offers the best kind of accurate information system possible to make sure that scarce resources for development are well used and not dribbled off in government incompetency, waste and corruption" (Power).

The divisions that separate the information rich and the information-poor, both internationally and nationally, as Anthony Smith makes clear,

> . . . could become almost inexorable, far harder to overcome than the divisions founded upon economic exploitation. Information wealth is difficult to sequestrate or tax or render equitable once it has been acquired. . . . Information gaps create further gaps in wealth and social status. They are intangible but self-replicating. (113)

Although I have written about illiteracy and about distinctions between North and South, black and white, rich and poor, it is essential to note that the individual does not necessarily fit into a stereotype. It is the individual and his or her functioning literacy with which we must ultimately be concerned. Research is accumulating that demonstrates a causal relationship among literacy, exposure to the mass media, and a person's readiness to engage in activities that promote personal and social change:

- As individuals gain reading skills, they extend the scope of their experience through the print media. Messages in the print media tend to promote change.
- Literacy permits the individual receivers, rather than the senders, to control the rates at which messages are received, stored, and interpreted.
- Literacy unlocks more complex mental abilities. Whereas the illiterate individual is largely dependent on memory, the literate individual is able to manipulate symbols.

For these reasons, "many experts view literacy instruction as the best possible means for an underdeveloped nation to break the vicious cycle of low income, high birth rates, and slow development, and make progress along the path toward modernization" (Rogers and Herzog 203).

Works Cited

Eberstadt, Nick. "Recent Declines in Fertility in Less Developed Countries, and What 'Population Planners' May Learn from Them." *World Development* 8(1980):37-60.

Habte, Akliku. *Proceedings of the International Literacy Day Conference*. Ed. Stuart Diamond. Washington, D.C.: National Endowment for the Humanities, 1978.

"Literacy, Gateway to Fulfillment." Special issue of *UNESCO Courier,* June 1980.

McCully, Bruce. *English Education and the Origins of Indian Nationalism*. New York: Columbia Univ. Press, 1965.

Najar, Ridha. "A Voice from the Third World: Towards a 'New World Order of Information.' " *UNESCO Courier* 30(April 1977):21-33.

Pinch, Edward T. "The Flow of News: An Assessment of the Non-Aligned Agencies Pool." *Journal of Communication* 28.4(1978):163-71.

Power, Philip H. "Third World vs. the Media." Unpublished draft for *New York Times Magazine* article, 1980.

———, and Elie Abel. "Third World vs. the Media." *New York Times Magazine,* 21 Sept. 1980, 116-23, 128, 133.

Rogers, Everett M., and William Herzog. "Functional Literacy among Colombian Peasants." *Economic Development and Cultural Change* 14(1966):190-203.

Smith, Anthony. *The Geopolitics of Information*. New York: Oxford Univ. Press, 1980.

"Women and Illiteracy." *UNESCO Courier* 28(March 1975):18.

Literacy in English:
An International Perspective

Richard W. Bailey

English now occupies a special place among the 4,500 languages of the world. Though second to Mandarin Chinese in the number of its native speakers, it is widely dispersed and is the sole official or semiofficial language of twenty-one countries and the co-official language of another sixteen (Conrad and Fishman 7). English, the most commonly used language in international organizations, serves as a lingua franca in many domains of international communication— trade and technology, diplomacy, telecommunications, air-traffic management, tourism, and a wide variety of other domains that affect the lives of millions of people who may not themselves speak English. The present state of affairs has a long tradition; even in the sixteenth century, when (among the languages of Europe) Dutch, Portuguese, and Spanish were more common than English in exploration and trade, Richard Mulcaster could describe the international use of English as a matter of national pride. "If the spreading sea, and the spacious land could vse anie speche," he wrote, "theie would both shew you where, and in how manie strange places, theie haue sene our peple" (90).

When Mulcaster wrote in 1582, English was barely established outside the British Isles. Today it is spoken around the globe by more than 300 million people, and a nearly equal number make some use of it as a language in addition to their own native tongue. Large as this number is, however, the total constitutes only fifteen percent of the world's population, a share that is likely to decrease in the next decade. Though many English users are literate (in comparison with other major language communities), this number too is likely to decrease if literacy is defined as effective control of the skills of reading and writing.

In contemplating the future of literacy in English, we need to take a wider view than that afforded by the 225 million English users in North America. In the next decade, the role of English is likely to change, and teachers and policy-makers need answers to these questions:

- Who will use English and for what purposes?
- What will be the role of reading and writing?

Informed speculation about the future of English is necessarily based on knowledge of the past. English is not the first language to spread as a lingua franca over a large territory, to lands where other languages were already established. Latin spread with the Roman Empire, took root in new territory, and, with the spread of successor empires, reached around the globe in the form of French, Portuguese, and Spanish. Similarly, Arabic spread over a huge territory as Islam gained adherents, and today it is the sixth most commonly spoken language. A more recent example of the same phenomenon is provided by the spread of Bahasa Indonesia, a language spoken by only a tiny minority at the turn of this century but now the national language of one of the most populous nations in the world (see Quirk 61-62). English, then, is merely one more in a series of world languages, and it is likely to grow or diminish, change or remain relatively stable, for the same reasons that affected its predecessors.

All the major languages that spread beyond their national boundaries in the past did so as a consequence of military, economic, or ideological conquest. Like them, English was dispersed by the impulse toward empire, and if the circumstances of its introduction were not always accompanied by military force, it is certainly true that English speakers arrived in new lands with the conviction that they had come to colonize and rule. Even when these immigrants came in peace, they were convinced that they were called to bring benefits to peoples who could only profit from new trade and technology, new religion, and a new language.

People bent on imposing their ways on others have no difficulty in contriving arguments to justify their doing so. The historical and present-day spread of English is no exception to that principle. Surprising as it may seem to those of us who have struggled with the vagaries of its spelling and the mysteries of its written conventions, English is sometimes promoted abroad on the grounds of its "intrinsic" efficiency and economy (see, for instance, Tunstall 126-27). Additional arguments on behalf of the intrinsic goodness of English are supported by appeals to a long and excellent literary tradition and to the wealth of its vocabulary. (While discussions of vocabulary typically acknowledge that the Inuit language has a richer vocabulary for *snow*—a natural resource of virtually no economic value—English ethnocentrism routinely assumes that anything worth saying or thinking can be efficiently articulated in English.)

There are dozens of testimonials to the intrinsic value of English, not only from native speakers of English who testify to its virtues—even though they command no other language—but also from those who have embraced English with the fervor of the converted. Among the latter, President Leopold S. Senghor of Senegal celebrates "its richness and flexibility, . . . the ideal of life it expresses, the humanist ideal of freedom of thought":

> One last remark on the English language: it has, since the eighteenth century, been one of the favourite instruments of the New Negro, who has used it to express his identity, his *Négritude*, his consciousness of the

African heritage. An instrument which, with its plasticity, its rhythm and its melody, corresponds to the profound, volcanic affectivity of the Black peoples. (85)

Senghor's praise of English concentrates on the intrinsic qualities of the language—"plasticity, rhythm, melody, and affectivity."[1] For him and for others in the third world, such features are sufficient in themselves to justify the use of English for national life and artistic expression.

A second set of arguments on behalf of English is more commonly invoked and is perhaps more persuasive: English is the language of the "developed" world, and nations and peoples who wish to participate fully in development must use English to gain access to valuable technology and precious information. While it is true that much of the world's science is made known through English, any language contains the potential for developing a technical vocabulary and a scientific style. Nonetheless, the national investment required to develop new linguistic domains is substantial unless a community is content to adapt international scientific vocabulary and masses of borrowed words. As the revival of Hebrew as a living language in our century shows, the conditions for "modernizing" a language according to puristic principles include a strong allegiance to that language and vigorous action by a language academy in developing and disseminating innovations. In many countries, the easier course has been followed: training a cadre of specialists who use one of the languages of wider communication, particularly English, to conduct the business of modernization and development.

The use of English for national development is no more inevitable than the acceptance of the idea of development itself. Recent political events remind us that evolution of the global village is not progressing along a single path. Western technology and the use of English were brought to an abrupt halt in Tehran by the Ayatollah's revolution, and English and French are no longer the lingua francas of Ho Chi Minh City (formerly Saigon). Less newsworthy, but no less important, was the decision of the Malaysian government to reduce greatly English-medium instruction for school children and to replace it with programs employing Bahasa Malaysia, the language of national unity. Such dissents from the Englishing of the world are not isolated or temporary diversions from the road to a uniform world order; rather, I believe, they foreshadow developments that are likely to reduce the spread of English in the third world.

In addition to arguments for English based on its intrinsic virtues and its role in development, a case for English has often rested on its potential for creating national unity. In many former British colonies, English continues to serve as an official language of government, although such uses of English have not been maintained uncritically as a postcolonial heritage. In the struggle for Indian independence, for instance, Gandhi argued that it was necessary to reject English along with the British raj. "The necessity of English training," he wrote, "has enslaved us" (14:122). Constitutional provisions adopted at the time of independence in 1948 allowed a fifteen-year interim in which English would serve as the language of national affairs. But as the time drew near for English to be replaced, urban riots led the government to postpone any change in language policy. Those who fought the change were not necessarily partisans of English; most of them were defending their own minority languages against Hindi, the majority language of northern India and the likely replacement for English in affairs of government. Should Hindi replace English, they reasoned, speakers of other languages would have distinctly diminished opportunities to participate in the management of the country. Such arguments for English are not based on its intrinsic worth or its utilitarian values; English is viewed simply as a lesser evil.

Other countries employ English for the same reason that it continues to be used in India. There, English serves as a national language because there is no significant group of local native speakers. All language communities within the nation are thus positioned equally to take part in government, since all must conduct the business of government in a language other than their own. In Nigeria, for instance, the constitution of 1963 asserts that "the business of Parliament shall be conducted in English," and many other former colonies in Africa— among them Ghana, Sierra Leone, Tanzania, Uganda, and Zambia—have adopted similar policies.

In many of these countries, however, the use of English in the national legislature is likely to be temporary, though changes may be repeatedly postponed, as has happened in India. In 1977, Nigeria adopted a National Policy on Education that is a harbinger of such change. Though this policy is written in English, it anticipates a day when multilingualism will make the continued use of English unnecessary:

> In addition to appreciating the importance of language in the educational process, and as a means of preserving the people's culture, the Government considers it to be in the interest of national unity that each child should be encouraged to learn one of the three major languages other than his own mother tongue. In this connection, the Government considers the three major languages in Nigeria to be Hausa, Ibo and Yoruba. (Federal Republic of Nigeria 5)[2]

Significantly, the rationale for this policy invokes both "national unity"—with the implication that a trilingual policy is preferable to the use of English in maintaining that unity—and the desirability of "preserving the people's culture." However excellent English may be for expressing African "identity," as Senghor asserted, the alien ideas that erode "the people's culture" come at least in part from the continued use of English in national affairs.

To this point, I have examined three principal rationales for the spread and maintenance of English around the world: its intrinsic virtues, its utilitarian value in economic development, and its role as an ostensibly neutral language in the internal affairs of multilingual nations. All three are profoundly political, and the future of English will itself be a matter of overt or unconscious policy decisions.

If English is merely another in a long series of "world languages," we need to examine the political events that accompanied the preservation, decline, or change in those other languages. In every case, their fate was directly connected with political affairs. Turkish, for example, disappeared from the territory of the Ottoman Empire (where it had been used for five hundred years) because local leaders in Palestine and Egypt perceived few benefits in abandoning their own languages in favor of it. The use of Turkish in such places was limited to matters of government and military command, and the political and social order did little to encourage its use in artistic endeavors, family settings, and other areas where it could have displaced the established, indigenous languages. With the collapse of the Ottoman Empire, local elites were still obliged to cope with foreign governors, this time ones speaking English or French, until those colonial rulers were likewise displaced and the Arabic of Cairo and Damascus finally emerged as the language of independent governments. Such an example suggests that if a world language is restricted to dealings between local leaders and a foreign elite, it will not take root unless the acquisition of that foreign language appears to benefit the local population and gives them access to significant political power (see Brosnahan).

Not all world languages necessarily follow the pattern of Turkish, eventually becoming extinct in areas freed from the influence of an empire. Languages may come to occupy a permanent and central place in the affairs of nations quite far removed from the political and cultural domain to which they were originally attached. For such languages to remain in use, however, the speakers of indigenous languages must be driven far from the sources of wealth and power, a situation well illustrated by several of the languages of northwestern Europe—Irish, Welsh, Scots Gaelic, Breton, and Basque. In their place, the languages of invaders have taken hold and effectively displaced or severely restricted them, a West Germanic language evolving into English and Latin into French and Spanish. Yet while the speakers of these world languages took up permanent residence in new territory, their languages were subject to significant change. Their history followed the linguistic principle articulated by Edward Sapir:

> No known language, unless it be artificially preserved for liturgical or other nonpopular uses, has ever been known to resist the tendency to split up into dialects, any one of which may in the long run assume the status of an independent language. (169)

In forming estimates about the future development of English, we need to guess just what time might be encompassed by Sapir's notion of "the long run." British English and American English, for instance, have been politically separated for more than two hundred years, and each of them constitutes a distinct dialect of English. Yet despite the nationalistic opinions of such linguistic patriots as Noah Webster and H. L. Mencken, no one would argue seriously that American

English constitutes an "independent language" and presents significant barriers to communication for a speaker of British English. Nonetheless, it would be a serious mistake to adopt an anglocentric view in which English in Britain, Ireland, and North America is seen as the norm of linguistic evolution. At least ten percent of those who make daily use of English live in Asia and Africa, and the relative proportion of that group will increase in the future. To judge by the experience of the recent past, the rate of change in the Northern Hemisphere will probably be relatively slow, while the rate in the Southern Hemisphere is likely to be relatively rapid, thus increasing the overall diversity of English and leading to the emergence first of new local standards and subsequently of one or, more likely, several independent languages.

Most observers view the splitting up of English into dialects as a threat to the welfare of the English-using community. The following characterization of that process by the British Council, the government agency charged with promoting English language and culture abroad, captures the tone of such pronouncements:

> In becoming a world language English, some say, like any other common currency, runs the risk of becoming worn, debased and subject to counterfeit. Its stamp is no longer authentic; it loses its clarity; it may become unrecognisable. Purists may claim that the quality of English spoken abroad must necessarily degenerate as it spreads, so that eventually the English of different overseas groups will become unintelligible to other users of English, including the English themselves. Alternatively, some think the potential resources of common communication provided by world-English may shrink to those of a global pidgin—a mere ghost of the English we know. (5)

The comparison drawn by the council between language and coinage is no accident; it fits the fears of generations of English users that, by some sort of linguistic Gresham's law, the circulation of "bad language" will debase English by driving out the "good language." Anxiety about "unintelligible" English has perplexed observers for nearly four hundred years; the catastrophe is not yet upon us. The range of diversity in the English of Africa, Asia, and the Caribbean, however, has increased in postcolonial times and is likely to increase still further in this decade.

Contending forces in the separate communities of English users promote or retard linguistic change. In many former British colonies, members of the ruling elite vehemently deny that the "best English" of their nations deviates from the norms of educated London usage. Local varieties, they say, even those institutionalized in written English, result from "imperfect learning," interference arising from local languages, or "slovenly" linguistic habits; however, local innovations abound: words borrowed from the languages of the country, new coinages from the existing word stock of English, distinctive pronunciations that result from additions to or deletions from the inventory of English sounds, differing distribution of sound segments, and archaic or novel uses that affect the grammatical system. Such distinctive local characteristics, however, seldom gain much currency outside the nation or region, usually because the persons whose speech or writing has the most distinctively local flavor have the fewest opportunities to communicate with outsiders who might in turn mimic these usages and introduce them into the mainstream.[3]

A picture of the present state of English in the third world resembles the pyramid figure used by sociologists to represent social class. Those near the apex of the pyramid—the social, cultural, and political elite—are likely to have international contacts and to communicate regularly with persons of similar social class from other English-using communities. Since the elite draws its linguistic norms from the prestige dialect of England, its English tends toward relative uniformity and supports the impression of a relatively uniform English language around the world. Individuals lower on the pyramid, however, are likely to diverge in their usage from the elite and to represent more localized varieties of English. It is from members of this group, then, that divergent standards begin to emerge, and from their innovations English will eventually divide into dialects that will take on "the status of independent languages" that Sapir saw as inevitable.

The varying rates of change in the different varieties of English depend on the extent to which English becomes associated with distinct and localized national identities. For many English users in the third world, English is both a source of prestige and a source of conflict with important cultural values. As long as English is seen as merely a vehicle through which science and technology are received by specialists in development, local cultural values are not necessarily disturbed. Yet even in the technical domain, the choice of accent in spoken English (and the parallel use of spelling conventions) depends on an ideological choice. Many third-world countries continue to promote accents and spelling from British sources, not only because many of them are emerging from the status of British client states but also because the decline of Great Britain as a world power makes British English less clearly value-laden than American English is. The same principle applies to countries in which English is primarily acquired as a second language; the Soviet Union, for instance, promotes British norms in its schools since those conventions seem less in conflict with its national objectives than American pronunciations and spellings are. Continued use of British English, then, however remote the linguistic connections, diminishes or at least delays the conflict between local and foreign values that is implicit in the use of English in the third world.

The conflict of values between local identity and foreign ideology will also have an important influence on the extent to which English is learned and used in third-world countries. The present situation is clearly illustrated in Singapore, where English is one of four official languages recognized in the Independence Act of 1965.[4] By 1975, fifty-six percent of the adult population could "understand" English, and English was especially common as the second language of those receiving the highest incomes (77.5% of the high-income group but only 35.3%

of the low-income group understood English). Despite the relatively wide knowledge of English in the country, the conflict between local and foreign values inherent in its use produces a startling paradox. English, as Eddie C. Y. Kuo explains,

> is associated with Western culture and Western values, and thus is perceived to be the language of modernity, progress, technology and economic development. At the same time, a prevalent view in Singapore sees that English is related to the decadent "Western" values of materialism, hippyism, sex, drugs and violence. (23)

These contending values animate policy discussions in third-world governments that will have far reaching effects on the use of English. Whatever balance is achieved between the positive and negative implications of speaking and writing English, the choice of any foreign language in government and education is a product of the equation between national and international forces. What the prime minister of Singapore, Lee Kuan Yew, recognized a decade ago will shape the future of all world languages: the "detrimental effects of deculturalization" that accompany the choice of *any* foreign language. Prime Minister Lee foresaw that general use of any such language may result in "anaemic, uprooted floating citizens without the social cohesiveness and the cultural impetus that give the people the drive and the will to succeed as a group" (quoted by Kuo 25).

Any estimate of the future of English must necessarily take into account likely developments in the growth and distribution of world population. Data compiled by the United Nations estimated that population at 3.6 billion in 1970, when three fourths of the world's people lived in "less developed countries." By the year 2000, the population is likely to reach 6.2 billion, with the greatest increase in those nations. As Philip M. Hauser points out, the less developed countries "may, in the course of little more than one human generation, between 1970 and 2000, increase by almost as many people as were on the entire globe in 1950" (13). Urban areas in particular will be subject to growth through migration and normal population increases. In 1960, four of the ten most populous urban areas in the world were predominantly English-speaking; by 1990, only one of these cities will remain among the top ten (Tapinos 23).[5]

Educational institutions in the United States and Great Britain are now struggling to maintain their present level of success in teaching citizens the skills of literacy, and even if additional funds make it possible to mount special programs to increase the proportion of the literate population, the incremental costs of such efforts will require a major investment. How much greater the problems will be on a global scale is only suggested by the population estimates. Third-world countries are increasingly unable to provide food and shelter for growing populations. Even their most effective literacy programs must compete for the scarce resources that provide basic necessities, and many countries will be unable to provide increases in education proportionate to their growth in population.

Short-term predictions—ones that deal only with people now alive—are characterized by a kind of Malthusian gloom, particularly when the need for increasingly sophisticated literacy is more and more important in postindustrial economies. Physical labor, supported by basic nutrition, contributes a smaller share of a nation's gross national product than at any time in the past; intellectual labor, supported by specialized forms of literacy, is more valuable to a nation's well-being than at previous times. And while the allocation of food is a closed system (bounded on the upper limit by the number of calories that the population can consume), the allocation of literacy is effectively an open system (with the upper bound of human memory indefinitely extended by the technology of information processing).

World literacy, like other components of the world economy, appears to be afflicted by increased demand and declining resources. Yet two factors suggest a solution to what now seems to be a literacy "shortage": ideology and technology. All literacy programs in the past have succeeded when large numbers of the population became convinced that acquiring literacy would result in dramatic improvements in their economic and political well-being. As Carlo M. Cipolla explains in his history of literacy, most Western nations increased their investments in literacy in response to a need for skilled workers who could be trained more efficiently with the help of written materials to supplement the oral tradition of apprenticeship. Open-sea navigation required literate sailors; artillery required soldiers who could consult tables designed to calculate the proper aim for long-range gunnery.[6] In each case, nations invested in literacy to ensure that they would participate in new or more efficient technology.

A recent impulse that has animated literacy campaigns is more overtly political than the acquisition of technical skills. Among the most influential examples for third-world countries is that provided by the Soviet Union in the years following the October revolution.[7] In a decree signed in December 1919, Lenin set in motion a program by which "the entire population of the Republic between the ages of eight and fifty, incapable of reading or writing, [was] obliged to study their own or [the] Russian language." To implement that decree, all literate adults were required to take part in the instruction of illiterates, and a massive investment of time and resources helped to transform the Soviet Union from an agricultural and illiterate nation to an industrial and literate one. Yet while "modernization," the impulse that had motivated the spread of literacy in Europe, was an important factor in the campaign, the rationale for the effort was based on the relation between literacy and self-government: the goal of the edict was "to enable the entire population of the Republic to participate consciously in the country's political life" (quoted from Lenin's decree by Zinovyev and Pleshakova 92). Literacy campaigns were similarly essential, for Gandhi, in his efforts to replace the historic caste system by the institutions of a democratic government, and more recently the Brazilian educator Paulo Freire has formulated an influential "pedagogy of the oppressed" as a means of transforming totalitarian states to ones that promote human freedom.[8]

While basic literacy may well be essential for political consciousness, increasing dispersion and sophistication of literacy are not necessarily accompanied by greater freedom and more participation in governmental affairs. Though literacy may create the potential for political transformation, the institutions through which it is transmitted—the schools—promote the traditional values of a society, foster obedience to authority, and socialize the young to accept roles within the established order. Revolutionary activity, well illustrated by recent events in Kampuchea, is likely to be carried out by the marginally literate rather than by learned ideologues. With rapid increases in the numbers of people least likely to have access to schools, the overall level of literacy in the world may decline as economic and social inequality foster political instability. A century ago, only ten percent of the world population were literate; today, about seventy percent have some claim to the skills of reading and writing. Despite the profound changes that literacy has made possible, however, mass literacy may prove to be a temporary episode in human history.

In many third-world countries, unemployment among educated persons creates significant social problems. Those who are "credentialed" by secondary or higher education have difficulty in finding socially useful roles in which to exercise their literacy. At the same time they are unwilling to pursue traditional tasks for which literacy is relatively superfluous. Citizens are often unwilling to pay taxes for the education of others if they do not perceive a possibility of direct return on their investment for themselves or for their children. In such circumstances, the potential profits from the "information industries" cannot be realized. Although the technology of information has become cheaper and more generally available, it is increasingly difficult for nations to participate in the international flow of information—with its great potential for transforming economic life—since the investment in production called for by new information is drained away by competing social demands.[9]

The future of literacy in general, then, will be shaped by population growth and economic conditions. Its distribution will depend upon the investments that nations make in universal primary education and in selective secondary and higher education. Yet most third-world countries will not be in a position to develop simultaneously both universal and selective educational systems. Universal education enhances general literacy but at a level too low for citizens to function in roles that lead to increased national wealth; selective education yields economic benefits but at the expense of the egalitarian ideals that are espoused by many third-world nations.

If there are solutions to the problem of world literacy, they must be found in an ideology that both fosters literacy and transforms economic and social life so that its benefits can be achieved. In order for that ideology and the consequent rewards to be realized, however, educational systems must be made more efficient so that the same proportionate investment can serve larger numbers of people. To balance the cost-benefit equation, educational systems will need to draw on inexpensive technology to multiply the effect of teachers and to reach students who are enjoying education while participating productively in the economic life of the society. The innovations that are now being made in educational technology can have a profound effect on literacy around the world.[10]

The ways in which nations choose to respond to economic and social conditions will profoundly affect the distribution of literacy in local languages and in world languages. Mass primary education in the third world will increase literacy in national languages and decrease the role for English; selective secondary and higher education will maintain or increase the role of English as long as its use does not overtly conflict with local values and national ideals. Perhaps the most likely future role for literacy in English will involve a further reduction in the functional domains in which it is used. In East Africa, for instance, the number of families using English in the home has decreased almost to the vanishing point; English is the language of school and of public affairs for many members of the elite, but it is not the vehicle for communication in their most cherished personal relations. In the oil fields of the Middle East, English is limited to fewer and fewer engineers and technicians, who use it only for the narrowly constrained purposes of their occupations. Instructional programs for foreign teachers in the United States and Great Britain have replaced their former emphasis on the skills of spoken English with the more limited domain of "English for special purposes," those connected with the written language and with the fields of science and technology. Literature written in English by third-world authors may continue to appeal to an international audience, but the contending claims of English and a local language are likely to be resolved in favor of the indigenous language or of so local an English that it will not be accessible to readers abroad.[11]

The questions posed at the beginning of this essay cannot easily be answered. It is likely, however, that in the next decade proportionately fewer persons will use English on the international scene and that those who do will limit their speaking, reading, and writing of English to a smaller number of functional domains. In the developed world, English is likely to expand as a lingua franca at the expense of other languages that now have some currency outside their traditional territory (just as it has already replaced German as the language essential for participation in international scientific work). In the less developed world, English may continue as an important international language, but it is likely that fewer national leaders and legislative bodies will employ it in the affairs of government. Reading and writing in some language will be more important as economies move toward greater technical sophistication, but the use of English is likely to diminish as work is rationalized into well-defined tasks and local languages are adapted to technical domains, perhaps through loanwords from English, to accommodate the need for written communications in the workplace. The hegemony of English that has steadily grown with the increase in global communications is now beginning to diminish and will shrink further in the immediate future.

If these speculations are correct, we need to increase our national investment in instructing American citizens in foreign languages. Historically, humble sellers have learned the languages of their powerful customers; as the United States becomes more dependent on foreign goods and raw materials and as we attempt to compete as a supplier in international trade, our citizens will no longer be able to assume that English is the dominant language of the world.

Notes

[1] Two extrinsic circumstances provide a context for Senghor's remarks: they were made on the occasion of his receiving an honorary degree from Oxford; and when he first published the text of his speech, he chose to write in French.

[2] I am grateful to Abiodun Goke-Pariola for bringing this document to my attention.

[3] For a detailed account of the present-day diversity (and unity) of English around the world, see Bailey and Görlach. These matters were vigorously debated at the beginning of this century by Matthews, Schinz, and Guérard.

[4] The other official languages are Malay, Mandarin, and Tamil. Malay, however, is the national language and is used, for instance, in military commands and for the national anthem.

[5] The ten most populous urban areas in 1960 were those surrounding New York, London, Tokyo, the Rhine-Ruhr valleys, Shanghai, Paris, Buenos Aires, Los Angeles, Moscow, and Chicago; 84.7 million people lived in these cities. In 1990, the ranking of the most populous urban areas is expected to be: Tokyo, Mexico City, New York, São Paulo, Shanghai, Seoul, Peking, Rio de Janeiro, Calcutta, and Bombay; 168.2 million people will live in these metropolitan areas. In 1970, thirty-eight percent of the world's population lived in cities; by 1990, the United Nations estimates that forty-five percent of the population will live in them (Tapinos 33).

[6] The same demand for aiming tables inspired the development of computers during World War II.

[7] In an overview of literacy campaigns in India, S. V. Ayyar opens his remarks with the sentence "It was Lenin who stated that education and electricity would transform the economy of a country from an agricultural one to an industrialised one" (68).

[8] Literacy campaigns are usually motivated by ideological themes in societies that are (or aspire to be) democratic or socialist. The following, from an act adopted by the government of Iraq in 1974, is typical:

> The high rate of illiteracy among citizens, particularly in rural areas, is considered to be the most serious and dangerous constraint impeding the political, economic, and social progression of the country. With the present high rate of illiteracy, it is impossible to raise the standard of the masses, build up an advanced revolutionary society capable of confronting the problems of the age and its complicated requisites. It is also not possible for our country to contribute to the building up of a united socialist Arab nation. Therefore, the fight against illiteracy within the shortest possible time is considered the most important sphere of our struggle and activities. (quoted by Oxenham 17)

Modern statements in opposition to mass literacy are uncommon, but the attack in 1807 by the president of the Royal Society on a proposal to introduce universal elementary education in England doubtless receives tacit approval in some modern nations:

> However specious in theory the project might be of giving education to the labouring classes of the poor, it would in effect be found to be prejudicial to their morals and happiness; it would teach them to despise their lot in life, instead of making them good servants in agriculture, and other laborious employment to which their rank in society had destined them; instead of teaching them subordination, it would render them factious and refractory, as was evident in the manufacturing counties; it would enable them to read seditious pamphlets, vicious books, and publications against Christianity; it would render them insolent to their superiors; and in a few years the result would be that the legislature would find it necessary to direct the strong arm of power toward them. (quoted by Cipolla 65-66)

[9] In *Education for Self-Reliance* (1967), President Julius K. Nyerere of Tanzania recognized the difficulties of adapting the structures of mass education found in developed countries in the conditions to the third world:

> Every penny spent on education is money taken away from some other needed activity— whether it is an investment in the future, better medical services, or just more food, clothing and comfort for our citizens at present. And the truth is that there is no possibility of Tanzania being able to increase the proportion of the national income which is spent on education; it ought to be decreased. (quoted by Blaug 376-77)

Some appreciation of the magnitude of the investment required for an effective literacy campaign may be gained from a recent decision by the government of Menufia province in the Nile delta in Egypt:

> The local council of the Menufia Governorate took a decision considered to be the first of its kind, stipulating the cancellation of literacy classes till the law of combatting illiteracy is amended by official authorities.
> Members of the Menufia governorate local council said that results of these classes are not conforming with their volume of expenditures. According to Dr. Abdul Dayem el Ansari, member of the NP Education Committee, 29,100,000 are still illiterate [in Egypt as a whole], 70 per cent of whom are youths.
> The number of illiterates is increasing by 500,000 annually and the numbers of primary schools drop-outs is rapidly growing each year, reaching 250,000 in 1981, Dr. Ansari said. ("New Approach to Literacy Drive" 3)

[10] In one of the most penetrating investigations of the social impact of computers and satellite communication, Simon Nora foresees significant changes in educational systems that may result from new technology:

> The development of computerizations on a mass scale may transform pedagogy and thereby the status of teaching personnel. . . . Specialization will fade away and levels of teaching will become more diversified, modifying the rigid statutory requirements on which diplomas and grades are based. Education will see its function distilled to one of coordinations, while more routine pedagogical tasks will be carried out by assistants. Looking at the matter from this point of view, a whole sociological world will undergo transformation. Given the state of mind of the teaching profession, it is not surprising that this development is not self-evident; it would not in any case be rapid. (62-63).

[11] Typical of this trend is the recent work of the Kenyan novelist Ngugi wa Thiong'o. Writing of Ngugi's novel *Petals of Blood* (1977), Clifford B. Robson states:

Ngugi's tendency in this novel, then, to adopt the frequent use of Gikuyu and Swahili words and phrases without feeling the need to explain them, is important not only for Ngugi's writing but for African literature as a whole, since it will ultimately fashion the "new English" that Achebe refers to in *Morning Yet on Creation Day*, "altered to suit its new African surroundings." (106)

See also Ngugi's essay "On the Abolition of the English Department."

Works Cited

Ayyar, S. V. "Literacy and Socio-economic Development." In *Seminar on Eradication of Illiteracy*. New Delhi: India International Centre, 1968, 68-75.

Bailey, Richard W., and Manfred Görlach, eds. *English as a World Language*. Ann Arbor: Univ. of Michigan Press, 1982.

Blaug, Mark. "The Quality of Population in Developing Countries, with Particular Reference to Education and Training." In *World Population and Development: Challenges and Prospects*. Ed. Philip M. Hauser. Syracuse, N.Y.: Syracuse Univ. Press, 1979, 361-402.

British Council. *The English Language Abroad*. London: The British Council, 1961.

Brosnahan, L. F. "Some Historical Cases of Language Imposition." 1963; rpt. in *Varieties of Present-Day English*. Ed. Richard W. Bailey and Jay L. Robinson. New York: Macmillan, 1973, 40-55.

Cipolla, Carlo M. *Literacy and Development in the West*. Harmondsworth: Penguin, 1969.

Conrad, Andrew W., and Joshua A. Fishman. "English as a World Language: The Evidence." In *The Spread of English*. Ed. Joshua A. Fishman, Robert L. Cooper, and Andrew W. Conrad. Rowley, Mass.: Newbury House, 1977, 3-76.

Federal Republic of Nigeria. *National Policy on Education*. Lagos: Federal Ministry of Information, 1977.

Freire, Paulo. *Pedagogy of the Oppressed*. 1967. Trans. Myra Bergman Ramos. New York: Seabury, 1979.

Gandhi, M. K. *The Collected Works of Mahatma Gandhi*. Delhi: Ministry of Information and Broadcasting, 1958—.

Guérard, Albert Leon. "English as an International Language." *Popular Science Monthly* 79(1911):337-45.

Hauser, Philip M. "Introduction and Overview." In *World Population and Development: Challenges and Propects*. Ed. Philip M. Hauser. Syracuse, N.Y.: Syracuse Univ. Press, 1979, 1-62.

Kuo, Eddie C. Y. "The Status of English in Singapore: A Sociolinguistic Analysis." In *The English Language in Singapore*. Ed. William Crewe. Singapore: Eastern Universities Press, 1977, 10-33.

Matthews, Brander. "English as a World-Language." *Century Magazine* 76(1908):430-35.

Mulcaster, Richard. *The First Part of the Elementarie Which Entreateth Chefelie of the Right Writing of Our English Tung.* 1582. Rpt., ed. E. T. Campagnac. Oxford: Clarendon, 1925.

"New Approach to Literacy Drive." *The Egyptian Mail* (Cairo), 1 Jan. 1983, 3.

Ngugi wa Thiong'o. "On the Abolition of the English Department." 1968. In *Homecoming: Essays on African and Caribbean Literature, Culture and Politics.* By Ngugi wa Thiong'o. New York: Lawrence Hill, 1972, 144-50.

Nora, Simon, and Alain Minc. *The Computerization of Society: A Report to the President of France.* 1978. Cambridge: MIT Press, 1980.

Oxenham, John. *Literacy: Writing, Reading and Social Organisation.* London: Routledge and Kegan Paul, 1980.

Quirk, Randolph. "Language and Nationhood." In *The Crown and the Thistle.* Ed. C. Maclean. Edinburgh: Scottish Academic Press, 1979, 57-70.

Robson, Clifford B. *Ngugi wa Thiong'o.* New York: St. Martin's, 1979.

Sapir, Edward. "Dialect." 1931; rpt. in *English Linguistics: An Introductory Reader.* Ed. Harold Hungerford, Jay Robinson, and James Sledd. Glenview, Ill.: Scott, Foresman, 1979, 168-74.

Schinz, Albert. "Will English Be the International Language?" *North American Review* 189(1909):760-70.

Senghor, Leopold S. "The Essence of Language: English and French." *Culture* 2.2(1975):75-98.

Tapinos, Georges. "The World in the 1980s: Demographic Perspectives." In *Six Billion People: Demographic Dilemmas and World Politics.* Ed. Georges Tapinos and Phyllis T. Piotrow. New York: McGraw-Hill, 1978, 21-79.

Tunstall, Jeremy. *The Media Are American: Anglo-American Media in the World.* London: Constable, 1977.

Zinovyev, M., and A. Pleshakova. *How Illiteracy Was Wiped Out in the U.S.S.R.* Moscow: Progress Publishers, n.d.

Literacy and Cultural Change: Some Experiences

A. L. Becker

> One thinks that one is tracing the outline of the thing's nature over and over again, and one is merely tracing round the frame through which we look at it.[1]
>
> —LUDWIG WITTGENSTEIN

This essay is a set of variations on Wittgenstein's observation about the scope of language, particularly the scope of the language one thinks with. The variations have to do with other kinds of literacy and are grounded in sometimes painful experience.

I was recently reading an essay by the anthropologist Elizabeth A. Brandt, who has spent many years studying the languages of the Native Americans of the Southwest. In her essay "Native American Attitudes toward Literacy and Recording in the Southwest," she says, "Until I was able to distance myself a little from graphocentrism, I could not conceive how anyone could seriously question the value of writing, recording, and literacy." Such an experience can only intensify one's understanding of Wittgenstein's observation. But how does one distance oneself from graphocentrism, even a little? It is very difficult to do as a mind experiment—just thinking about it. I suspect that few of us know what giving up graphocentrism entails. I won't try to retell Elizabeth Brandt's stories about the proud and secure orality of some Native Americans in the Southwest; I will turn instead to some of my own experiences in Southeast Asia, not with oral people, but with people with a different kind of literacy from the one I learned in America and took completely for granted until I began to learn Burmese, Indonesian, and, now, Javanese.

(I almost wrote that my experience was not with preliterate people but with people at a different stage of literacy than we are in. Notice how ethnocentric that is: are there stages of literacy? I recall Jean-Paul Sartre: "Progress, that long steep path which leads to me" (21). What I would like to call into question is just that powerful plot: that "progress" proceeds, and must proceed, from orality to writing to printing to secondary orality, which is what Walter Ong calls our television culture. To call that plot into question is to doubt our own version of history—our own "tracing round the frame through which we look at" things—

but perhaps that is what distancing oneself a little from graphocentrism may require, right at the start.)

One of my first experiences with literacy I didn't understand until nearly twenty years later.[2] It was in Burma, and I was a young Fulbright teacher with an M.A. in English and an uninformed attraction to Buddhism. I began to learn Burmese from a very kind old scholar who remained my teacher for three years— and ever after. I was asking him words for things, and he would pronounce them, and I would write them down. He kept staring at my writing. I said, "How do you say 'speak?' " And he answered. I wrote down /py ɔ/. He got quite upset, more upset then than at any other time in the years he taught me. "No," he said, "you write ᒡᔥᑭ . If you want to learn from me, you must write it that way." I said, in my half-taught arrogance, "But it makes no difference." I believed, and I don't think I was the only linguist to believe it, that phonemic writing was "language neutral," as we used to put it. Fortunately, my teacher prevailed and I learned Burmese writing. What difference did it make?

It made several differences, some of which I am only beginning to understand. First of all, it was impossible to do linguistics on his writing. /p/ is in the center, /y/ is wrapped around /p/, and /ɔ/ is half in front and half behind /p/. How do I segment that? How do I do linguistics and not segment the stream of speech into units? In order to study Burmese I had to put it into phonemic notation, behind my teacher's back. It was my problem, not his.

His problem, I came much later to realize, was much deeper. A decade later, in Bali, I learned that all knowledge is arranged around one figure: a center and four (or more) points around it; above, below, and on the two sides of the center.[3] (I won't say "before" and "after" since that reverses in translation.) A compass rose is one of its manifestations. On that figure, besides the directions North, South, East, West, and Center, there are overlaid parts of the body, days of the week, stages of life, colors, illnesses, places, professions, and much else— all the categories of knowledge, in fact. It is, until today, the mnemonic and rhetorical framework for the many Southeast Asians who retain the old writing. The basic iconography of that framework is the written symbol. It is divine beyond even gods—the essence of divinity in Bali. Mary Zurbuchen has carefully unfolded some of the implications of that epistemology, so radically different from our own. Here are some excerpts from her translation of the invocation of a Balinese shadow play, a traditional theater which is taught and performed orally. It is a declaration of obeisance to the written symbol as a source of power.[4]

> Just as the boundaries of awareness become perceptible,
> There is perfect tranquillity, undisturbed by any threat,
> And even the utterances of the gods subside.
> It is none other which forms the beginning of my obeisance to the Divine.
> Greatly may I be forgiven for my intention to call forth a story.
> And where dwells the story?
> There is a god unsupported by the divine mother earth,

Unsheltered by the sky,
Unilluminated by the sun, moon, stars, or constellations.
Yes, Lord, you dwell in the void, and are situated thus:
You reside in a golden jewel,
Regaled on a golden palanquin,
Umbrellaed by a floating lotus.
There approached in audience by all the gods of the cardinal directions. . . .

These last lines, after locating the written symbol outside time and space, describe metaphorically the shaping of the written symbol as a focal point for natural order. Zurbuchen's translation continues, describing the implements of writing:

There, there are the young palm leaves, the one *lontar,*
Which, when taken and split apart, carefully measured are the lengths and
    widths.
It is this which is brought to life with *hasta, gangga, uwira, tanu.*
And what are the things so named? *Hasta* means 'hand'
Gangga means 'water'
Uwira means 'writing instrument'
Tanu means 'ink'.
What is that which is called 'ink'?
That is the name for
And none other than
The smoke of the oil lamp,
Collected on the bark of the kepuh-tree,
On a base of copper leaf.
It is these things which are gathered together
and given shape on leaf.
'Written symbol' is its name,
Of one substance and different soundings. . . . (vi-viii)

The translation, which I have taken the liberty of arranging in lines (mainly to slow down the reader), goes on slowly to evolve the story from the written symbol.

My point, however, is not to explore this image further or to recount Zurbuchen's stories but to try to understand why my teacher insisted on my learning Burmese his way. I think it was that traditional learning was organized around that shape, that it was a root metaphor,[5] the stuff that holds learning together—just as our sequential writing lines up so well with our sequential tense system and our notions of causality and history. That is a great deal to ask anyone to give up—the metaphoric power of his writing system. And I had tried to argue with that wise old man that it didn't matter.

One of the most subtle forces of colonialism, ancient or modern, is to undermine not just the substance but the framework of someone's learning. As Gregory Bateson put it, in his oft-quoted letter to the other regents of the University of California, "Break the pattern which connects the items of learning and you necessarily destroy all quality" (8).[6] I see now that what I had been suggesting to my teacher, though neither of us could articulate it, was that we break the pattern that connects the items of his learning. Going from one literacy to another, like going from orality to literacy, as many have pointed out, is not mere technology but a major break in the pattern that connects the items of learning.

What replaces that pattern is something deeply alien. As Spolsky and Irvine put it in describing American colonialism:

> the functions of literacy among the Navaho have been directly linked to religious beliefs alien to their culture, information about colonial government policies such as stock reductions and relocation, and now transitional programs.

Writing has come to Southeast Asia several times,[7] each time with a different religion, a different calendar, a different understanding of language, and a different philology (a different collection of canonic or classical texts, and texts about texts—that is, grammars and dictionaries—to explain old, distant texts).[8] The differing experiences of Sanskrit, Arabic, and English-French-Dutch-Portuguese (hyphenated by their Roman writing system) are too vast to even outline here. One might note as but one important difference that with Sanskrit the language itself is divine, not, as with the others, only certain texts. In the Sanskritic set of beliefs about language, the writing, the grammar, and the categories of language are true and eternal: the ground of all being as the Balinese quotation earlier told us. Imagine powerful aliens arriving here and telling us, with the support of some strange new medium, that the rest of the universe spoke their language, Classical Universe. But my point is not that. It is that writing involves more than technology, and more than what most would call language.

A writing system affects, deeply, the whole of what Walter Ong has called the noetic process—the shaping, storage, retrieving, and communication of knowledge. We in the literate West have had the luxury of long, cumulative noetic stability. Our philology is vast and relatively accessible, and change has been cumulative rather than replacive. We are not unique in this (and it should not form the basis for a new superiority myth), yet for many in the world the modes of shaping, storing, retrieving, and communicating knowledge have changed at least once in their lifetimes. That is, they have learned a new writing system—and its attendant philology—in replacement (as a source of truth) of their birthright noetic modes. In much of the former colonial world, literacy today means exclusively literacy in the Roman writing system.

My goal is not to argue for or against literacy, Roman or Pallava, but to explore what it means to distance oneself from a particular graphocentrism and to learn from what are, after all, my own mistakes. I give the examples not to romanticize Southeast Asia but to expose those mistakes. The unquestionably beautiful and once powerful Sanskritic cultures of Southeast Asia may be just relics, but try to convince a modern Balinese of that. I have tried and have received smiles of ageless patience.

Few of us know what it entails to distance ourselves from our particular brand of graphocentrism: it entails giving up powerful modes of analysis; giving up a basic mnemonic framework; giving up basic images of nature, icons, and root metaphors; and breaking the pattern that connects the items of learning. I am sure that as we explore comparative philology in the coming years, this list of entailments will seem short. Many of the implications of Wittgenstein's observation have yet even to be recognized.

Notes

[1] The original German reads as follows:

> Man glaubt, wieder und wieder der Natur nachzufahren, und fahrt nur der Form entlang, durch die wir sie betrachten.

Note the person shift (in both English and German) and what it does to the force of the sentence.

[2] In studying "the frame" (in Wittgenstein's sense) it is difficult to avoid discussing personal experience, since the frame is as important to observe as the thing framed. One becomes aware of the frame each time one enters another language, particularly one distant from one's own, and this is a uniquely personal experience, I suspect. At this point it is difficult to separate personal constraints on the frame from cultural (i.e., lingual) ones. And this is also why I must move from one language to another in this essay: I am studying cross-cultural understanding, and many lessons only came after one language had already been "learned." The essay has always been the genre for learning through personal experience.

[3] I am deeply indebted to Patricia Henry and Mary Zurbuchen for a great deal of my understanding of this image. Henry first gathered together prior research that discussed this issue in an unpublished essay. Much of this work was based on Clifford Geertz's "Person, Time and Conduct in Bali."

For further elaboration and insight into this image, see, among others, Covarrubias 296, Mershon 57-66, Hooykaas *Agama Tirtha* 133-37 (explanation of fig. 12). In Java, the image is related to verse form and village layout; see Pigeaud 1:20 and Kartomi 44. On the notion of an image as a focus of research, see Kenneth Boulding.

[4] Zurbuchen's dissertation describes in detail Balinese thought about language. See also Hooykass, *Kama and Kala,* for translations and explanations of similar invocations.

[5] For a detailed study of root metaphors in English, see George Lakoff and Mark Johnson.

[6] Note that transliterating Southeast Asian texts into Roman letters necessarily breaks the pattern that connects the items of learning, from the perspective of the Southeast Asian, necessary as it may be for Western scholars.

[7] For details of the history of writing in Southeast Asia, see Casparis, Chhabra, Holle, and Pigeaud 3:1-80.

[8] On the use of philology to mean a set of classical and canonical texts and commentaries, see Kroeber 215-35.

Works Cited

Bateson, Gregory, *Mind and Nature*. New York: Dutton, 1979.

Boulding, Kenneth. *The Image*. Ann Arbor: Univ. of Michigan Press, 1956.

Brandt, Elizabeth A. "Native American Attitudes toward Literacy and Recording in the Southwest." *Journal of the Linguistic Association of the Southwest,* forthcoming.

Casparis, J. G. de. *Indonesian Palaeography*. Leiden: E. J. Brill, 1975.

Chhabra, B. Ch. *Expansion of Indo-Aryan Culture during Pallava Rule*. Delhi: Munshi Ram Manohar Lal, 1965.

Covarrubias, Miguel. *The Island of Bali*. New York: Knopf, 1937.

Geertz, Clifford. "Person, Time and Conduct in Bali." In his *The Interpretation of Cultures*. New York: Basic, 1973, 360-411.

Henry, Patricia. " 'The Image' in Javanese Myth and Music." (1977). Unpublished essay.

———. "The Old Javanese Kakawin Arjuna Wiwaha." Diss. Univ. of Michigan 1981.

Holle, K. F. *Tabel van Oud- en Nieuw-Indische Alphabetten*. Batavia: W. Bruning, 1882.

Hooykaas, C. *Agama Tirtha: Five Studies in Hindu-Balinese Religion*. Amsterdam: N. V. Noord-Hollandsche Uitgevers Maatschappij, 1964.

———. *Kama and Kala*. Amsterdam: North Holland Publishing, 1973.

Kartomi, Margaret. *Matjapat Songs in Central and West Java*. Canberra: Australian National Univ. Press, 1973.

Kroeber, A. L. *Configurations of Cultural Growth*. Berkeley: Univ. of California Press, 1944.

Lakoff, George, and Mark Johnson. *Metaphors We Live By*. Chicago: Univ. of Chicago Press, 1980.

Mershon, K. "Five Great Elementals: Pancha Maha Buta." In *Traditional Balinese Culture*. Ed. Jane Belo. New York: Columbia Univ. Press, 1970.

Ong, Walter J. "African Talking Drums and Oral Noetics." In his *Interfaces of the Word: Studies in the Evolution of Consciousness and Culture*. Ithaca, N.Y.: Cornell Univ. Press, 1977, 92-120.

Pigeaud, Theodore G. Th. *Literature of Java*. The Hague: M. Nijhoff. Vol. 1, 1967; Vol. 3, 1970.

Sartre, Jean-Paul. *The Words*. Trans. Bernard Frechtman. Greenwich, Conn.: Fawcett, 1964.

Spolsky, Bernard, and Patricia Irvine. "Sociolinguistic Aspects of Literacy in the Vernacular." In *Speaking, Singing, and Teaching*. Proceedings of SWALLOW VIII. Anthropological Research Papers. Arizona State Univ. 1980.

Wittgenstein, Ludwig. *Philosophical Investigations*. Trans. G. E. M. Anscombe. New York: Macmillan, 1958.

Zurbuchen, Mary. "The Shadow Theater of Bali: Explorations in Language and Text." Diss. Univ. of Michigan 1981.

The Insiders

Edwin J. Delattre

All humanity is made up of two classes of people: the insiders and the outsiders. The insiders of the world have the power to learn their way about and to gain access to the meaning and significance of ideas and events. The outsiders are eternally strangers to such meaning.

We all enter life as beginners. The insiders are those whose beginnings lead them beyond themselves to overcome the ignorance that typifies beginners. They are the ones who can learn for themselves but are not constrained to learn all by themselves, because much of the intelligibility of the world is given to them through the experience, expression, and insight of those who have gone before. The outsiders are those who must, from beginning to end, rely almost entirely on their own devices. The fundamental bond that unites progressive generations of insiders is language and the knowledge and skills that language delivers. The key to getting inside is literacy, the ability to read and write and, with it, to listen and speak.

The advancement of reading and writing is not a sufficient goal of education, but it is a necessary one and must not be neglected. Current uses of the word "reading" explain this necessity. We now speak of "reading" defenses in football, of "reading" situations in police work, of "reading" facial expressions, of "reading" a person like a book. These uses of "reading" remind us that the ability to read is akin to the ability to make sense of or find meaning in events or circumstances of any imaginable kind. Failure to read amounts to a kind of isolation, a sort of solitary confinement that promises deprivation of much of what is fine and instructive in the heritage of human beings.

Mark Van Doren observed that a genuinely educated person is one who could refound his or her own civilization. To be unable to read is to be farthest away from this ideal, to be cut off throughout life from a basic understanding of civilization. It was not always so, and it is not entirely the case where rich oral traditions flourish and where oral literature is part of the life of a community. But in large measure it is so. And for those who are so exiled, so distinctly outsiders, experience and grasp of the world are destined to be frail and disjointed; people, events, principles, policies are likely to appear forever as "buzzing, blooming confusion." Worse, they may never be able to identify things that are sensible and clear or to distinguish them from things that are truly confusing or perplexing. And so they are not likely to be able to identify worthwhile problems or set out to solve them.

Thus, in the sense that literacy gives access, it is a blessing; it lets us inside where we have an opportunity to see and appreciate what is possible for us. It lets us reach each other. It makes us the heirs and beneficiaries of civilization.

The problem for education, of course, is that many outsiders do not even know they are outsiders; they think the world is for everyone as it is for them. The challenge for teachers (parents, relatives, friends, classroom teachers) is to draw the outsiders far enough inside to detect the difference. Learners must have the chance to know with brilliant clarity what it feels like to be outsiders and to know that they are outsiders. This experience is central to the passion to learn.

To experience this feeling for a poignant moment, look at a page in a language that is utterly foreign to you or in an alphabet you do not know or look at a page of equations beyond your present grasp. Watch a game whose rules and practices you do not know or look at a painting or sculpture by an artist you do not understand. Inspect a complex scientific experiment where the hypothesis being tested is unknown to you or watch a skilled craftsman perform a task unfamiliar to you. These sorts of moments constitute the experience of recognizing oneself as an outsider, and if teachers choose them well they generate healthy interest rather than idle curiosity in the student. They nurture the desire, the earnest desire, to know and understand—to get inside.

The principal tasks of educators and families are to show that there is an inside and an outside, to enable outsiders to recognize themselves for what they are, and to invite them warmly and humbly to the inside. The opportunities to succeed at these tasks are limitless—telling fascinating stories, providing toys that raise questions, teaching how to read a chessboard or a pool table and moving by analogy to books and works of art, solving a problem by using a manual, finding engaging places to visit by securing written information about local geography and history, reducing grocery costs by reading unit prices, examining catalogs to discover the best available bicycles or skates, reading directions of how to assemble and fly a kite or a model rocket. Offering worthwhile and engaging invitations takes imagination, patience, time, and, for youngsters who are outsiders only because of their youth, very little else. For youngsters and others who are outsiders because of deprived backgrounds or willful refusal to learn, invitations must be even more engaging, since the admission even to oneself that one is an outsider is painful and threatening. But the principles are the same.

Powerful arguments can be made that quality of life, possibilities for enriching experience and work, and financial opportunity depend in some measure on literacy. This dependence is clear too in the well-being of a social order and in the preservation of the force and power of a constitutional heritage. Without literacy, the constitutional foundations of America would have been impossible.

Without literacy, the understanding of law, authority, rights, and limits necessary for the ideals of constitutional government to remain alive in a public cannot be maintained or secured.

But these arguments have been made in detail elsewhere, and often, and need not be rehearsed here. What needs to be emphasized is the simple, often overlooked fact that being literate is just more fun, more joyful, than being illiterate. It is more fun to be an insider than to be excluded, more fun to read than to see meaningless shapes on signboards, menus, train schedules, and the like. It is more fun to grasp language with sufficient skill to be able to understand ideas—one's own and those of others—than to be limited to a shapeless, rough vagueness about nearly everything.

It is more fun to share the intimacy made possible by the written word than to be limited to the intimacy of the spoken word, more fun to be in direct communication through their writings with human beings now long dead than to be confined to the companionship of those who can reach us only in speech. It is more fun to be able to have a telephone conversation and to read or write a love letter than to be reduced to the intimacy of telephone conversations so highly overrated by advertisements of telephone companies. No one who ever treasured a love letter or a letter from a parent or devoted friend could possibly be persuaded otherwise.

In the end, this is one of the most compelling arguments for learning itself: in general, life is more fun when we can bring powerful habits of learning into play than when we cannot. It is more fun to read Shakespeare than never to do so, more fun to understand the Declaration of Independence than not, more fun to cultivate one's mind than to waste it. It is more fun, and it is immeasurably less boring.

Habits of learning give meaning to time; they make it precious, for they reveal so much that fascinates us and leads us into the future. Even though establishing these habits of learning can be difficult and arduous (a fact that is an obstacle to becoming an insider), the established habits disclose so much that is interesting that through them life can become an ongoing and emotionally moving intellectual adventure.

John Stuart Mill observed that if you ask a man and a pig whether they would rather be a man or a pig, the man will always say a man, and the pig will always say a pig. Mill insists that the man is a better judge, because he is capable of a pig's experience while the pig is not capable of the man's. So it is with literacy and illiteracy. Ask a literate person and an illiterate one which they would rather be and the literate person will always say literate. The illiterate person's answer is not predictable; it depends on whether he or she recognizes the plight of being an outsider. Everyone who is literate has been illiterate and is accordingly qualified to judge. But the reverse is not true. And everyone is inevitably illiterate about something—some language, some system of symbols— and can accordingly be reminded by experience how much better literacy is. The ignorance of the pig may be bliss, and for the pig's sake we should hope that it is, but it is not so among us. For us, the ignorance of illiteracy amounts in practice to a combination of helplessness, impotence, and futility. It reduces to terribly limited proportions the domain of possible experience and understanding.

If the arguments of experience are not enough, the arguments for overcoming the frailty, weakness, and helplessness of being an outsider are. Examples of such frailty have always existed in abundance, and our time is no exception.

We may pause, for example, to note that there are twenty thousand practicing astrologers in America today. It is estimated that some 32 million Americans believe to some extent in the predictive value of astrology and support these astrologers. Yet the arguments that astrology is not a science, that it does not rely for its conclusions on logical procedures or publicly observable data, have been conclusive since the case against astrology was made by Favorinus and reported by Aulus Gellius in *The Attic Nights* over eighteen hundred years ago.

How is it possible that these overwhelming arguments could be in print for so long and yet be so widely without influence? How could people have access to the arguments for so long and still be duped by the charlatanry of astrology? How can it be that the wonderful exchange about astrology between Gloucester and Edmund in *King Lear* has not laid to rest forever the arrogant claims of astrology?

GLOUCESTER.   These late eclipses in the sun and moon portend no good to us. Though the wisdom of nature can reason it thus and thus, yet nature finds itself scourg'd by the sequent effects. Love cools, friendship falls off, brothers divide: in cities, mutinies; in countries, discord; in palaces, treason; and the bond crack'd 'twixt son and father. This villain of mine comes under the prediction; there's son against father: the King falls from bias of nature; there's father against child. We have seen the best of our time. Machinations, hollowness, treachery, and all ruinous disorders follow us disquietly to our graves. Find out this villain, Edmund, it shall lose thee nothing, do it carefully. And the noble and true-hearted Kent banish'd! his offence, honesty! 'Tis strange!
[Exit]
EDMUND.   This is the excellent foppery of the world, that when we are sick in fortune—often the surfeits of our own behavior—we make guilty of our disasters the sun, the moon, and stars, as if we were villains on necessity, fools by heavenly compulsion, knaves, thieves, and treachers by spherical predominance; drunkards, liars, and adulterers by an enforced obedience of planetary influence; and all that we are evil in, by a divine thrusting on. An admirable evasion of whoremaster man, to lay his goatish disposition to the charge of a star! My father compounded with my mother under the Dragon's tail, and my nativity was under Ursa Major, so it follows I am rough and lecherous. [Fut,] I should have been that I am, had the maidenl'est star in the firmament twinkled on my bastardizing.
(1.2.103-33)
". . . an admirable evasion of whoremaster man, to lay his goatish disposition

to the charge of a star." How is it possible for people to fail to be arrested by such a point?

The answers to these questions, of course, are not difficult. There are those who cannot read, and to them the insights of Favorinus and Edmund are closed. There are those who have no principles for selecting what to read, for deciding what deserves to be read, and for them most of the greatest writing ever done will never have appeal. There are those who never learn to read slowly or patiently enough to be arrested by anything, and for them, reading never takes on its full magnificence, never moves by the beautiful cogency of what is before the reader. And there are those who learn to read and write, listen and speak, but never learn to think reliably, and to them the power of evidence, the force of compelling argumentation, is largely lost. As usual, the outsiders, by these characteristics, are the victims of charlatans. They are the easy prey of the manipulators of human beings.

It is imperative to see that mere literacy is by itself not enough to get all the way inside; if it were, newspapers and books—which have appeal only to people who can read—would not include sections devoted to horoscopes and astrological signs.

Literacy is no blessing when it is attended by the vulnerability of an undisciplined mind. For this reason conscientious parents build their young children's libraries with care and deliberation. The vulnerability is eloquently described by Dorothy L. Sayers in *The Lost Tools of Learning:*

> For we let our young men and women go out unarmed, in a day when armour was never so necessary. By teaching them all to read, we have left them at the mercy of the printed word. By the invention of the film and the radio, we have made certain that no aversion to reading shall secure them from the incessant battery of words, words, words. They do not know what the words mean; they do not know how to ward them off or blunt their edge or fling them back; they are a prey to words. . . . (12)

Access to the inside, to the intelligibility of the world, calls for more than literacy. It requires critical, intelligent literacy—the ability to read slowly, to think reliably, and to select readings that are worth the candle. Access to the world of genuine understanding turns on the ability to assess arguments correctly, to see the connections between principles and the relevant circumstances of their application, and to gather evidence for oneself. Without these, the literate and the illiterate alike are truly "a prey to words"—one to the written and spoken word, the other to the spoken word alone. It is not clear which suffers the worse fate.

The same general conclusions about thinking apply to writing as well as to reading: it is not enough to be able to string words together; what is called for is a grasp of language adequate to say just what one means, in the manner of the *Federalist No. 10,* or *King Lear,* or the Sermon on the Mount, or Lincoln's letter to Mrs. Bixby, or *Madame Bovary,* or the correspondence of Adams and Jefferson, or the "I have a dream" speech of Martin Luther King, or "The Bee" of James Dickey. Clarity with eloquence is obviously not the only end of language, but it is ignored in the learning of any generation at the peril of civilization.

These are the reasons that the so-called back-to-basics movement is so shallow and so dangerous. The movement does not sufficiently emphasize mathematics, the paradigm of conclusive reasoning and certainly among the foundations of the most sophisticated universal languages of the future; it neglects logic, the study of reliable patterns of thought generally, in both technical and nontechnical discourse; it does not support forcefully the study of foreign languages; it does not encourage the study of language itself as a social and public achievement of humanity whose power goes far beyond banal exchanges of information or opinion, nor does it insist on selecting texts, for learners of all ages, that give evidence of this power; and it disdains the importance of scientific and aesthetic literacy as though they were somehow not basic. At best, it offers students a shortsighted and drab vision of the utility of learning, and, like most attempts to reduce value to utility, it diminishes the future. We do not need to go back, we need to go forward, taking advantage of the lessons of the history of education and therefore striving for intellectually and emotionally mature literacy. We need to be thorough about what is basic to becoming an educated person.

Otherwise, either we allow illiteracy to flourish by ignoring what is basic or we teach a version of the basics so simplistic and so narrow that we condemn many students to the limits of our own pale expectations of what they can learn. We condemn them to irreverence for language, indifference to the liberal and fine arts, and to distance from the most powerful disciplines of discovery and reflection known to us. Bases and foundations matter because they are places to stand, and they must be designed so as to allow students to step from them progressively onto the shoulders of giants.

We must insist of ourselves that we have high expectations of students, and we must make demands on them that follow from these expectations. To teach less thoughtfully, with less aspiration, is to run the risk of leaving the impression or the conviction that study in the liberal and fine arts is an unnecessary frill and that really learning mathematics is worthwhile only if one has a taste for it, and so on. Nothing could be further from the truth.

Obviously, there are greater horrors than illiteracy, greater terrors than uncritical literacy. Starvation, abject poverty, child abuse, and being a victim or perpetrator of genocide come to mind. But educationally, few things are more terrifying than programs of instruction that do not even aspire to scientific, humanistic, and aesthetic literacy. Such programs teach students that education is not really of much consequence, and they thereby thrust the students outside the community of insiders, the community where the students belong—where everybody belongs. Too many people will be condemned to the outside by facts of life beyond the control of educational institutions; it will not do for schools and colleges to contribute to more of the same by doing anything whatsoever that is shallow and unmindful of the fullest conception of literacy.

My experience as a teacher during the past fifteen years, with secondary and college students, brings to mind a host of commonplace examples of the sort of things students are taught, in school and out, that obscure for them the power of language and the ideals of scientific, humanistic, and aesthetic literacy.

Frequently, in discussions that demand clear and full understanding of the meanings of words and in which accurate definitions are sought, students say, "That's just semantics." They mean that examination of the meanings of words is not really necessary and is somehow trivial. Wherever they learn such nonsense, their misunderstanding reveals that they do not see that unless words have public, articulable meanings that are shared by the users of language, then intelligent and fruitful discourse is impossible. They do not grasp that how we use words is directly connected to what we believe, what conclusions we reach, and that what we believe is directly connected to what we do and how we behave. The prejudice against language disclosed in "That's just semantics" denies the undeniable fact that language use, belief, and action make up an interwoven fabric that can be rent only if action is to be divorced from thought—with all the resulting effects of thoughtless action.

The same prejudice is embodied in the saying of some students when discussing the meaning of a word, "Well, you mean what you mean, and I mean what I mean." Clearly some disagreements about what words mean are genuinely instructive, but any student who is left with the view that the meanings of words are a matter of individual choice is destined to share the silly view of Humpty-Dumpty that language is a question not of what the words mean but, rather, of "who is to be the master, us or the words." The prospects in such students for mastery of reading, writing, or even the art of conversation are minimal; most of them are condemned to shallow and fruitless talk precisely because they have been taught that language, the vehicle of talk, has no real, public authority.

These misleading ideas come fully to life when students say such things as "I know what I mean, but I can't say it." Again, it is as though language were not necessary for thought, as though one could think clearly, have a lucid understanding of one's ideas, without even using language. Students who are taught that such a thing is possible have effectively been told that the effort required to have a clear thought, and therefore a thought they can express clearly in words, does not need to be made. Their thinking is often limited to vague, largely ineffable sentiments or preferences rather than to ideas. Their sense of language, unless it matures into a more thoughtful one, will keep them outside forever.

Those who have this vague sense of language and of thought do not grasp literacy itself. They do not get the full-blooded experience of what it feels like to understand an argument, let alone to anticipate the conclusion of one; they tend to be excluded from the experience of understanding a work of art because they do not know the intellectual means by which works of art are understood, and so they are left appealing to what they like and what they don't like. The barrenness of such illiteracy, the deprivation of opportunities to look or listen and understand, is grounds for those who love the young to weep. Condemnation to the outside is pitiable.

The goal of education, one of the fundamental goals of civilization, is to make it the case that the only outsiders are the beginners, the newcomers to human life. This goal is to make it possible to say of all but the newborn, "They are becoming insiders." It is to bring in from the cold and away from the terrible judgment that the world normally visits on the uneducated, everyone to the extent that they will accept the invitation. We are not likely to succeed altogether, but we must bend every effort to succeed where we can. And we must remember and remind others that there is room inside for all of us.

Works Cited

Sayers, Dorothy L. *The Lost Tools of Learning*. London: Methuen, 1948.

Shakespeare, William. *King Lear*. In *The Riverside Shakespeare*. Ed. G. Blakemore Evans. Boston: Houghton, 1974, 1249-304.

Forms of Literacy

Literacy: Who Cares?

Robben W. Fleming

The literacy problem has many faces. If literacy means the ability to read and write, the problem includes far more of our fellow Americans than most of us realize. It is a continuing source of worry to parents who wonder why children in primary and secondary schools can't read and write very well. Likewise, instructors in colleges and universities see in many of their students an erosion in these same abilities, and business executives complain that their management personnel do not easily write coherent, well-organized reports. In view of the number of hours that the American public now devotes to watching television, there is a great deal of speculation about what this activity is doing to both our ability to think and our interest in reading and writing.

The answer to the question I have posed in my title is, I think, that a great many of us care, but we care in different ways. If we are concerned with unemployment of unskilled workers and the frequent mismatch between available jobs and employee qualifications, we may be concerned about functional literacy. If we have children, we care about the caliber of the training they receive in schools. If we spend our lives in universities, we are concerned about the quality of the education we are giving our students. If we ponder the impact of our national obsession with television, we wonder what it is doing to us as a people. One could spin out a whole series of additional concerns.

My own special concerns about literacy are twofold. One is long-standing, the other recently acquired. The long-standing concern has to do with problems of achieving full employment and the ways in which those problems intertwine with literacy and training. The newly acquired interest is in how the telecommunications media—by which I mean broadcasting, videotapes and discs, cable connections, interactive computers, direct satellite service, and so forth—can be used to help address problems of literacy. To a considerable extent these interests are related because telecommunications technology is essentially a delivery system that is available for application to many problems, one of which may be literacy.

Western industrial societies, among which Japan is now generally included, have made their great gains in productivity through mechanization. Mechanization is, in turn, most easily applicable to unskilled, repetitive jobs. Such jobs, of course, are easiest for the uneducated and unskilled to acquire. To the extent that people are eliminated from such jobs, the market for the unskilled to find gainful employment is reduced, and that is exactly what has happened. Farm employment has dropped dramatically; manufacturing lends itself increasingly to sophisticated automation; and computer applications are increasingly invading even the service area.

Meanwhile, it is estimated that there may be as many as 57 million adult illiterates in the United States. How are they to be employed in an economy that offers less and less of what we used to call common labor? If we are to have anything like full employment, part of the answer involves trying to find ways to make this group functionally literate. Doing so is complicated and costly. We have spent a large number of state and federal dollars subsidizing training programs and offering employers an incentive to provide programs in the workplace. Such programs have met with mixed success, and we now seem to have concluded that we must reduce our expenditures in this area in order to help bring the federal and state budgets under control.

Could we find a less costly but effective way of addressing this problem through the telecommunications system? Public radio can reach roughly sixty-eight percent of the country. Public television can reach at least ninety percent of the country. Schools frequently have the equipment to use videotapes and discs. Cable coverage is spreading rapidly, frequently with channels available for public service needs.

In a report entitled *Adult Literacy and Broadcasting: The BBC Experience,* David Hargreaves describes Great Britain's efforts to address the problem of functional illiteracy through the media. The report gives a detailed and fascinating account of the BBC's experience with functional illiteracy from 1974 to 1979. Part of what the BBC found out was what all of us, in various cultures around the world, have also found out about socioeconomic problems. They are seldom simple, and progress can only be made by a multifaceted approach. The illiterate are frequently shamed by their inadequacies and therefore reluctant to identify themselves. Self-discipline in matters of learning is not easily acquired. Volunteers who will give time and effort to the project are essential, not only to reduce the high cost of the program but also to supply the human element.

The BBC story is not one of such overwhelming success that others may simply imitate it as a universal solution to the problem of functional illiteracy. It was a thoughtful, dedicated, disciplined effort, and it taught both its participants and the rest of us who are interested some lessons. But one unalterable fact remains: the telecommunications media have an unrivaled capacity to deliver programming to the home. The chances of reaching an audience in the home through radio, television, and some of the newer technology are infinitely greater than through any other method we can identify. We must learn to use them effectively.

Another example of an effort to raise the level of literacy is provided by the English Composition Board's student writing program at the University of Michigan. The program came about in 1974 because of concern among both faculty and students about the caliber and quality of student writing. It worked its way through faculty and administrative channels and finally emerged with strong support from both the university and foundations. The president of the Mellon Foundation, John Sawyer, has been a particularly steadfast advocate of the program.

Michigan's student writing program has now had several years in which to experiment, refine, adjust, and perfect its approach. So far as one can see, it appears to be working well, and the question, therefore, is whether it is transferable elsewhere. The need for improved student writing is universal, but it is expensive to mount a first-rate writing program, and it is not always a high priority. Consideration, therefore, should be given to whether and how the Michigan program can be replicated in other places.

Given my interests in what can be done through the media, I am naturally inclined to reflect on the possibilities of putting the Michigan writing program on videotape for use elsewhere. In no other way could it possibly achieve such an outreach.

At the Corporation for Public Broadcasting, there is now a CPB-ASC project, more widely known as the Annenberg Project, which is the result of a $150 million gift from the Annenberg family through the Annenberg School of Communications at the University of Pennsylvania. It provides $10 million annually for the next fifteen years to fund the preparation of courses to be offered by interested colleges and universities largely for credit toward their degrees. A specific effort will be made to exploit the latest and most innovative technology in connection with such courses.

How much of a writing program like Michigan's is reducible to tapes and cassettes? Is there a way to incorporate the interactive computer with the program? Would that part of the Michigan program which involves writing courses in the field of one's major, during the junior and senior years, have to be separated from the program in order to make it work elsewhere? What about the very important interaction that has taken place with the high schools? How would one handle that through a media approach? Does the institution wishing to replicate the Michigan program, using some part of it on tapes or cassettes, supply the human element without which no technological delivery system is likely to work? Who trains the personnel to participate in such a course? Does each user make adaptations for its clientele?

The point of these questions, of course, is to determine whether we can find ways to use the incredible outreach of the new telecommunications technology to improve some of our educational processes. The proposition can be put rather simply. There is a serious need throughout our high schools and colleges for an improvement in student writing. The University of Michigan has developed what seems to be a successful program. Is the program unique to that university or can it be duplicated elsewhere? If it can be duplicated, can the media play a significant role in that process? If so, how? Do we have the tact, the persuasiveness, the sensitivity, the creativity, and enough knowledge of the strengths and limitations of the media to put together learning programs and technological delivery? The academic world will be uneasy because the telecommunications delivery system may seem threatening. It need not be a threat and, in my view, is unlikely to be so. There are problems of learning that are universal, costly, dependent on mobilization of specialized personnel, and badly needed. My plea, my conviction, is that we are going to have to be innovative and daring in trying to deal with such problems.

Some will feel that television is a part of the problem, that it contributes to a deterioration in the reading and writing abilities of students. If it is part of the problem, how can it possibly be part of the solution?

Television can indeed be a part of the problem. It absorbs an enormous number of hours for the growing child and even the college student. Television watching may well have become a substitute for family conversations, which contributed to habits of literacy. We might all benefit from fewer hours of exposure. But even if all these things are true, does anyone think the problem is going to go away? or that we are going to improve it by simply lamenting television's shortcomings?

Literacy is an educational problem, but we are not going to solve it solely through the traditional school system. Our resources are limited; our reach is not. We have in the telecommunications technology a delivery system that can reach most of our people. What we need is the imagination to link it to programs that attack the problem of illiteracy.

Declining literacy in the United States is a pervasive problem. We all care about it, but in different ways according to how it confronts us. Because we do care about it and because it confronts us in so many ways, we have an almost unlimited range of possibilities for attacking it. My particular approach is to try to find ways to tie together the outreach of modern telecommunications techniques and the educational process, a far more complex problem than many of us believe. If there are difficulties in bringing about the marriage of media and education, and there are, is it because we lack the creativity to do so, or is it because it is difficult and we don't want to try?

Work Cited

Hargreaves, David. *Adult Literacy and Broadcasting: The BBC Experience*. New York: Nichols, 1980.

Television Literacy and
Television vs. Literacy

Gavriel Salomon

The title of this paper rests on two assumptions: first, that "literacy" varies according to the mode in which information is presented (i.e., television, like print, music, or ballet, is assumed to require its own kind of literacy); second, that varieties of literacy may compete with each other (for instance, tv-related literacy may develop at the expense of print literacy). The notion of tv literacy—a set of skills that develops to match the medium's demands—has been dealt with extensively, but only in recent years has it been submitted to empirical study. The findings have been somewhat inconsistent. Rice, Huston, and Wright, Gardner and Meringoff, and my own work *Interaction of Media, Cognition, and Learning* present evidence that special skills are required for the comprehension of television and that these skills can be developed and cultivated by the medium, just as print literacy and picture reading require particular skills to be developed. Other evidence offered by Stauffer, Frost, and Rybolt, however, suggests that these skills are closely related and that one's success in school and skill with print literacy determine the sophistication with which one comprehends television. With such conflicting reports, it is not obvious whether tv literacy requires a separate set of abilities.

Claims concerning the way in which tv-cultivated skills affect other abilities are also inconsistent. In recent years it has been popularly argued that televiewing has adverse effects on the development of reading abilities, but as Hornik shows, research findings to support this view are far too few and weak. How much evidence is there to support the claims that SAT scores decrease because of extensive tv viewing or that nonreading-related skills become cultivated at the expense of reading-related ones?

Is There a Television Literacy?

Literacy traditionally has been associated with the mastery of language skills, although it has not always been exclusively associated with reading and writing. Ong points out that until quite recently in history, discussions of literacy were shaped by a tradition primarily concerned with oration. Still, reading and writing were already of some concern in biblical times, if not earlier, and became a matter of widespread concern by at least the seventeenth century.

Whether defined in terms of oration or script, literacy requires the ability to extract information from coded messages and to express ideas, feelings, and thoughts through such messages. Broadly defined, then, literacy is the mastery of specific mental skills that are cultivated in response to the specific demands of coded messages within a particular cultural context. Indeed, it is the nature of the coding, the structure of a symbol system, and the nature of the cultural activities associated with it (e.g., writing, editing) that determine what skills are needed for a literate handling of messages. Since symbol systems differ in their semantic and syntactic structures and in the activities they demand and allow, we might safely assume that they also differ in the sets of skills they require; for example, the skills needed to read a text and the skills needed to read a musical score appear to be different.

Television differs from other media primarily in terms of its "language" or symbol system (see Salomon, *Interaction;* Meringoff; and Rice, Huston, and Wright). Like film, as Kjørup points out, it combines several symbol systems—pictures, speech, music, and movement—and generates messages with an overall structure unique to the medium. The uniqueness of the medium is evident from single shots (e.g., zooms) to a sequence of shots, from the production of a single program (compare *Sesame Street* to other programs) to the arrangement of a series of programs.

Since tv involves a complex symbol system composed both of elements common to other media (e.g., pictures) and of unique elements (e.g., commercial interruptions, zooms, split screens), it should require a unique literacy. Rice, Huston, and Wright suggest that there are three levels of symbolic representation in tv. The first level involves both visual and auditory portrayals of real-world information and hence does not require tv-specific literacy. The second level entails the medium's special elements (zooms, dissolves, and other effects) and thus requires special decoding processes for comprehension. Some such elements can serve as models for mental representational skills (see Salomon, *Interaction*). When copied, internalized, and used as "mental tools," they are likely to enable a youngster to become more sophisticated with the medium and perhaps with other message systems as well. The third level of representation involves symbols that are shared by other media (for instance, a red light symbolizing danger) and thus requires a general literacy.

Research shows that certain skills must be mastered to extract information from quick cuts, spatial fragmentation, and other elements unique to television (see Salomon and Cohen). The mastery of some of these skills is not correlated with the mastery of reading-related skills, and this fact suggests that a specific kind of literacy is needed to comprehend at least some tv messages. Such tv literacy is required not only for simple elements (e.g., cuts, fades, and zooms) but also for more complex elements that blend the simpler ones together into a whole plot. But how important are these special skills to the overall comprehension of tv programs? How much variance in comprehension can be attributed to varying levels of tv-unique skills? To what extent is a youngster's understanding of, for instance, a news program dependent on such skills? The answers to these questions depend on how television comprehension is defined and measured.

Consider the definition and measurement of print literacy. If, as Resnick and Resnick point out, writing one's name were the criterion for print literacy (an important criterion until well into the nineteenth century), then illiteracy would not be a problem in the United States. If reading aloud a simple and well-known passage were the criterion for literacy, the number of illiterates in the United States would still be minimal. But "the number would start to rise . . . if unfamiliar texts were to be read and new information gleaned from them. And if inferential rather than directly stated information were to be drawn from the text, we would probably announce a true crisis in literacy" (371). Thus a change in criterion often involves a change in the kinds of skills required to be literate. The skills needed to comprehend a familiar passage are closely related and specifically tailored to the coding and decoding demands of the text. But the more general skills needed to draw inferences from a new text reflect to a far larger extent one's general intellectual abilities.

The same may apply to tv literacy. If the criterion for tv literacy requires one to decipher or mentally recode symbolic elements that are unique to tv, then "tv skills" (that is, skills used only for tv viewing) will be needed, as Salomon and Cohen, Rice, Huston, and Wright, and Gardner and Meringoff suggest. But if the criterion for tv literacy requires one to make inferences or to generate connections between causes and consequences or motives and deeds, then tv skills are unlikely to be as significantly involved. Research by Rice, Huston, and Wright and by Roberts and Bachen shows that children gradually become more skillful in drawing inferences from tv programs and better able to distinguish fact from fiction and information from persuasion. Such developments do not appear to be related, however, to the amount of time spent viewing tv; rather, they most likely reflect general developments in cognitive ability.

Let us assume for a moment that the comprehension of tv entails three sequential phases: (1) mentally recoding (or deciphering) a coded message into a parallel mental representation (for example, identifying objects in a picture or reading the sounds of printed letters and generating a meaningful word from them); (2) chunking or integrating these components into meaningful units; and (3) elaborating the material to make inferences, new attributions, new associations, new questions, and so on.

The first phase—deciphering a coded message—involves processes that are largely dependent on the symbolic nature of a coded message, and this phase therefore requires skills that are uniquely tailored to the demands of the symbol system. When a sequence of close-ups and long shots appears on tv, viewers must interrelate the components to make them meaningful. Similarly, when viewers are confronted with spatial fragmentation, they must generate a whole image. Such processes are called "bottom-up" processes because the viewer starts with a concrete stimulus and mentally transforms it.

Rice, Huston, and Wright observe that prior to mastering the first phase of tv comprehension, young children are very attentive to salient features—e.g., fast pace, sudden changes in tempo, camera techniques—without putting such features into a context. Young children enjoy forms more than content while they are acquiring the skills necessary to recode such elements. Only later on do they become more selective and begin to disregard those features that are uninformative.

The second phase involves chunking the recoded material that has been stored in one's short-term memory. The skills involved in this phase are more general than those in the first phase. There is a growing body of research that shows how children gradually learn to chunk tv messages. For example, Collins provides evidence that young children are insensitive to the structure of televised drama and comprehend it piecemeal, regardless of how well or poorly it is structured. Only later on do they connect the pieces and become disturbed with a poorly edited program. Wright, Watkins, and Huston-Stein show that as children mature they begin to be interested in the content of programs and develop a structural framework to integrate the units of content. Note, however, that such changes reflect to an important extent a child's general cognitive development, not an improvement in tv skills.

The third phase involves "top-down" processes of elaboration, which reflect to an even greater extent one's general abilities, world knowledge, expectations, and hypotheses concerning the nature of the material. These processes are quite different from the processes of recoding and chunking in that they depend very little on the original symbolic attributes of the material. Indeed, processes of elaboration are applied to the material as already stored in one's short-term memory, and such internal representations are not replicas of the original message; the symbolic nature of the original message is lost during the processes of recoding and chunking. Thus elaboration is influenced not by the symbolic nature of the original message but by such factors as content, the task to be performed on it, one's expectations, previous knowledge, and mastery of general elaboration skills.

What phase involves those skills we most commonly associate with literacy? Wolf argues that reading entails more than "a mental interaction with the written word" (411) and claims that it is "the ability to interpret diverse sorts of information" (417). Guided by such a conception, Wolf finds that available research shows "remarkable similarities . . . in the way people read texts, the way they view pictures, the way they read music, and the way they study maps" (412). Given that Wolf addresses himself mainly to the third phase of interpreting a message, he may be correct in collapsing all kinds of literacy into one, since interpretation involves general "top-down" processes.

If, however, we posit literacy not as the ability to go beyond the information given but as the more mundane activity of coding and recoding, we are more likely to find remarkable differences in the skills people use to read texts, view tv, and study maps. Scribner and Cole studied the cognitive processes of literate but unschooled members of the Vai people in Liberia and found highly specific differences in cognitive ability between these literates and their illiterate peers: for instance, differences in their ability to analyze speech and to give clear instructions. Abstract interpretations are not demanded by the Vai texts, nor is there a tradition of text production for mass distribution. Literacy in that culture requires only the ability to code and recode specific scripts. No wonder that the skills involved and cultivated by practice pertain only to the first and second phases of the process.

I am led to the hypothesis that different kinds of literacy exist and are manifested in the earlier phases of processing a message. The initial phase of processing a picture, map, film, or text is carried out by skills that closely reflect the specific demands of each symbol system. Such skills are cultivated by repeated practice with the medium. As processing continues, more general, "top-down" skills are required (for instance, relating discrete elements, solving problems, and making inferences). Specific literacy gives way to general knowledge and ability, which are equally applicable to different symbol systems. Thus, tv literacy, like print literacy, is evident mainly at the coding and recoding phase of processing. When processing becomes more complex, variance in comprehension can be attributed no longer to variance in the mastery of skills used specifically for the medium but to the amount and nature of the elaborations performed on messages.

This hypothesis is based on the assumption that processing is a sequential activity that begins with specific skills and progresses to more general skills. While a reasonable assumption, it does not address the question of how important that first phase of processing is to a "literate" televiewer. The relative importance of tv literacy depends on who the televiewer is. It is much greater for a beginner, who is still acquiring recoding skills, than for a more advanced viewer, who uses these skills automatically.

Gombrich points out that a proper reading of black-and-white photographs involves understanding that such photographs are not renderings of a colorless world. Once this fact has been learned and automatically assumed, the weight of literacy shifts to the interpretation of photographs (as done, e.g., by intelligence officers, surveyors, or archaeologists who study aerial photos). The skills such professionals employ in the interpretation of photographs are general. Thus good picture interpreters should also be good text interpreters.

Recent findings by Gardner and Meringoff suggest that children are quick to acquire many of the elementary skills that constitute tv literacy. Although they neither receive direct tutelage from adults nor practice expressing ideas through tv, they are capable of making important distinctions concerning the medium by the time they enter school. At a somewhat older age they learn to process complex narratives, according to Collins, and at about age nine they can identify the commercial intentions behind advertisements, as Roberts testified.

As children mature, they become better able to apply to tv increasingly more general skills in a "top-down" fashion. They are less attentive to salient formal features that carry no information, increasingly guided by conceptual anticipations, and more selectively attentive to features that carry specific kinds of comprehensible information (Rice, Huston, and Wright).

It thus appears that tv literacy per se is acquired easily and is applied automatically by most children at a relatively early age. Subsequent developments derive from this and other kinds of literacy and reflect children's more general abilities. Except for young children, then, tv literacy is of little importance to one's comprehension compared to other, more general skills that are applicable to many modes of presentation. As with reading, perhaps the "bottom-up" processes that are typical of beginners give way to "top-down" processes once the former become automatized (see LaBerge and Samuels and McConkie and Rayner).

My formulation must be qualified by two considerations. First, I have argued that tv literacy belongs to the initial phases of processing and develops earlier in life than more general skills. But tv skills are not acquired independently of other cognitive developments. It is reasonable to assume, after all, that a child's comprehension of a cut, a zoom, or a separator or a child's ability to evaluate the lifelikeness of the *Bionic Woman* depends on the development of more general abilities. Wartella, for example, gives evidence that a child's ability to carry out some of the more complex mental processes depends on his or her general ability to center and decenter attention. And my research (in "Cognitive Skill") shows how exposure to the novel and mentally demanding elements of a tv program such as *Sesame Street* affects mastery of those skills that children are already capable of acquiring (e.g., analytic skills) but not more advanced ones (e.g., skills of synthesis).

Second, I have suggested that no further development of tv literacy is needed once children have acquired and begun to apply automatically the basic skills necessary to handle television's symbolic forms. Only the application of more general abilities is then called for. But this position is based on a questionable assumption: that the set of skills uniquely required for tv comprehension is finite and narrowly restricted in scope. The symbolic, structural nature of tv material is quite complex. Compounding and orchestration are common within a shot and across shots, within one symbolic modality (speech) and across modalities (picture, movement, music) (see Salomon, *Interaction,* and Kjørup for more detail). Thus, as one's general cognitive capabilities grow, one can address increasingly complex elements and recode them. By so doing, additional and more complex tv skills may be mastered. I have found (*Interaction*) that when sixth graders take tv seriously and try to extract from it more than basic pleasurable information, they show improved visual memory (i.e., chunking). It appears that youngsters can master new tv-related skills even after they have acquired the basic necessary literacy, provided they are motivated (for whatever reason) to extract increasingly complex information from television.

The furthering of one's tv literacy beyond the basics is apparently a matter of interplay between "bottom-up" and "top-down" inference-making processes. Epistemically guided by a conception, expectation, hypothesis, or tentative inference, one addresses new and more complex elements in a program and recodes them to extract the additional information that is sought. Thus, "top-down" processes can guide one to encounter novel elements, and the practice of recoding them leads to improved mastery of tv skills. Improvements of this kind (e.g., learning to chunk selectively larger amounts of visual information) lead to additional inferences and other high-order cognitive products.

In sum, tv literacy pertains to the coding and recoding of the medium's complex symbol systems and serves as a basis for more elaborate and more general processes. The more general processes can be applied to all kinds of materials. As the basic literacy is mastered and carried out automatically, more general processes become dominant. If tv literacy is defined and measured as one's ability to "go beyond the televised information," it is much the same as other kinds of literacy, using more or less the same general cognitive processes. Such processes can continue to guide information extraction addressed at increasingly complex elements of tv symbol systems and by so doing, can cause a further cultivation of tv literacy. Thus, general and specific abilities guide the development of each other. The thesis presented above is schematically shown in figure 1.

Television Literacy versus Other Literacies

While much has been said in recent years about the adverse effects of televiewing on school performance, SAT scores, reading ability, and the like, rhetoric far exceeds evidence. As Hornik points out, there is hardly any clear-cut, strong, and consistent evidence to support—or reject—such claims.

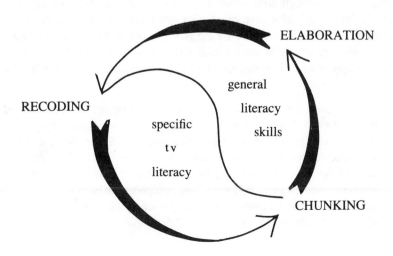

Figure 1.   The interrelations of processing phases and levels of literacy.

Thus far I have argued that tv literacy involves specific skills that are cultivated in response to the demands of the medium's symbolic nature and are used mainly, if not exclusively, to extract information from tv messages. Other systems may demand other skills, and thus we speak of script literacy, musical literacy, and the like.

How can such diverse literacies relate to and influence each other? Can the development of one literacy enhance or hinder the development of another? Two schools of thought have evolved over the years. One argues literacies involve general abilities (as does Greenfield); the other, that literacies involve specific, nontransferable skills (Scribner and Cole).

According to the first view, written language, in contrast to oral language, is context-free and cultivates abstract thought that transfers to a wide array of new tasks. It would follow logically from such an approach that continuous exposure to television, with its emphasis on the pictorial, the concrete, and the fleeting experience, should transfer to other domains, such as reading and writing. To the extent that self-generated imagery facilitates prose comprehension, as Pressley argues, and perhaps even production, prolonged exposure to tv should benefit other kinds of literacy. Whether facilitating or debilitating, tv skills should be generalized and become transferable to other activities.

According to the second school of thought, cultivation of skills is highly specific to the tasks that demand them. Thus skills are not transferable to dissimilar tasks. As Scribner and Cole argue, writing poetry has different consequences for literacy than writing business letters, and the respective skills thus practiced and mastered are not easily transferable. It would follow that if tv cultivates medium-specific skills, such skills would be limited to televiewing and have no effect on other activities.

As with other dichotomies, the two approaches just described need not be mutually exclusive. Skills promoted by the demands of some activity with one symbol system, though well suited to perform that activity, may also become useful for other activities performed with other symbol systems. For example, I have observed that some specific skills improved in response to tv demands and became transferable to other visual and nonvisual materials (Salomon, "Effects"). Scribner and Cole suggest a similar conclusion in their discussion of writing:

> As practice in any activity continues, we would expect the range of materials which engage it to be extended and skills to become increasingly free from the particular conditions of the original practice. Skills, then, will be more available for what has been called "far transfer," including tasks and situations that do not involve the written modality. When skill systems involved in literacy are many, varied and complex, and have wide applicability, the functional and general ability approaches will converge in their predictions of intellectual outcomes. (458)

When can such "far transfer" take place? As I pointed out above, literacy consists not only of basic and specific skills but also of other, more general skills, such as cue attendance, inference making, and other logical processes. General skills can certainly be transferred from one medium to another. But we might also expect certain specific skills to transfer to new materials when similar kinds of activities are performed.

In a recent study by Tidhar, children planned, shot, and edited eight-millimeter films. The effects of each of these activities were measured against the mastery of such mental skills as imagery, spatial construction, story completion, and chunking. Filmmaking had profound cognitive effects. But the activity of greatest influence was editing, and the skills most strongly affected were the most general and least tv-specific ones (story completion, story construction, headline generation). It appears, then, that the activity of communicating through film, particularly when it involves editorial activity, cultivates generalizable skills. The activity of editing is of course itself a transferable activity.

Literacy, however, consists not only of newly mastered skills. It also consists of certain habits and perceptions of when and where the skills are to be employed. Texts, it appears, are perceived as demanding more elaboration than tv programs (even if the same content is presented by both). As a result, people devote more attention to reading texts than to viewing tv. Possibly for reasons of pictoriality (thus, attributed lifelikeness), youngsters learn to process tv at only the recoding and chunking levels and do not invest much effort in elaborating televised material (Salomon, *Communication*). Thus, they come to use only automatic skills in viewing tv.

Perhaps unlike print, tv is a medium that allows such shallow processing. Singer even claims that the "crowdedness" of tv—its pictorial-holistic nature—inhibits deeper processing. It is not impossible that children acquire the expectation that pleasurable information can be obtained effortlessly, an expectation they then carry over to written material. As Morgan and Gross speculate:

> because watching television is "easier" than reading, in that it does not require the same degree of sustained concentration for comprehension, heavy television viewing could reinforce impatience with reading; and reading skills hence would remain underdeveloped. (131)

Indeed, Morgan shows that intelligent, heavy tv viewers come to read more material that "reflects common television programming." Morgan and Gross suggest that such children exhibit poorer reading ability than similar children who watch tv less often.

We are not concerned here with tv literacy replacing print literacy. Rather, children may be learning from tv to invest little effort in material and to forgo the employment of more general skills; they may bring the same attitudes to print and fail to develop their reading skills. As LaBerge and Samuels point out:

> When a person does not pay attention to what he is practicing, he rules out opportunities for forming higher units because he simply processes through codes that are already laid down. (315)

For other children, possibly those with poor language skills, the perceived "ease" of tv makes the difficulty of reading and writing appear even greater.

As our recent research tends to show, the shallow, nonelaborative processing of tv material is more a matter of perception and acquired habit than a necessary outcome. When programs demand the elaboration of material, youngsters can and do invest more mental effort in elaborating tv material and thus come to learn more from it.

It follows, then, that practice in applying more general skills to tv could benefit other literacies. Children who practice inference making, internal chunking, or integration of many discrete units of information with tv material should reflect the results of such practice in, say, their writing. But this expectation assumes that they actually apply such skills to tv. Our initial research suggests that unless tutored or guided, they do not do so, and thus they miss the opportunity to practice these skills while televiewing. Moreover, we entertain the hypothesis that the acquired expectation for "easy" material on tv transfers to non-tv tasks.

An important, though tentative, implication follows from the discussion above. There seems to be no reason to fear that tv skills, cultivated by the continuous practice of televiewing, will interfere with the development of skills needed for reading and writing. There is more reason to be concerned that more general abilities are not being practiced while watching tv. Thus there is a growing need to tutor and coach youngsters to invest more (rather than less) mental effort in tv by applying to its programs the same general skills we urge them to apply to print material. By so doing, we can help them to perceive tv as less "shallow" and thus witness the cultivation of skills that, as Tidhar's research shows, are transferable to non-tv domains.

We are now involved in a series of studies designed to test some of the ideas presented here. We want to see whether comprehension of television material gradually becomes a matter of employing general rather than tv-specific skills. We are also involved in the development of tutorials to change youngsters' way of perceiving and handling tv. We hope that by improving their generalizable skills through television, we can help them improve their reading and writing.

Works Cited

Collins, W. Andrew. "Children's Comprehension of Television Content." In *Children Communicating: Media and Development of Thought, Speech, Understanding*. Ed. Ellen Wartella. Beverly Hills, Calif.: Sage, 1979, 21-52.

Gardner, H., and L. K. Meringoff. *Children Stories Media, Fourth Annual Review to the Markle Foundation.* Harvard Project Zero, Dec. 1980.

Gombrich, E. H. "The Visual Image." In *Media and Symbols: The Forms of Expression, Communication and Education.* Ed. David R. Olson. Chicago: Univ. of Chicago Press, 1974, 241-70.

Greenfield, Patricia M. "Oral or Written Language: The Consequences for Cognitive Development in Africa, the United States and England." *Language and Speech* 15(1972):169-78.

Hornik, Robert. "Out of School Television and Schooling: Hypotheses and Methods." *Review of Educational Research* 51(1981):193-214.

Kjørup, Søran. "Film as a Meetingplace of Multiple Codes." In *The Arts and Cognition.* Ed. David Perkins and Barbara Leondar. Baltimore: John Hopkins Univ. Press, 1977, 20-47.

LaBerge, David, and S. Jay Samuels. "Toward a Theory of Automatic Information Processing in Reading." *Cognitive Psychology* 6(1974):293-323.

McConkie, George W., and Keith Rayner. "Identifying the Span of the Effective Stimulus in Reading: Literature Review and Theories of Reading." In *Theoretical Models and Processes of Reading.* Ed. Harry Singer and Robert B. Ruddell. 2nd ed. Newark, Del.: International Reading Assoc., 1976, 137-62.

Meringoff, Laurene Krasny. "Influence of the Medium on Children's Story Apprehension." *Journal of Educational Psychology* 72(1980):40-249.

Morgan, Michael. "Television Viewing and Reading: Does More Equal Better?" *Journal of Communication* 30(1980):159-65.

————, and Larry Gross. "Television Viewing, IQ and Academic Achievement." *Journal of Broadcasting* 24(1980):117-33.

Ong, Walter J. *Interfaces of the Word: Studies in the Evolution of Consciousness and Culture.* Ithaca, N.Y.: Cornell Univ. Press, 1977.

Pressley, Michael. "Imagery and Children's Learning: Putting the Picture in Developmental Perspective." *Review of Educational Research* 47(1977):585-622.

Resnick, Daniel P., and Lauren B. Resnick. "The Nature of Literacy: An Historical Exploration." *Harvard Educational Review* 47(1977):370-85.

Rice, M. L., A. C. Huston, and J. C. Wright. "The Forms and Codes of Television: Effect on Children's Attention, Comprehension and Social Behavior." In *Report of the Surgeon General's Scientific Advisory Committee on Television and Social Behavior.* Rev. ed. National Institute of Mental Health, in press.

Roberts, Donald F. Testimony before the Federal Trade Commission's Rulemaking on Children and TV Advertising. San Francisco, 1979.

————, and Christine M. Bachen. "Mass Communication Effects." *Annual Review of Psychology* 32(1981):307-56.

Salomon, Gavriel. "Cognitive Skill Learning across Cultures." *Journal of Communication* 26(1976):138-45.

————. *Communication and Education: Social and Psychological Interactions.* Beverly Hills, Calif.: Sage, 1981.

————. "Effects of Encouraging Israeli Mothers to Coobserve *Sesame Street* with Their Five-Year-Olds." *Child Development* 48(1977):1146-51.

————. *Interaction of Media, Cognition, and Learning.* San Francisco: Jossey-Bass, 1979.

————, and A. A. Cohen. "Television Formats, Mastery of Mental Skills, and the Acquisition of Knowledge." *Journal of Educational Psychology* 69(1977):12-619.

Scribner, Sylvia, and Michael Cole. "Literacy without Schooling: Testing for Intellectual Effects." *Harvard Educational Review* 48(1978):448-61.

Singer, Jerome L. "The Power and Limitations of Television: A Cognitive-Affective Analysis." In *The Entertainment Functions of Television*. Ed. Percy H. Tannenbaum. Hillsdale, N.J.: L. Erlbaum Assocs., 1980, 31-65.

Stauffer, John, Richard Frost, and William Rybolt. "Literacy, Illiteracy, and Learning from Television News." *Communication Research* 5(1978):221-32.

Tidhar, C. "Cognitive Effects of Communicating through Films' Codes." Diss. Hebrew Univ. of Jerusalem 1981.

Wartella, Ellen. "Children and Television: The Development of the Child's Understanding of the Medium." In vol. 1 of *Mass Communication Yearbook*. Ed. G. Cleveland Wilhoit. Beverly Hills, Calif.: Sage, 1980, 516-54.

Wolf, Thomas. "Reading Reconsidered." *Harvard Educational Review* 47(1977):411-29.

Wright, John C., B. A. Watkins, and Aletra Huston-Stein. *Active vs. Passive Television Viewing: A Model of the Development of Television Information Processing by Children*. Monographs of the World Federation of Mental Health, 1980.

Oral and Literate Strategies in Spoken and Written Discourse

Deborah Tannen

What Is Discourse?

The term "discourse" has been used by many people in many different ways, some using the term to refer to face-to-face conversation (e.g., Coulthard); others, to refer to two hypothetical sentences in a row (e.g., Bolinger). I use it to mean anything "beyond the sentence"—any two or more sentences taken together to form a text in any mode.

Charles Fillmore once opened a class on text analysis with the following demonstration of textness. Imagine a sign posted at a swimming pool that says, POOL FOR MEMBERS' USE ONLY. Now imagine a sign posted at a swimming pool that says, PLEASE USE REST ROOMS, NOT THE POOL. And now imagine these two warnings placed together: PLEASE USE REST ROOMS, NOT THE POOL. POOL FOR MEMBERS' USE ONLY. These two sentences are funny when they are juxtaposed in this order because the interpretation of "use" is carried over from the first sentence to the second. Meaning spills beyond words and sentences when they are joined in discourse.

Thus I am using the terms "discourse" and "text" interchangeably,[1] and although I use "discourse" in this essay, I might just as well have chosen to use "text." The point is simply to refer to a stream of language as opposed to sentences taken out of context. I should also add that in my own studies of discourse and in the work of others that I refer to, I only concern myself with actual discourse—spoken or written language that has actually been produced and used by people in real contexts.

Why Spoken versus Written Language?

If discourse is a stream of language, spoken or written, why talk about spoken versus written language? In addressing questions of literacy with a view to helping educators meet future social requirements for reading and writing, we immediately confront the question of what it is about reading and writing that

79

makes them so difficult to master. Why is it that every child learns to talk fluently, while many never learn to write with anything near fluency?

Investigating the relation between spoken and written language is crucial to understanding how language works for people. Theoretical linguists of many different traditions continually seek to understand the underlying structures and recurrent patterns that distinguish the two by analyzing different kinds of discourse. In what follows, however, I suggest that the distinction between writing and speech, literacy and orality, is not primary but that the differences between them may in fact grow out of other factors: specifically, communicative goals and relative focus on interpersonal involvement.

Past studies of spoken versus written language have typically compared conversation to expository prose (or "essayist literacy" [Olson]). These genres have not been the focus of such research by chance. There is something typically spoken about conversation and something typically written about expository prose. But by limiting our analysis to these genres, we are likely to draw conclusions about spoken and written language that are incorrect. For instance, contrary to what a comparison of these genres suggests, strategies typically associated with spoken discourse can be and are used in writing, and strategies typically associated with written language are likewise realized in speech.

In this essay I show how both spoken and written discourse can each reflect both oral and literate strategies. Further, I make the perhaps radical suggestion that oral strategies may underlie successful production of written discourse. Before proceeding, however, I will sketch briefly what these oral and literate strategies are.

Two Hypotheses about Spoken versus Written Discourse

Two general hypotheses have been made about spoken versus written discourse: one is that written language is decontextualized while spoken language is highly context-bound; the other, that spoken discourse establishes cohesion through paralinguistic cues while written discourse relies more on lexicalization.

The Contextualization Hypothesis

Three major arguments have been introduced by scholars in support of the view that spoken discourse is highly context-bound. First, a speaker can refer to the context of immediate surroundings visible to both speaker and hearer. For example, I can say, "Look at this!" and rely on hearers to see what "this" refers to. A writer and a reader, however, are generally separated in time and place, so immediate context is lost. Second, speakers are free to be minimally explicit since confused hearers can ask for clarification on the spot.[2] Readers, however, can't ask for clarification when confused, so writers must anticipate all likely confusion and head it off by filling in necessary background information and all the steps of a logical argument. Third, speakers normally share similar social backgrounds and hence all sorts of assumptions about the world, their mutual or respective histories, and so on. Writer and reader, however, are likely to share minimal social context, so the writer cannot make assumptions about shared attitudes.

Clearly, in such a schema, "spoken discourse" is typically spontaneous face-to-face conversation, and "written discourse" is typically expository prose. For these genres it makes sense to hypothesize that spoken language is highly context-bound, while written language is decontextualized. But I suspect that the differences between conversation and expository prose are due not to the fact that one is spoken and the other written, but to the communicative goals inherent in each. In face-to-face spontaneous conversation (e.g., dinner-table conversation), the fact of speaking is relatively more important than the content of the message conveyed. That is, what Malinowski calls "phatic communion" is relatively significant in the interaction. It is almost a form of talk for talk's sake. In fact, most of what is said in social settings is not new information. But that is not to say that the communication is not important. Quite the contrary, something very important is communicated—what Bateson calls the metamessage: a statement about the relation between interactants.[3] Far from being unimportant, such messages (e.g., "I am well disposed toward you," "I'm angry at you," and the like) are the basis for carrying on the interaction.

Expository prose is a special genre in which content is relatively important. Thus Kay points out that the form of discourse that has been associated with writing—what he aptly calls "autonomous language"—has come with technological advancement. A complex technological society has need for much communication, typically among strangers, in which interpersonal involvement is beside the point, and communication is more efficiently carried out if such involvement is conventionally ignored. (This convention may be peculiarly American or at least Western. It certainly creates misunderstandings when American business executives try to ignore personal involvement and get right down to business with Japanese, Arabs, or Greeks, for whom the establishment of personal relations must lay the groundwork for any business dealings.)

Thus, it is not a coincidence that the genres of conversation and expository prose have been the focus of study for linguists interested in spoken versus written language. There is something typically "written" about content-focused communication; indeed it was the innovation of print that made communication with people in other social contexts popular. And there is something typically "oral" about interpersonal involvement. In communicating with friends or family, it is hard to focus exclusively on content. (Hence the common observation that one should not take driving lessons from spouses and parents, and the fact that any comment can touch off a fight between speakers or any comment can seem particularly charming, depending on the place of the interaction in the history of the relationship between participants.)

But a look at other genres will show the conclusions discussed above to be faulty. In some personal letters, for example, the fact of communication is more important than content. Certainly it is just as possible and common to *write* a lot of nothing as it is to whisper sweet nothings with just as much satisfaction for all concerned. Note passing in school is another example of written communication that contradicts the contextualization hypothesis since the copresence of writer and reader makes it possible for the writer to refer to the context of immediate surroundings and for the reader to ask for clarification on the spot. Similarly, oral communication is often minimally context-bound and very content-focused, as in lectures and radio or television broadcasts.[4] Ritual language also makes use of literate strategies in that the speaker performs a chant or ceremony that was composed long ago by authors far away, addressed to a large and impersonal audience (see Chafe, "Integration").

Thus, the above discussion makes possible two sets of observations. First, while the contextualization hypothesis is applicable to certain types of discourse, it does not apply to written and spoken language per se. Second, differences in discourse types spring not from their status as written or spoken language but from their communicative goals. And it appears that the goals of one-way communication differ as a rule from those of two-way communication.[5] One-way communication is typically associated with relatively more focus on conveying a message (i.e., content is important), while two-way communication is typically associated with relatively more focus on interpersonal involvement.

A final observation about the close connection between interpersonal involvement and speaking on the one hand and between focus on content and writing on the other concerns the differing levels of "immediacy" involved in each mode. The slowness of writing makes it an ill-formed medium for the communication of nonsignificant content. In communicating with deaf people, for instance, when writing is the only medium available for communication, I have found myself choosing not to communicate all sorts of relatively unimportant asides because they didn't seem worth the trouble of writing.[6] And yet it is just such seemingly meaningless interchange that creates a social relationship. That is precisely why deafness is such a terrible handicap: it is socially isolating.

Cohesion in Spoken and Written Discourse

A second hypothesis that has been made about spoken versus written discourse is that cohesion is accomplished in spoken discourse through paralinguistic and prosodic cues, whereas in written discourse, cohesion must be lexicalized (Chafe, "Integration"; Cook-Gumperz and Gumperz; Gumperz, Kaltman, and O'Connor; Ochs).

In spoken communication, everything is said at some pitch, in some tone of voice, at some speed, with some expression or lack of expression in the voice and on the face. All these nonverbal and paralinguistic features reveal the speaker's attitude toward the message and establish cohesion—that is, show relations among ideas; show their relative importance; foreground and background information, and so on. Just as Bateson observes that in a social setting one cannot not communicate (the act of keeping silent is a communication within the frame of interaction), one cannot speak without showing one's attitude toward the message and the speech activity.

In contrast, nonverbal and paralinguistic features are not available in writing. You may wrinkle your face up until it cracks while you write, but this expression will not show up on the written page. You may yell or whisper or sing as you compose sentences, but the words as they fall on the page will not reflect this behavior.[7] Therefore, in writing, the relations among ideas and the writer's attitude toward them must be lexicalized. There are a number of ways to make those relations clear: for example, (1) by making outright statements (e.g., instead of laughing while saying something one may write "humorously" or instead of winking while speaking one may write, "I don't mean this literally");[8] (2) by carefully choosing words with just the right connotation; or (3) by using complex syntactic constructions, transitional phrases, and so on. Thus a number of linguists have found that in spoken narrative (and here the genre narrative is important) most ideas are strung together with no conjunctions or the minimal conjunction "and" (Chafe, "Integration"; Kroll; Ochs). In contrast, in written narrative, conjunctions are chosen that show the relation between ideas (e.g., "so," "because") and subordinate constructions are used to do some of the work of foregrounding and backgrounding that would be done paralinguistically in speaking.[9]

Thus we have the second hypothesis: spoken discourse typically relies on paralinguistic and nonverbal channels whereas written discourse relies on lexicalization for the establishment of cohesion. An examination of varied discourse types shows this hypothesis to be valid.

Oral and Literate Strategies in Discourse

The idea that spoken discourse can exhibit strategies associated with orality and literacy (that is, with typically spoken- or writtenlike discourse) can be traced to Bernstein's research into children's use of language.[10] Bernstein found that children's discourse, as elicited by experimental tasks, fell into two stylistic types, which he identified as restricted and elaborated "codes." In describing a picture, a child using restricted code, for example, might say, "They hit it through there and he got mad." A child using elaborated code might say, "The children were playing ball and hit the ball through the window. The man who lived in the house got mad at them." The second version is easier to understand only when the picture is not in view. Though Bernstein did not associate these two codes with orality and literacy, Cook-Gumperz and Gumperz point out that the overt lexicalization of background material in the elaborated code is akin to literacy.

I would now like to cite some of my own and others' work to demonstrate that both written and spoken discourse can reflect either oral or literate strategies. First I will show some uses of oral and literate strategies in spoken discourse, and then I will do the same in written.

Preparation for Literacy in Oral Discourse in School

Let us assume that typically oral strategies are those that are highly context-bound, that require maximal contribution from the audience in supplying background information and doing interpretive work, and that depend on paralinguistic and nonverbal cues instead of on lexicalization for cohesion and evaluation. Literate strategies, we will suppose, are more decontextualized, require less audience contribution in supplying necessary information and connections, and rely on lexicalization to show the author's attitude toward material and the relationship among parts of the text.

Cook-Gumperz and Gumperz suggest that children make a "transition to literacy" when they go to school. Michaels and Cook-Gumperz analyzed in detail an oral discourse activity in a first-grade classroom that prepares children for a literate approach to information: "sharing time." During sharing time, children are expected to address the entire class and tell about one thing that is very important. Although the children are in face-to-face communication and they share context in many ways, the teacher encourages them to repeat known information in order to give a "complete" discourse appropriate to sharing time. Michaels and Collins, in a similar study, give the example of a child who brought to class two candles she had made in day camp and began to talk about them "using highly context-bound expressions and gestures." She said, for example, "This one came out blue and I don't know what this color is." The teacher encouraged the child to produce a more literate-style discourse: "Tell the kids how you do it from the very start. Pretend we don't know a thing about candles." The teacher's use of "from the very start" and "pretend" emphasizes the counter-intuitive nature of literate discourse. The injunction to "pretend we don't know a thing about candles" sets up the reader-as-blank-slate idealization that underlies much expository writing.

Michaels and Cook-Gumperz observed that the children in this first grade class fell into two groups with respect to how they performed during sharing time and consequently how much reinforcement from the teacher and practice in literate-style discourse they received. Some children tended to lexicalize connections and focus on the main point, whereas others usually accomplished this cohesion with special intonation patterns. To better document these differences, Michaels and her coworkers showed a short film to the children and had them tell someone what they saw in the film.[11] These experimentally elicited narratives also exhibit oral-based and literate-based strategies in spoken narratives (Michaels and Collins).

Michaels and Collins found that literate-style speakers used complex syntactic constructions and lexicalization to identify the man, whereas oral-style speakers used special intonation patterns. For example, a literate-style speaker said,

.. there was a man /
... that was ... picking some ... pears //

Notice that she introduced the man by using an independent clause ("there was ...") and then identified him by using a relative clause ("that was picking some pears"). In contrast, a child characterized as oral-style introduced the same character by using two independent clauses:

it was about / ... this man /
he was um / ... um ... takes some um ... peach—/
... some ... pea:rs off the tree /

Even more striking is the difference in the way these two speakers identified the man when he reappeared in the last scene. The literate-style speaker used a restrictive appositive, a relative clause beginning with "who":

... and then / ... they ... walked by the man /
who gave / ... wh-who was picking the pears //

In contrast, the oral-style speaker again used two independent clauses, identifying the man as the same one previously mentioned by using what Michaels and Collins describe as a high rise-fall intonational contour on the word "man":

... and when that ... when he pa:ssed /
by that ma:n /
... the man ... the ma:n came out the tree /

A special intonational contour on "man" signaled, "You know which man I mean, the one I mentioned before."

Michaels and Collins further wanted to compare children's speech style with their written discourse styles, so they included in their study fourth-grade children who saw the film and both told and wrote narratives about it. Oral-literate style differences appeared in the oral narratives of the fourth graders, very much like those described for first graders; furthermore, the children who used literate style strategies in speaking were able to write unambiguous prose, whereas the children who relied on paralinguistic channels in speaking were more likely to write discourse that was ambiguous. In other words, the children neglected to make the switch and lexicalize connections that were lost with the paralinguistic channel.

Oral and Literate Strategies in Conversational Style

I turn now to my own research on conversational style. By tape-recording and transcribing two and a half hours of naturally occurring conversation at Thanksgiving dinner among six participants of various ethnic and geographic backgrounds, I was able to describe the linguistic and paralinguistic features that made up participants' speaking styles in this setting. I focused on such features as pacing, rate of speech, overlap and interruption, intonation, pitch, loudness, syntactic structures, topic, storytelling, irony, humor, and so on (Tannen, *Conversational Style*). Many of these features turned out to cluster in the styles of participants such that three of them seemed to share what might be called one style, while the other three clearly did not share this style.[12] I have called the "dominant" style high-involvement, since many of the features that characterize it can be understood as serving the goals of interpersonal involvement. In this sense the style can be associated with oral strategies. The others, who did not share this style, expected speakers to use strategies that may be seen as more literatelike in style.

One way in which the different patterns of speech emerged was in the speakers' attitudes toward and tendency to use overlapped or simultaneous speech. Three of the participants in the conversation I studied were what I call "cooperative overlappers." That is, two or more of them often talked at the same time, but this overlapping speech did not mean they were not listening to each other, and it did not mean that they wanted to grab the floor—that is, to interrupt each other.[13] Often, a listener talked at the same time as a speaker to show encouragement, or showed understanding by uttering "response cries" (Goffman), told ministories to demonstrate understanding, or finished the speaker's sentences to demonstrate that the listener knew where the sentence was headed. All this overlapping gives the speaker the assurance that he or she isn't in the conversation alone. The active listeners often asked questions of the speaker, which the speaker obviously would have answered anyway, not to indicate that they thought the speaker would not get to that point but to assure the speaker that the information was eagerly awaited. (Space does not permit the presentation of examples to demonstrate this type of interaction, as they require detailed discussion and line-by-line explication, but such examples and analysis can be found in many of my articles on conversational style.)

The preference for overlapping talk in some settings has been reported among numerous ethnic groups—Armenian-American, Black-American, West Indian, Cape Verdean–American, to name just a few. This preference sacrifices the clear relay of information for the show of conversational involvement, and in that sense, it is typically interactive or oral as opposed to literate in style. The effect of overlapping or "chiming in" with speakers who share this style is to grease the conversational wheels. But when speakers use this device with others who do not expect or understand its use, the effect is quite the opposite. The other speaker, feeling interrupted, stops talking. A paradoxical aspect of this style clash is that the interruption is actually created by the one who stops talking when she or he was expected to continue. Yet this reaction is natural for anyone who assumes that in conversation only one person speaks at a time. Such a strategy is literate in style in the sense that it puts emphasis on content, on uttering a complete message, on a kind of elaborated code.[14]

Another aspect of the differences between oral and literate strategies that emerged in this study of conversational style is how speakers got to the point of their stories (i.e., narratives of personal experience), and what the point of their stories was likely to be. In the conversation of speakers whose style I have characterized as oral-like: (1) more stories were told, (2) the stories were more likely to be about their personal experiences, (3) the point of the story was more likely to concern their own feelings about those experiences, and, perhaps most important, (4) the point of the story was generally not lexicalized but was dramatized by recreating the speaker's own reaction to or mimicry of the characters in the narrative.

These differences in storytelling styles left all participants feeling a bit dissatisfied with the narratives told by those who used a different style. Both tended to react to stories told in the other style with a variant of "What's the point?"—the rejoinder Labov has aptly called "withering."

Only the briefest examples can be given here, but detailed examples and discussion can be found in Tannen, "Implications" and *Conversational Style*.

The following is an example of a story told during Thanksgiving dinner by Kurt.[15]

> (1) **K:** Í have a little sèven-year-old student ... a little gírl who
> p
>
> wears those. ......   Shé is *too* →
>
> (2) **T:** └She wears those? [chuckle] ┘
>
> **K:** múch. Can yóu imagine? She's séven years old, and she síts in her
> acc
>
> chair and she goes .... [squeals and squirms in his seat.]
> acc ─────┤
>
> (3) **T:** Oh:: Go::d. ... She's only SEVen?
>
> (4) **K:** And I say well .. hów about let's do sò-and-so. And she says
> acc ─────┤
>
> ... ⌈Okay. ...⌈Jùst like thát.
> [squealing]
>
> (5) **T:** ⌈Oh:::::
>   p
> (6) **D:** └What does it méan.
>   p, acc
> (7) **K:** It's just so ...⌈she's acting like such a little gírl already.
>   p

It is clear from the transcript that the two listeners, David and I (represented in the transcript as D and T respectively), have different reactions to the story. In (3) and (5) I show, through paralinguistically exaggerated responses, that I have appreciated the story. In contrast, David states in (6) that he doesn't understand what the story is supposed to mean. When I played this segment of the taped conversation to David later, he said that Kurt hadn't said what it was about the girl's behavior that he was trying to point out. Moreover, when Kurt answered David's question in (7), he didn't explain at all; David said that "such a little girl" to him means "such a grown-up," whereas what Kurt meant was "such a coquette." David seemed to feel that Kurt wasn't telling the story right; he should have said what he meant. To Kurt, the point was obvious and should not be stated.

At other times in the transcript David tells about his experiences, and there the reactions of Kurt and the other oral-strategy-stylists indicate that they feel David is unnecessarily stating the obvious and not getting to the point quickly enough (see Tannen, *Conversational Style,* for examples and analysis).

By expecting the point of a story to be made explicit and by finding events more important than characters' feelings, some of the participants in this conversation were exhibiting expectations of literatelike strategies in speech. By expecting the point of a story to be dramatized by the speaker and inferred by the hearer and by finding personal feelings more interesting than events, the other speakers were exhibiting oral-like strategies.

It is particularly significant that the speakers in my study who used oral strategies are highly literate. Many of the studies that have distinguished oral and literate strategies in spoken discourse have done so to explain the failure of children of certain ethnic groups to learn to write and read well. The speakers I have found using oral strategies in speaking are New Yorkers of East European Jewish background, a cultural group that has been documented as having a highly oral tradition (Kirshenblatt-Gimblett) as well as a highly literate one. Thus, individuals and groups are not either oral or literate. Rather, people have at their disposal and are inclined to use, based on individual habits as well as cultural conventions, strategies associated with literacy and orality both in speech and in writing.

Oral and Literate Strategies in Spoken Discourse

I will present one final example of how both oral and literate strategies surface in spoken discourse, suggested by recent work by Fillmore on fluency. Fillmore distinguishes four different types of oral fluency: the abilities to (1) talk at length with few pauses; (2) have appropriate things to say in a wide range of contexts; (3) talk in semantically coherent, reasoned, and dense sentences; and (4) be creative and imaginative with language. I suggest that the first two types of fluency are associated with strategies that have been called oral. They grow out of interactive or social goals—the need to keep talk going—where the message content is less important than the fact of talk. In contrast, the last two types of fluency are literatelike, as they depend on the intratextual relations (3) and build on words as carrying meaning in themselves rather than triggering social meaning (4).

Oral and Literate Strategies in Written Discourse

If one thinks at first that written and spoken language are very different, one may think as well that written literature—short stories, poems, novels—are the most different from casual conversation of all. Quite the contrary, imaginative literature has more in common with spontaneous conversation than with the typical written genre, expository prose.

If expository prose is minimally contextualized—that is, the writer demands the least from the reader in terms of filling in background information and crucial premises—imaginative literature is maximally contextualized. The best work of art is the one that suggests the most to the reader with the fewest words. Rader demonstrates this claim, suggesting that maximal contextualization is not incidental to the nature of literature but is basic to it. The goal of creative writers is to encourage their readers to fill in as much as possible. The more the readers supply, the more they will believe and care about the message in the work. As Rader puts it, "The reader of a novel *creates* a world according to the instructions given by the writer." The features we think of as quintessentially literary are, furthermore, basic to spontaneous conversation and not crucial to written expository prose. A few such features are repetition of sounds (alliteration and assonance), repetition of words, recurrent metaphors, parallel syntactic constructions, and compelling rhythm.

Analyzing a transcript of ordinary conversation among family members, Sacks shows that in determining why a speaker chose a particular variant of a word—for example, "because," "cause," or "cuz"—an analyst should look to see if the variant chosen is "sound coordinated with things in its environment." In the case presented, a speaker said (referring to fish they were eating), "*cause* it comes from cold water." A few lines later, the same speaker says, "You better eat something *because* you're gonna be hungry before we get there." In suggesting why the speaker chose "cause" in the first instance and "because" in the second, Sacks notes that "cause" appears in the environment of repeated /k/ sounds in "comes" and "cold," whereas "because" is coordinated with "be" in "be hungry" and "before."

Sacks goes on to suggest that another speaker chooses a rather stilted expression, "Will you be good enough to empty this in there," because at that point in the talk there are a number of measure terms (i.e., an extended metaphor) being used: in this sentence, the term "empty"; in nearby sentences, the words "more" and "missing." Hence the choice of "good *enough*," in which the measure term "enough" is metaphoric. (I have chosen a few representative examples. The work of Harvey Sacks is rich with examples of poetic processes in ordinary conversation.)

Examples of parallel constructions in natural conversation are also ubiquitous. Listen to individuals talk and you will notice how often they set up a syntactic construction and repeat it for several sentences. A brief example will suffice to suggest the process. It comes from a narrative I have analyzed at length elsewhere, comparing spoken and written versions of the same story (Tannen, "Oral and Literate Strategies"). In a spontaneous conversation with some friends, the speaker impressed her audience with a co-worker's linguistic ability by saying, "And he knows Spanish, and he knows French, and he knows English, and he knows German. And *he* is a *gent*leman." The rhythm of the repeated constructions sweeps the hearers along, creating the effect of a long list, suggesting even more than the four languages that are actually named. (Such parallel constructions are probably an aid to speech production, since the repeated construction can be uttered automatically while the speaker plans new information to insert in the variable slot. It is a technique public speakers can be heard to use frequently.) Furthermore, the speaker can use the established rhythm of the repeated construction to play off against, as in the phrase that follows the parallelism: "And *he* is a *gent*leman." Contrast this with the way the same speaker conveyed the same idea in writing: "He knows at least four languages fluently—Spanish, French, English, and something else."[16]

Rhythm, then, is basic to this highly oral strategy of parallel constructions. Erickson and Shultz and Scollon (in "Rhythmic Integration") have demonstrated that rhythm is basic to participation in face-to-face conversation. Erickson has shown that ordinary conversation can be set to a metronome, and verbal and nonverbal participation takes place on the beat. In order to show listenership and to know when to talk, one must participate in this rhythm. In conversation with speakers from another culture or with speakers who tend to take turns slower or faster than you are used to, you can't tell when they are finished and you don't know when to come in. The effect is like trying to enter a line of dancers who are going just a bit faster or slower than you expect; if you can't adjust to the beat, you have to either drop back or bumble along, spoiling everyone's sense of harmony.

Thus rhythm is basic to conversational involvement in the most mechanical sense. It also contributes in conversation, as it does in music, poetry, and oratory, to the impact of the discourse on the audience. The rhythm sweeps the audience along and convinces them by moving them emotionally. Saville-Troike quotes Duncan to the effect that Hitler, in his foreword to *Mein Kampf*, apologizes for writing a book, since he believes that people are moved not by writing but by the spoken word and that "every great movement owed its growth to great orators, not to great writers."

Why is it that literary language builds on and perfects features of mundane conversation? I believe it is because literary language, like ordinary conversation, is dependent for its effect on interpersonal involvement. It fosters and builds on the involvement between speaker and hearer instead of (conventionally) ignoring or underplaying it. And it depends for its impact on the emotional involvement of the hearer. In contrast, expository prose, associated with literate tradition in the way we have seen, depends for its impact on impressing the audience with the strength and completeness of its argument—that is, aspects of its content.[17]

Oral Strategies in Successful Spoken and Written Discourse Processes

A particularly fascinating aspect of the notion of oral and literate strategies is the possibility that strategies that have been characterized as oral may be the most efficient for both writing and reading. Successful writing requires not the production of discourse with no sense of audience but, rather, the positing of a hypothetical reader and playing to the needs of that audience. This is a sense in which writing may be seen as decontextualized: the context must be posited rather than being found in the actual setting. The ability to imagine what a hypothetical reader needs to know is therefore an interactive skill. Reading is a matter of decoding written words. But the act of reading efficiently is often a matter not so much of decoding (though this skill must underlie any reading) but of discerning a familiar text structure, hypothesizing what information will be presented, and being ready for it when it comes. By making maximum use of context, good readers may be using oral strategies.

Summary

I have suggested that previous work on the oral and literate tradition and spoken versus written language has led to two hypotheses. The first—that written language is decontextualized whereas spoken is context-bound—seems to grow out of the types of spoken and written discourse that were examined: face-to-face conversation on the one hand and expository prose on the other. I suggest therefore that the differences result not so much from the spoken and written modes as from the relative focus on interpersonal involvement on the one hand and relative focus on content on the other. In this sense, the features of discourse grow out of communicative goals.

The second hypothesis is that spoken language establishes cohesion by use of paralinguistic and nonverbal channels, whereas written language depends more on lexicalization. This observation indeed reflects differences between spoken and written discourse.

Given these views of oral and literate strategies in discourse, I then demonstrated that strategies associated with both modes can be found in both spoken and written discourse. Finally, I have suggested—and this may be the most radical of my assertions—that oral strategies may underlie successful discourse production and comprehension in the written as well as the oral mode.

Notes

[1] I recently organized a conference entitled "Analyzing Discourse: Text and Talk." I intended "text" and "talk" to be overlapping categories: "talk" is a kind of text, and "texts" can be talk. Most people understood this to be a dichotomy, however, and understood text and talk as two different and mutually exclusive kinds of discourse.

[2] My own research on interaction suggests, however, that when signals or references are misunderstood, hearers are not likely to ask for clarification. Rather, they take their misinterpretation for a correct interpretation and construct an understanding based on it. Only when the understanding they so construct becomes completely untenable do they stop the interaction to question meaning.

[3] This point always brings to mind the line from T. S. Eliot, "How much it means to me that I say this to you." The impression of such metamessages is often opaque to teenagers, who become disillusioned with their parents for "saying what they don't mean" and "talking empty talk," which they mistake for hypocrisy and replace with conventionalized talk of their own, which in turn strikes their parents and other adults as "meaningless."

[4] Though current radio and tv seems to be getting more interactive than content-focused, including the news.

[5] In teaching writing, I used to demonstrate the difference between one-way and two-way communication by use of a diagram that two students tried to recreate without looking at or talking to each other. One faced the back of the room and gave instructions, while the other followed the instructions and drew the diagram as proficiently as possible without asking questions. I then allowed two other students to reproduce the diagram in the same way—only they were allowed to talk to and watch each other. Of course the second pair negotiated a fairly reasonable approximation of the diagram, whereas the one-way communication always produced something very different. The students then concluded, in discussion, that the one-way situation was more like writing, and so in writing they had better anticipate and preclude some of the confusion that might arise in the mind of the reader. (I am grateful to Marcia Perlstein for teaching me this exercise.)

[6] This reaction is likely when confronting any impediment to effortless communication: having to whisper because of laryngitis, shout because your addressee is hard of hearing or in another room, or take pains to translate because of language differences. Since I am hard of hearing, I have experienced this response from other people innumerable times, when a request for repetition elicits the maddening "it wasn't important."

[7] What I am saying is completely true only for print. In handwriting, one can capture hints of these attitudes by varying size and manner of writing, underlining, using capitalization, and so on.

[8]In fiction, as I will discuss, writers attempt to create the impact of spoken language and so may write, "She said with a wink," or "He said, laughing," instead of telling outright, "This was a joke."

[9]The question of whether spoken or written language is more "complex," and even whether one has more or less subordination, is still unsettled. Some have asserted that written language is more complex (Chafe, "Integration"; Ochs); others, that spoken language is more complex (Halliday 1979). A likely explanation is that these scholars are employing different definitions of "complexity."

[10]One always hesitates to cite Bernstein because of the pernicious application his theories have inspired to the effect that some children spoke restricted code and in effect didn't have language. Bernstein should be credited, however, with the identification of different uses of language conventions in discourse. He was in error in calling these different "codes," a term used by linguists to refer to different languages or registers (Hill and Varenne).

[11]The children told their narratives to an adult research assistant, but one who had been participating in the classroom over the entire year. The film is the one (affectionately) called "the pear film" which was commissioned for a project directed by Wallace Chafe at the University of California, Berkeley. Narratives told about this film form the basis of much research on discourse including Chafe's "Flow of Thought," the papers collected in Chafe's *Pear Stories,* and Tannen's "What's in a Frame?" "A Comparative Analysis," and "Spoken and Written Narrative." In the film, a man is seen picking pears. A boy comes along, takes a basket of pears away on his bike, and later falls off his bike. He is helped by three other boys to whom he gives pears. At the end, the three boys eating their pears walk past the man who was picking them in the first scene. These scenes were designed to set up a problem for the narrators: they needed to identify the man in the last scene as the same man who appeared in the first scene.

Transcription conventions used by Michaels and Collins: three dots (...) = measurable pause; a colon (:) = lengthening of vowel; a slash(/) = minor tone group boundary; two slashes (//) = major tone group boundary. Lines above and below words indicate intonational contours.

[12]I could not say whether the other three shared a style, as it was the pattern of the faster-paced speakers that "dominated." This will always be the case when one or more speakers are faster relative to the others. I have stressed in my writing, as have others (e.g., Scollon, "The Machine Stops"), that it is always the interaction that is crucial; conversation is a joint production. Speakers' styles are never absolute but always partly a response to the styles of the other participants, which are simultaneously created as a response to theirs.

[13]Note that this pattern is somewhat different from a related pattern that Erickson and his collaborators have elegantly demonstrated (Erickson; Shultz, Florio, and Erickson) of conversations that have multiple floors. In the conversation I have been describing there is one floor (though at other times there are multiple ones), but more than one speaker can speak at a time without wresting the floor; the role of listener is not a silent one.

[14]It is important to note, however, that this is simply one kind of elaboration, that of the message channel. The other style is using elaboration of another channel: the emotive or interpersonal one. See Tannen "The Oral/Literate Continuum" and "Indirectness."

[15]K = Kurt, D = David, T = DT (the author)

Transcription conventions: p = pianissimo (soft); acc = accelerando (fast); a colon (:) indicates lengthening of vowel; ⌐ indicates high pitch; ⌐⌐ indicates very high pitch; → indicates speech continues uninterrupted (look for continuation on next line). Brackets show simultaneous speech. Three dots (. . .) indicate half-second pause. Each additional dot indicates another half-second pause. Line over "okay" shows intonation contour.

[16]It may seem surprising that the writer wrote "and something else." She had all the time she needed to think of what "something else" was and put it in. But this writer in this case was writing something very much like a short story, so she combined features of spokenlike and of writtenlike discourse. Elsewhere I analyze in detail which features she uses (Tannen, "Oral and Literate Strategies"). The present example is one in which she uses a writtenlike device in writing, by collapsing the information into a more efficient though less compelling construction, as well as an oral-like device in the vague referent "and something else."

[17]This distinction underlies a comment in a column by Meg Greenfield in *Newsweek*. She ended the column about arms control by suggesting, "We need to look at the [arms-control] agreements we have made and are going to embark on in a much more intelligent, critical, and unsentimental way" (29 June 1981). Note that the notions "critical" and "intelligent" go along with "unsentimental."

Works Cited

Bateson, Gregory. *Steps to an Ecology of Mind.* New York: Ballantine, 1972.

Bernstein, Basil. "Elaborated and Restricted Codes: Their Social Origins and Some Consequences." *American Anthropologist* 66.6.2(1964):55-69.

Bolinger, Dwight. "Pronouns in Discourse." In *Discourse and Syntax.* Ed. Talmý Givon. New York: Academic Press, 1979, 289-309.

Chafe, Wallace L. "The Flow of Thought and the Flow of Language." In *Discourse and Syntax.* Ed. Talmy Givon. New York: Academic Press, 1979, 159-81.

———. "Integration and Involvement in Speaking, Writing, and Oral Literature." In *Spoken and Written Language: Exploring Orality and Literacy.* Ed. Deborah Tannen. Norwood, N.J.: Ablex, 1982, 35-53.

———. *The Pear Stories: Cognitive, Cultural, and Linguistic Aspects of Narrative Production.* Norwood, N.J.: Ablex, 1980.

Cook-Gumperz, Jenny, and John J. Gumperz. "From Oral to Written Culture: The Transition to Literacy." In *Variation in Writing: Functional and Linguistic-Cultural Differences.* Ed. Marcia Farr Whiteman. Vol. 1 of *Writing: The Nature, Development, and Teaching of Written Communication.* Hillsdale, N.J.: Lawrence Erlbaum Associates, 1981, 89-109.

Coulthard, Malcolm. *An Introduction to Discourse Analysis.* London: Longman, 1977.

Duncan, Hugh Dalziel. *Communication and the Social Order.* London: Oxford Univ. Press, 1962.

Erickson, Frederick. "Money Tree, Lasagna Bush, Salt and Pepper: Social Construction of Topical Cohesion in a Conversation among Italian-Americans." In *Georgetown University Round Table on Languages and Linguistics 1981, Analyzing Discourse: Text and Talk*. Ed. Deborah Tannen. Washington, D.C.: Georgetown Univ. Press, 1982, 43-70.

————, and Jeffrey Shultz. *The Counselor as Gatekeeper: Social Interaction in Interviews*. New York: Academic Press, 1982.

Fillmore, Charles. "On Fluency." In *Individual Differences in Language Ability and Language Behavior*. Ed. Charles J. Fillmore, Daniel Kempler, and William S.-Y. Wang. New York: Academic Press, 1979, 85-101.

Goffman, Erving. "Response Cries." *Language* 54(1978):787-815. Rpt. in his *Forms of Talk*. Philadelphia: Univ. of Pennsylvania Press, 1981, 78-123.

Goody, Jack. *The Domestication of the Savage Mind*. Cambridge: Cambridge Univ. Press, 1977.

Gumperz, John, Hannah Kaltman, and Mary Catherine O'Connor. "Cohesion in Written and Spoken Discourse." In *Coherence in Spoken and Written Discourse*. Ed. Deborah Tannen. Norwood, N.J.: Ablex, 1983.

Halliday, M. A. K. "Differences between Spoken and Written Language: Some Implications for Literacy Teaching." In *Communication through Reading: Proceedings of the Fourth Australian Reading Conference*. Ed. Glenda Page, John Elkins, and Barrie O'Connor. Vol. 2. Adelaide, S.A.: Australian Reading Assoc., 1979, 37-52.

Hill, Clifford, and Herve Varenne. "Family Language and Education: The Sociolinguistic Model of Restricted and Elaborated Codes." *Social Science Information* 20.1 (1981):187-227.

Kay, Paul. "Language Evolution and Speech Style." In *Sociocultural Dimensions of Language Change*. Ed. Ben G. Blount and Mary Sanches. New York: Academic Press, 1977, 21-33.

Kirshenblatt-Gimblett, Barbara. "The Concept and Varieties of Narrative Performance in East European Jewish Culture." In *Explorations in the Ethnography of Speaking*. Ed. Richard Bauman and Joel Sherzer. Cambridge: Cambridge Univ. Press, 1974, 283-308.

Kroll, Barbara. "Combining Ideas in Written and Spoken English: A Look at Subordination." In *Discourse across Time and Space*. Ed. Elinor O. Keenan and Tina Bennet. Southern California Occasional Papers in Linguistics no. 5. Los Angeles: Univ. of Southern California, Linguistics Dept., 1977, 69-108.

Labov, William. *Language in the Inner City*. Philadelphia: Univ. of Pennsylvania Press, 1972.

Malinowski, Bronislaw. "The Problem of Meaning in Primitive Languages." Supplement 1 in *The Meaning of Meaning*. Ed. C. K. Ogden and I. A. Richards. New York: Harcourt, 1923, 296-336.

Michaels, Sarah, and Jim Collins. "Oral Discourse Style: Classroom Interaction and the Acquisition of Literacy." In *Coherence in Spoken and Written Discourse*. Ed. Deborah Tannen. Norwood, N.J.: Ablex, 1983.

Michaels, Sarah, and Jenny Cook-Gumperz. "A Study of Sharing Time with First Grade Students: Discourse Narratives in the Classroom." In *Proceedings of the Fifth Annual Meeting of the Berkeley Linguistics Society*. Univ. of California, Berkeley, Institute of Human Learning, 1979, 647-59.

Ochs, Elinor. "Planned and Unplanned Discourse." In *Discourse and Syntax*. Ed. Talmy Givon. New York: Academic Press, 1979, 51-80.

Olson, David R. "From Utterance to Text: The Bias of Language in Speech and Writing." *Harvard Educational Review* 47.3(1977):257-81.

Ong, Walter J. *The Presence of the Word*. New Haven: Yale Univ. Press, 1967.

Rader, Margaret. "Context in Written Language: The Case of Imaginative Fiction." In *Spoken and Written Language: Exploring Orality and Literacy*. Ed. Deborah Tannen. Norwood, N.J.: Ablex, 1982, 185-98.

Sacks, Harvey. Lecture notes, 11 March 1971.

Saville-Troike, Muriel. *The Ethnography of Communication*. London: Blackwell, 1982.

Scollon, Ron. "The Machine Stops: Silence in the Metaphor of Malfunction." In *Perspectives on Silence*. Ed. Deborah Tannen and Muriel Saville-Troike. Forthcoming.

———. "The Rhythmic Integration of Ordinary Talk." In *Georgetown University Round Table on Languages and Linguistics 1981, Analyzing Discourse: Text and Talk*. Ed. Deborah Tannen. Washington, D.C.: Georgetown Univ. Press, 1982, 335-49.

Shultz, Jeffrey J., Susan Florio, and Frederick Erickson. "Where's the Floor? Aspects of the Cultural Organization of Social Relationships in Communication at Home and at School." In *Children in and out of School: Ethnography and Education*. Ed. Perry Gilmore and Allan A. Glatthorn. Washington, D.C.: Center for Applied Linguistics, 1982, 88-123.

Tannen, Deborah. "A Comparative Analysis of Oral Narrative Style." In *The Pear Stories: Cognitive, Cultural, and Linguistic Aspects of Narrative Production*. Ed. Wallace L. Chafe. Norwood, N.J.: Ablex, 1980, 51-87.

———. *Conversational Style: Analyzing Talk among Friends*. Norwood, N.J.: Ablex, 1983.

———. "Indirectness in Discourse: Ethnicity as Conversational Style." *Discourse Processes* 4.3(1981):221-38.

———. "The Machine-Gun Question: An Example of Conversational Style." *Journal of Pragmatics* 5.5(1981):383-97.

———. "New York Jewish Conversational Style." *International Journal of the Sociology of Language* 30(1981):133-49.

———. "Oral and Literate Strategies in Spoken and Written Narratives." *Language* 58.1(1982):1-21.

———. "The Oral/Literate Continuum in Discourse." In *Spoken and Written Language: Exploring Orality and Literacy*. Ed. Deborah Tannen. Norwood, N.J.: Ablex, 1982, 1-16.

———. "Spoken and Written Narrative in English and Greek." In *Coherence in Spoken and Written Discourse*. Ed. Deborah Tannen. Norwood, N.J.: Ablex, 1983.

———. "What's in a Frame?" In *New Directions in Discourse Processing*. Ed. Roy Freedle. Norwood, N.J.: Ablex, 1979, 137-81.

Literacy and Cognition:
A Developmental Perspective

Frank J. D'Angelo

During the past six or seven years, articles in the popular press and in professional publications have focused on what has come to be called the "crisis in literacy." According to one of the earliest articles, written in 1974 by Malcolm Scully for the *Chronicle of Higher Education,*

> stories of students who "can't write" or who are "functionally illiterate" come not only from two-year colleges and four-year institutions with open admissions, but also from private colleges and major public institutions that have traditionally attracted verbally skilled students. (1)

A part of Malcolm Scully's evidence came from a survey of English department chairpersons conducted by the Association of Departments of English. The ADE found that there was a widespread concern that students coming to college, middle-class students as well as disadvantaged students, "had a far less firm grasp on fundamentals" than students in previous years (Scully 1). Some of the evidence was anecdotal. Among the comments the ADE received from teachers in private colleges, major state universities, urban colleges, and a prestigious women's school were these:

- Students are less prepared than ever for articulating thoughts in writing. They are affected by antilinguistic assumptions of our culture.
- We have to offer more remedial composition as a result of poor high-school training. In 1970, we had 106 remedial students; now we have 376. These are not minority kids but WASPs from supposedly good high schools.
- We're getting verbally gifted students who can't organize their thoughts in writing.
- We are faced with an increasingly desperate attempt to overcome the semi-literacy of most incoming students, who have had little or no practice in reading or writing.

It did not take long for the popular press to take up the cry that the level of literacy of students entering college was alarmingly low. For example, in an article entitled "College Essays: Freshmen Ain't So Good, Mostly" that appeared in the 3 November 1974 edition of the *Los Angeles Times*, Philip Hager noted:

> of the 2,718 new students admitted to Berkeley this year [1974] a record number—48%—was found to need remedial instruction in basic English composition on the basis of a three page essay test. At other UC campuses, the percentages ranged from 40 to 65. (1)

These are not "boneheads or dolts," reported Hager, but students taken from the top of their respective high school classes. Yet they seem unable to express their thoughts in writing. Not only do they make the usual errors that one might expect of less educated students (errors in subject and verb agreement or lack of agreement between a pronoun and its antecedent), but they misuse words with distressing frequency. They use nouns when verbs are needed. They misspell words. They invent incorrect or inappropriate words (e.g., "uneducation"), because their own vocabularies are either impoverished or nonexistent (Hager 6).

Hager's article was followed by an outpouring of other articles from newspapers and magazines such as the *Christian Science Monitor*, the *Wall Street Journal*, the *New York Times*, *Time*, *Newsweek*, the *Yale Alumni Magazine*, *Harper's*, and the *National Observer*. The *Newsweek* article especially, titled "Why Johnny Can't Write," caused a nationwide clamor. The opening paragraph set the tone for the whole article:

> If your children are attending college, the chances are that when they graduate they will be unable to write ordinary, expository English with any real degree of structure and lucidity. If they are in high school and planning to attend college, the chances are less than even that they will be able to write English at the minimal college level when they get there. If they are not planning to attend college, their skills in writing English may not even qualify them for secretarial or clerical work. And if they are attending elementary school, they are almost certainly not being given the kind of required reading material, much less writing instruction, that might make it possible for them eventually to write comprehensible English. Willy-nilly, the U.S. educational system is spawning a generation of semiliterates. (Skels 58)

The *Yale Alumni Magazine* ran a series of articles called "The Writing Gap" with an editorial preface that began in this way:

> Anyone who reads student writing today knows that students can't write. The students know it themselves—their eagerness to take writing courses is a desperate cry for help. It is easy to blame the schools and colleges for so fundamental a failure, and some of the blame is properly theirs. But the causes are rooted far more deeply in a society which rears its children on sentimental and shoddy reading matter, which bathes them in the linguistic sludge of television, and which debases the English language in the place where all learning begins: at home. (15)

There were some, however, who doubted that a crisis in literacy actually existed. But the evidence began to mount. For example, verbal scores on achievement tests declined precipitously between 1963 and 1977, as studies by Harnischfeger and Wiley and by Bishop show. The peak score of the Scholastic Aptitude Test in 1963 was 478. This score declined to 444 in 1974 and to 434 in 1975. By 1977, the scores on the SAT declined 49 points on a scale of 600. Scores on the ACT English Aptitude Test also declined from a mean score of 18.7 in 1966 to a score of 17.6 in 1974. The National Assessment of Educational Progress in Writing reported that the writing of seventeen-year-olds declined markedly in quality between 1970 and 1974. These writers had difficulty writing coherent paragraphs. Their writing was filled with awkward sentences, fragments, and run-on sentences, and it showed signs of an impoverished vocabulary (see also Mellon's two studies on the National Writing Assessment).

According to a report in the *New York Times* (quoted in Bishop 2), publishers are resorting to simplified language in their textbooks because college students cannot read college-level materials. An editorial in the *Wall Street Journal* titled "Stone-Age Thinking" reported ironically that a pamphlet, written by the Association of American Publishers and intended to help students read college material, had to be rewritten on a ninth-grade level because many college freshmen couldn't understand it.

At the City University of New York, which began an open admissions policy in 1970, it was reported that almost all of the CUNY students took some kind of remedial instruction. Although many of these students graduated from high school with an average score of eighty percent, only about a third were prepared for college-level work in English and at least another third lacked even the rudiments of English. Two years ago, the City University of New York ruled that before students could enter their junior year, they would have to reach a twelfth-grade level in reading, and they would have to be able to write an acceptable essay of about three hundred words (Bishop 3).

Other evidence supporting the claim that there was a crisis in literacy came from Great Britain, where a six-hundred-page study of the state of English in the schools revealed that the level of literacy among British students had declined over the past few years (from about 1970 to 1975). A nineteen-member committee recommended "that a national center for language education be established, one concerned with the teaching of English from infancy to advanced studies" ("Report" 23).

The crisis, then, may be one of international import. And it concerns all kinds of students—bright students who have done well on SAT and ACT tests, poorly prepared students, semiliterate students, minority students, disadvantaged students.

Not all critics, however, accepted the notion that there was a crisis in literacy. Richard Lloyd-Jones, a former chair of the Conference on College Composition and Communication and chair of the English department at the University of Iowa, commented in the University of Iowa *Spectator* that "the sad truth is that the public wailing about the quality of writing has far more to say about the personality and motives of those who are moaning than it does about the quality of writing. We just don't know much about writing in bulk lots" (2). Richard Ohmann, who was at that time editor of *College English,* retained a healthy skepticism when in 1976 he called for manuscripts for a special issue of *College English:*

> Is there a decline in literacy? in writing ability?
>
> If so, what are its causes? To what extent is it accountable to changes in schooling? To changes in American society? What can—or should— college English teachers be doing about it? Are there college programs that successfully make up deficits in verbal skills? Is "bonehead English" an idea whose time has come again? Do competency requirements for graduation help? Should this be a problem of the English department, or the whole college or university? Can we distinguish between the traditional basis—spelling, usage, etc.—and some others that have more to do with intellectual competence? Can English teachers usefully shape the national concern with verbal competence, rather than simply respond to needs expressed by pundits, legislators, regents, and businessmen?
>
> If, on the other hand, there has been no significant decline in reading or writing ability among college students, what explains the outcry? What can English teachers do to correct public misconceptions? Is our responsibility confined to the classroom, or does it include social and political action? (819)

When the issue finally appeared in January 1977 Ohmann expressed his disappointment with the response. "We were . . . disappointed by the *scope* of the contributions," he wrote:

> A large proportion merely reiterated the public concerns and in terms very similar to those employed by the media. Others devoted most of their energy to suggesting better ways to teach writing. We might infer from these facts that the profession accepts not only the public assessment of the literacy "crisis" but also the blame for it. Our original call queried whether in fact there has been a significant decline in reading and writing ability among students. Yet not one contribution reviewed and analyzed in any detail the assumptions, methods, and statistics of the testing on which so much of the public outcry seems to be based. Are these assumptions, methods, and statistics as invulnerable to criticism as our professional silence suggests? (441)

Granted, it may be difficult to prove that "there has been a significant decline in reading and writing ability among students" over the past ten years. One reason is that we have not kept records of what the reading and writing abilities of students were like ten or fifteen years ago. But the decline in college admissions tests scores, the anecdotal evidence of teachers, and projects such as those of the National Assessment of Educational Progress do seem to suggest that something is wrong. J. Stanley Ahmann, in "A Report on National Assessment in Seven Learning Areas," maintains that there is "mounting evidence that too many children and adults have not achieved the language competencies required to cope successfully with life needs." To support this contention, he gives examples of the findings by the National Assessment of Educational Progress:

(1) Relatively few young Americans could read and interpret graphs, maps, or tables.
(2) Less than half of the nation's seventeen-year-olds and young adults could accurately read all parts of a ballot.
(3) Only 14 percent of the adults could write letters with no punctuation errors.
(4) Only 57 percent of the adults wrote adequate directions for making or doing something.
(5) Only 49 percent of the adults composed acceptable letters for the purpose of ordering a product. (63-64)

According to this report, Johnny is not the only one who cannot read or write; his parents cannot either.

If there has been some disagreement as to whether or not there is in fact a crisis in literacy, there has been even more disagreement about the causes of the problem. A. Bartlett Giamatti, then professor of English and comparative literature at Yale University and now its president, has attributed the decline in writing ability to the Free Speech Movement of the early sixties and seventies. In an article written for the *Yale Alumni Magazine,* Giamatti gave this profile of today's college students:

> They are the products of the anti-structures of that time. They have come and are coming out of the "open classroom," vertical grouping, modular buildings with 50 pupils to a room. They have come out of the "new math" and its concepts, its legos and blocks and set theory, not knowing how to multiply. They have come out of "individualized instruction" and "elective systems," not knowing how to listen to anyone else, not knowing how to take a direction.
>
> They have come out of the sentimental '60's, where "repressive" and "arbitrary" grades were done away with, not able to take the pressure of grading. They have come out of a primary and secondary world where "personal development" was said to be worth more than achievement, where "creativity" was the highest goal and was often completely divorced from one of its essential components: discipline. And they are arriving in college often completely at a loss about how to cope with their work, with their time, with themselves.
>
> But most of all, these present college students, and those now in

junior high and high school, cannot handle the English language, particularly as it is written. (18)

Others have attributed the decline in writing ability to "progressive" teaching. According to Neville Bennett of Lancaster University, progressive teaching is teaching done in informal classes where students can move around and gather into informal groups. They can talk when they please and choose only those subjects and tasks that interest them. There are no strict boundaries between subjects, and tests and homework are seldom given. By contrast, traditional teaching is done in structured situations where there are fixed subjects, little movement or talking, and plenty of tests and homework. In these schools, the teacher speaks to the class as a whole, instead of moving about from group to group. Bennett and a team of researchers at Lancaster University claim that children in traditional classes fare much better than do those in progressive classes. They are months ahead of the other children in reading ability, mathematics, and English.

In *The Literacy Hoax,* Paul Copperman puts the blame squarely on the public schools:

> The amount and quality of academic work demanded of public school students has been cut sharply. For one thing, students are simply not taking as many academic courses as they did in the early 1960s. As a percentage of high school enrollment, enrollments in English, history, science, and math are sharply lower. Even the enrollment figures underestimate the reduction in the academic course load of the average student. Many traditional and rigorous courses have been replaced with fare best described as educational entertainment. Courses in film literature and science fiction are replacing English composition; courses in contemporary world issues and comparative revolutions are replacing world history. In these courses the amount of work assigned and the standard to which it is held are considerably lower than in the courses they replace. (16)

Copperman contends that even in those classes where the subject matter and teaching are fairly traditional, the standards of grading and the amount of work required have been considerably reduced. The book includes Copperman's interviews with teachers and administrators from a wide range of high schools; "the consensus of these teachers," he states, "is that the average student is assigned 50 percent less reading and writing than in the early 1960s, and that standards for written work are correspondingly low" (16).

Not everyone puts the blame for poor student writing on high school teachers. In a provocative article in *Harper's* magazine, Gene Lyons, a former teacher of English at state universities in Massachusetts, Arkansas, and Texas, claims that all too often college professors balk at teaching college students to write. He laments:

> The business of the American English department is not the teaching of literacy; it is the worship of literature. After eight years' experience as a

student and seven more as a faculty member at five state universities, I am every day more astonished by the increasing distance between most English departments and the everyday concerns of the society that pays their bills. (35)

A special advisory panel appointed by the College Entrance Examination Board to investigate why student scores on the Scholastic Aptitude Tests have dropped so sharply had this to say about the decline in student performance:

An amalgam of social and educational changes—less emphasis on "critical reading and careful writing" in America's high schools, too much television-watching, more one-parent families, and tumultuous political upheavals that formed a "decade of distraction"—probably accounts for the present decline in the aptitude-test scores of college-bound high-school seniors in the 1970s. (Fields 1)

The panel was quick to add that it had only circumstantial evidence about the decline in literacy and acknowledged that there is no one cause of the decline in SAT scores. But it suggested that generally there has been a lowering of standards: "Acceptance of excessive student absenteeism, grade inflation, reduced homework, and automatic grade-to-grade promotion all are involved, the panel indicates" (Fields 13).

Despite the plausibility of many of the reasons given for the decline in literacy, unfortunately we cannot with certainty prove many of the hypotheses that have been offered as evidence. What we do know with some certainty is that composition requirements in high schools and colleges eroded during the sixties and early seventies, that the composition of student populations has changed (in some schools, for example, there are more disadvantaged students), and that more high-risk students, students who in past years may have dropped out before graduating from high school, are now staying in school longer (see Smith).

Attempts to improve the situation began around 1976. Many schools, convinced that their students had serious deficiencies in grammar, usage, and mechanics, advocated a return to the basics. In some schools, this trend has meant developing remediation programs, setting up writing laboratories, and expanding writing programs. In other schools, a return to the basics has meant intensive study in the fundamentals of spelling, punctuation, capitalization, formal grammar, sentence structure, and paragraph development.

Yet despite these attempts to help students cope with the written language, many of the same problems that teachers and the general public complained about in the early seventies persist. As in the past, some of the evidence is anecdotal, consisting of complaints from teachers and parents. But some of the evidence is more specific. For example, the College Board recently announced that test scores are still declining. The board indicated that high school seniors scored lower in the SAT in 1979-80 than they did in the previous testing period, continuing a decline that started seventeen years ago. The American College Testing Board stated that the ACT scores of college-bound students also dipped slightly in 1979-80. As I noted earlier, the average score on the verbal part of the SAT test in 1963 was 478; in 1979-80 it was 424. The average expected score is 500. The scale for the test is between 200 and 800. The average ACT verbal score in 1943 was 20.4. In 1979-80, it was 18.6. The scale of the ACT is between 1 and 36 (see "College Board Test Scores"). Even more recently, the National Assessment of Educational Progress reported that most of the nine-, thirteen-, and seventeen-year-old students it tested had serious difficulties with the written language. This report was based on writing exercises given to students three times between 1969 and 1979. Even though critics have attacked the validity of some of these tests, parents and educators worry about the declining scores and question the quality of education that students are getting.

If problems such as those I have pointed out continue to persist and if the remedies offered so far have failed to work, perhaps we should be looking elsewhere for underlying causes and for possible solutions. What we do know for certain is that the student population has changed. Many students come from what Walter Ong would call a "residually oral" culture, a stratum within the mainstream of society where oral modes of expression permeate thinking. They come from homes where speech is more widespread than reading or writing. These students have acquired some elements of literacy, but those habits of mind that depend on literacy are imperfectly or incompletely developed. Other students have mastered literate modes of thought, at least to the extent that they can function fairly well in the classroom, but their leisure time is dominated by media which reinforce oral modes of thinking. Walter Ong would describe the thinking of these students as being that of "electronic orality" or "secondary orality." Although these students move adequately between oral and literate modes of thinking, their thinking in some respects may be more like that of residually oral students or perhaps like the thinking of the nonliterate Russian peasants that A. R. Luria studied in the 1930s or the singers of tales that Eric Havelock writes about in his studies of preliterate Greek culture.

The thinking of preliterate and nonliterate people is concrete, syncretic, diffuse, perceptual, affective, situation-bound, additive, and digressive, concerned with everyday events, actions, and happenings rather than with abstract ideas. The thinking of literate people tends to be more abstract, discrete, definite, and articulated, consisting of generalizations, deductions, and inferences. Without writing, according to some scholars, the mind cannot participate in the kinds of analytical, sequential thinking necessary to develop even a single magazine article. Writing may be artificial, but it is also an artifice and an art that seems to be essential for the development of consciousness.

What I am suggesting is that one possible reason for the decline in literacy might be related to the incipient or undeveloped forms of literate thinking in some of our students. This point of view makes the solution to problems in literacy dependent upon our understanding of the cognitive development of our students, not on our understanding of the kinds of errors that such students make (although we might infer something about their thinking from the study of such errors).

A number of scholars have suggested that the problems of literacy may be intimately tied to the development of consciousness. For instance, Walter Ong has hypothesized that in the development of the individual consciousness, each person recapitulates the historical development of communications media. Ong depicts this development as a series of stages, moving from a primarily oral stage (as in preliterate Greek society), to a residually oral stage (a stage after the invention of literacy in which people continue to display habits of thinking that are predominantly oral), to a literate stage (a stage in which the symbol systems of literacy have been interiorized), and finally to an electronic stage of secondary orality. In each of these stages, the medium (the human voice, print, writing, books, television) is partially responsible for transforming thought processes.

My thinking about literacy and the evolution of consciousness has developed along lines similar to those of Ong and Havelock. In an article published in 1978 in the *Quarterly Journal of Speech,* entitled "An Ontological Basis for a Modern Theory of the Composing Process," I theorized that the series of stages through which the mind advances in the composing process is similar to the sequence of stages in the evolution of consciousness. "In this view, the composing process is analogous to universal evolutionary processes, in which an original, amorphous, undifferentiated whole gradually evolves into a more complex, differentiated one" (79). Applying this idea to writing, the writer moves from a felt intention, not clearly defined, amorphous, in unorganized congeries or heaps; to analysis, where the parts of the piece of writing are sorted out and differentiated, sometimes almost to the point of fragmentation; to synthesis, where the parts are brought together into an articulated whole. In each of these stages, there may be considerable overlapping.

These stages are similar in some respects to those outlined by Ong, but I came to them from other sources. In looking at the paradigms of different disciplines, especially those of comparative and developmental psychology, I noted that the principles underlying the systems of these disciplines were remarkably alike. These principles were often depicted as a series of developmental stages. For example, Piaget (3-73) depicts four stages in the mental development of children: the sensori-motor stage, the preoperational state, the stage of concrete operations, and the stage of formal or abstract operations. The Russian psychologist L. S. Vygotsky describes three basic phases of concept formation in children: putting together objects in unorganized congeries or heaps, thinking in complexes, and finally isolating elements and seeing them apart from the concrete experience in which they are embedded. Jerome Bruner (327-28) characterizes the course of cognitive growth in individuals as moving from action, through imagery, to language. Corresponding to these stages of mental development are three modes of knowing: enactive, iconic, and symbolic (327-28). Alfred North Whitehead traces three stages of intellectual growth in the individual: the stage of romance, the stage of precision, and the stage of generalization (28-30). Finally, Heinz Werner portrays the course of mental development "from the primitive to the civilized" as a movement from a global, diffuse, undifferentiated, and uncentralized stage to a stage of increasing differentiation and centralization, culminating in hierarchic integration (*Comparative Psychology* 40-51). The following scheme depicts the parallelism that exists among these formal systems:

Piaget	sensorimotor	preoperational	concrete operations	abstract operations
Vygotsky		diffuse grouping	thinking in complexes	abstracting
Bruner		action	imagining	symbolic thinking
Whitehead		romance	precision	generalization
Werner		global	analytic	synthetic

These are not exact correspondences, of course. But these systems do reveal a similar patterning (Piaget's first two stages could easily be assimilated to a single stage). Most important, however, all can be said to be manifestations of a basic assumption of developmental psychology:

> Whenever development occurs, it proceeds from a state of relative differentiation to a state of increasing differentiation, articulation, and hierarchic integration. This principle has the status of a heuristic law. Though itself not subject to empirical test, it is valuable . . . in directing inquiry and in determining the actual range of applicability with regard to the behavior of organisms. (Werner, *Developmental Processes* 86)

The stages of these various systems are in no sense separate but rather represent a fluid, ongoing process of development that serves to transform mental states into successively more differentiated processes. We focus on these stages as if they were discrete because they provide an interpretative framework that can direct our thinking to the underlying processes that are involved. Such an interpretative framework is needed, it seems to me, if we are to come to grips with the apparent conflict between literacy and orality in the writing of our students.

As far as I can determine, teachers and scholars trying to cope with problems in teaching writing most often have been influenced by those researchers who recommend error analyses of student writing (see Shaughnessy, Kroll and Schafer, and Bartholomae). This approach can be labeled "cognitive" to the extent that it attempts to get at the mental processes of the learner in order to discover why a student writer makes certain kinds of errors. But error analysis has limitations because, as Ney writes, it "deals with only part of the language competence which individuals possess, the part which is demonstrated by their performance" (10-12). In other words, proponents of error analysis look only at the mental processes that relate to the errors that students make. They do not look at the mental processes that relate to the language that students control. In addition, proponents of error analysis concentrate heavily on subskills to the relative neglect of global skills. These qualifications are not intended to detract from the considerable accomplishments of scholars working with error analysis. Rather, they are intended to suggest that a complementary approach to the teaching of developmental writing and to the problems of literacy is needed—an approach that will enable teachers of writing to look beyond the conventional errors that students make in order to determine whether the problem is merely not knowing the basics or whether it is really a problem that needs "cognitive restructuring." Such an approach might profitably be based on the principles of developmental and comparative psychology.

Andrea Lunsford is one scholar who has attempted to apply the principles of developmental psychology to the teaching of writing. In her studies of the mental processes of basic writers, she has found that

> they have not attained that level of cognitive development which would allow them to form abstractions or conceptions. That is, they are most often unable to practice analysis and synthesis and to apply successfully the principles thus derived to college tasks. In short, our students might well perform a given task in a specific situation, but they have great difficulty abstracting from it or replicating it in another context. (38)

She suggests that "the best way to move students into conceptualization and synthetic modes of thought is to create assignments and activities which allow students to practice or exercise themselves in these modes continuously" (41). This is certainly excellent advice, but how does one go about doing it? The biggest difficulty I have had in trying to apply the insights of developmental psychology to the problems of literacy is that the developmental framework seems to be too broad and general to be of significant practical value. Perhaps it needs to be refined or at least supplemented by principles from related fields. I believe that we can get additional heuristic help from the field of comparative psychology. What follows is an attempt to sketch a heuristic framework based on the principles of composition as they relate to the principles of developmental and comparative psychology. In this discussion I am relying heavily on the works of A. R. Luria and Heinz Werner. The interpolations and explanations that follow, however, are my own.

If we abstract the common elements from the conceptual frameworks of cognitive psychologists, we come up with three genetic levels of cognitive development: a sensorimotor level, a perceptual-imagistic level, and a conceptual level. These levels are to be considered not as discrete but as continuous, fluid, and organic and as analogous to one another. In terms of the evolution of consciousness, one level follows another, but when a subsequent level is reached, the previous level does not disappear but continues to operate. During the course of cognitive growth, not only does one's consciousness go through these stages but each level follows an orderly sequence. For example, on the sensorimotor level, sensorimotor activity is at first global, then analytic, and finally synthetic.

Similarly, perceptual-imagistic thinking progresses from the whole to the parts and finally to a stage where the parts are integrated into a whole. Conceptual thinking follows the same pattern.

Each genetic level is also subject to different kinds of mental processes, so that, for example, sensorimotor activity may be syncretic or discrete, diffuse or articulated, as may perceptual-imagistic mental activity and conceptual mental activity. By syncretic mental processes, I mean the kind of thinking in which mental functions, contents, or meanings are merged into one another, as images might be merged in a dream or as sense perceptions might be fused in synesthesia. By discrete mental processes, I mean the kind of mental activity in which the contents of thought are well defined, distinct, and explicit, set apart from other things. By diffuse mental processes, I am referring to a mode of thought in which the contents of thinking are profuse, digressive, widely spread out or scattered, not concentrated or localized. And by articulated mental processes, I mean the kind of mental activity made up of distinguishable parts that are distinct elements of a whole construction.

Thus far my discussion has been on a rather abstract level, but I want to introduce one last set of concepts before going on to consider specific applications of these principles. In addition to the kinds of cognitive activities previously mentioned, the most important forms of cognitive activity such as perceiving similarities and differences, classifying, discerning cause-and-effect relationships, abstracting, and thinking syllogistically can be found as analogous processes on the three genetic levels. For example, perceiving relationships on a sensorimotor level is analogous to perceiving relationships on a perceptual-imagistic level, and perceiving relationships on a perceptual-imagistic level is analogous to perceiving relationships on a conceptual level. Grouping on the perceptual level is analogous to classifying on the conceptual level, and abstraction (the mental activity whereby we detach parts of a unit from a whole) is a mental activity that exists on all three levels.

What is interesting about this last group of categories is their relationship to rhetorical and compositional categories. Classification, for example, is a mental process, a topos of classical invention, a nineteenth-century method of developing paragraphs, and a twentieth-century mode of discourse. Because these are such familiar categories and because they have been used in the teaching of writing, they can be eminently useful in developing a conceptual framework for the study of literacy. For what we discover on careful investigation is that what sometimes passes for error in student papers is really the product of mental activity that is in an incipient stage of development.

For example, there is an intimate relationship between the concrete, perceptual grouping of objects and events and conceptual classification. It is entirely possible, therefore, that in a writing assignment students might be grouping things together on the purely perceptual level and teachers who are accustomed to looking for scientific classification might conclude that students don't know how to classify, when in reality the student is using an analogous method of classifying. Do we label such attempts on the part of the student as errors, or do we instead try to point out that there are different methods of classifying appropriate for different purposes? Assuming that we want to teach scientific classification, the problem is how to move the student from concrete perceptual grouping to conceptual classification. The solution may be to make students more self-conscious about the strategies they are using by teaching both kinds of classification and showing the relationships that exist between the two.

Comparison is another mode that some students have difficulty with in their writing. Yet as teachers we would suppose this to be the easiest mode for students to use. What could be easier than comparing two things in order to determine a resemblance between them? Conceptual comparison is based on the ability to isolate and abstract the common features of two or more things and bring them together in the mind apart from their immediate context. This ability seems to depend upon verbal and logical operations made possible by literacy. The research by Werner and Luria on perceiving relationships suggests that there is a progression from the apprehension of relations on a sensorimotor level to the apprehension of relations on the perceptual-imagistic level to the understanding of relations on the conceptual level. Animals, for example, can perceive on the purely sensory level that one object is brighter than another. Children at a certain stage in their cognitive development exhibit a concrete grasp of relationships. It is possible that the concrete relating of two features on the basis of perception is a step that is necessary in order to make the abstract conceptual judgment. The latter is a derived form of relationship that is expressed in words.

What students who seem to operate more comfortably in a perceptual mode sometimes do is merely to list and describe the features of the objects to be compared, without necessarily trying to incorporate the features in a conceptual scheme. The act of listing features seems to presuppose some kind of abstracting process, but abstraction can be a concrete mental operation in which the features isolated are concrete and specific rather than formal (i.e., based on form alone). It is perceptually easier to describe the concrete appearance of things than it is to isolate features and hold them in the mind apart from any physical context. Other students will compare by isolating a single salient feature from the things to be compared, under the assumption that if one thing is like another in one respect, it must be like the other in all respects. In sum, students operating on the sensory or perceptual levels will isolate features of the things to be compared and group them into relatively undifferentiated paragraphs, with little or no attempt to incorporate these features into some larger scheme. They will sometimes pick out different features of the objects, believing that all they have to do to make a valid comparison is to list as many features of the respective subjects as they can and juxtapose them indiscriminately. Consequently, we might expect that the organization of their essays will reveal a kind of primitive syncretism and lack definite form. At the same time, we might expect to find a kind of diffuseness, in which the features are scattered throughout the essay, lacking centration, concentration, unity, and proper subordination of the parts to the whole.

Of all the compositional modes, that of cause and effect seems to give students the most difficulty. Ask a student of marginal literacy to write an essay using cause and effect as a means of explaining an idea or as a method of persuasion, and you will inevitably get essays that are narrative or descriptive in mode. The causes and effects are there all right, but they are buried in the narrative continuum. Students who give a narrative explanation of causality do not divide events into a discrete series of causes and effects but instead syn-cretically subsume the particular to the general. Their thinking is concrete and particular, and it proceeds in terms of undivided totalities. These students are aware that events follow one another in time, but they seem to be more interested in the narrative progression than in the causal sequence (i.e., why something has taken place). This is not to say that such students cannot make "lawful" explanations. It is to say, however, that they rely more heavily on modes of thought that depend upon concrete perception and sensorimotor action. Yet we expect them to be objective, impersonal, and abstract in their thinking, and when they are not, we criticize their papers as being incorrect, instead of trying to understand that they are operating in an analogous mode. In the earliest stages of causal thinking in language, children string together events by means of the narrative conjunction "and." At a later stage, they begin to use causal conjunctions such as "if," "then," "because," and "since," but even at this stage the ideas connected are apt to be concrete and embedded in a continuum of action. Finally, language and thought come together in a more meaningful way as the perception of cause-and-effect relationships becomes more discrete and explicit.

Definition would seem to be a mode that depends almost exclusively on verbal and logical mental operations. Yet many students are inclined to use concrete thinking to describe the physical attributes of the object to be defined rather than to think in classes. Others will describe the uses of the object or try to reconstruct a concrete situation in which the object might be found. When given an abstract term to define, some students will resort to tautologies (e.g., "a brave man is a man . . .") instead of a more generic term. The more literate students may occasionally think in visual terms, but they can also perceive the relationship between the general and the particular in a formal definition and see the genus and species as distinct entities.

Syllogistic thinking is a mode of thinking with which we would expect students to have some difficulty because it is based on abstract propositions. But all too often in looking at the deductive thinking of our students, we tend to judge such thinking in terms of logical errors, when in fact the problem might be that these students are operating on the sensorimotor or perceptual level. Luria, for example, has shown in his experiments with nonliterate Russian peasants that nonliterate people tend to perceive the parts of a syllogism as isolated, concrete judgments. They do not perceive syllogisms as unified systems but instead repeat each sentence of a syllogism separately, as if it had no relationship to the others, and when asked to repeat the syllogism, they would often change the wording. Consequently, they are not able to draw valid conclusions from the premises. Marginally literate students who fail to draw the proper conclusion from the premises of a syllogism are not always making the usual errors in logic but are engaging in thinking that is concrete, experiential, perceptual, and diffuse. They will accept a proposition provided that they can relate it to their own experience, but they will make judgments on each proposition as if each were a separate unit of experience.

Heinz Werner claims that there is an early form of inferential thinking that is neither induction nor deduction but transduction. Werner's description of this kind of thinking suggests that the thinking of some of our students is in this transitional stage. According to Werner, transduction is the "leading over" from one concrete, isolated judgment to another. In order to solve a problem that a literate adult would solve by logical inference, a student with marginal literacy might "imaginatively conceive" a situation in which such judgments would take place. To illustrate this kind of "imaginative" thinking, Werner gives the example of a child who concludes that a piece of rope strung across the iron railing of a balcony is "something to pin clothes on." Werner comments that this is not a true logical deduction because there is no inherent necessity in the situation (as there might be in syllogistic thinking) that allows the child to make this judgment. What the child apparently did was to react to a global situation with which he was familiar—that of seeing the family wash—and fit his conclusion into a concrete context. The child could easily have "imagined" a different conclusion.

The foregoing discussion of the relationship of developmental cognitive processes to the teaching of writing suggests that if we are to help both residually oral students and students having features of electronic orality in their thinking to improve their writing, then we will have to increase their conscious control of certain kinds of mental activities. The mere possession of such cognitive processes as perceptual grouping, classification, the apprehension of relationships on various cognitive levels, abstraction, and causal reasoning is not enough. Every day students abstract, classify, compare and contrast, and discern cause-and-effect relationships in the world around them. But these mental processes are embedded in the concrete activities of everyday life. And although students can use these processes intuitively, they cannot always use them self-consciously as rhetorical strategies in their writing. In order to develop what Jerome Bruner calls an "analytic competence," students must move beyond the stage of concrete mental operations toward a more self-conscious and context-free elaboration of ideas. The kind of conceptual framework that I have described may suggest teaching strategies that will enable us both to understand more fully the relationship between thought and language and to bridge the cultural gap between orality and literacy.

If we use a conceptual framework derived from cognitive psychology in the teaching and evaluating of writing, a number of questions readily suggest themselves:

(1) To what extent is the individual's development as a writer tied to his or her cognitive development?

(2) How can we get students to move effectively from one kind of analogous mental operation to another, from one cognitive level to another?

(3) Does the possession of "mere literacy" speed up cognitive development, or is it necessary, as Jerome Bruner maintains, that there be an "elaboration" of the use of language?

(4) If, as the Russian psychologist L. S. Vygotsky contends, instruction marches ahead of developmental processes and leads them, what kind of instructional strategies can we plan to facilitate this development and to increase the students' conscious control of language?

(5) Can instruction in the classical topoi and in the use of compositional modes facilitate cognitive development and writing competence?

(6) How can we determine the cognitive strategies that a writer is using so that we can plan better instruction? Can specific features of pieces of writing give us clues?

(7) Can a deductive model such as the one I am trying to develop give teachers heuristic help in knowing what to look for or is an inductive model better? Are these approaches mutually exclusive?

(8) Should sentence-level difficulties as determined by error analysis be placed in some perspective relative to the entire composing process?

Writing is a complex activity, and the conceptual framework I have discussed is tentative and exploratory. But some kind of developmental framework is necessary, I believe, to explain the crisis in literacy that continues to exist despite the efforts of our best teachers. Students coming to our classes today do not have mental capacities that are inferior to the mental capacities of students of bygone years. Their ways of processing information are simply different. To teach these students to read and write beyond a minimum level of competence is the central problem of education for a democratic society that depends on literacy for the free and meaningful exchange of ideas. Other pursuits are trivial in comparison.

Works Cited

Ahmann, J. Stanley. "A Report on National Assessment in Seven Learning Areas." *Today's Education* 64(1975):63-64.

Bartholomae, David. "The Study of Error." *College Composition and Communication* 31(1980):253-69.

Bennett, Neville. "Progressive Teaching Flunks Study in Britain." *Arizona Republic,* 26 April 1976, A20.

Bishop, Arthur, ed. "The Concern for Writing." *Focus 5.* Princeton: Educational Testing Service, 1979.

Bruner, Jerome S. *Beyond the Information Given.* New York: Norton, 1973.

"College Board Test Scores Still Sliding." *Arizona Republic,* 5 Oct. 1980, B14.

Copperman, Paul. *The Literacy Hoax.* New York: Morrow, 1978.

D'Angelo, Frank J. "An Ontological Basis for a Modern Theory of the Composing Process." *Quarterly Journal of Speech* 64(1978):79-85.

Fields, Cheryl M. "Why the Big Drop in S.A.T. Scores?" *Chronicle of Higher Education,* 6 September 1977, 1, 13.

Giamatti, A. Bartlett. "Sentimentality." *Yale Alumni Magazine,* Jan. 1976, 17-19.

Hager, Philip. "College Essays: Freshmen Ain't So Good, Mostly." *Los Angeles Times,* 3 Nov. 1974, 1, 6.

Harnischfeger, Annegret, and David E. Wiley. *Achievement Test Score Decline: Do We Need to Worry?* Chicago: Central Midwestern Educational Research Laboratory, 1975.

Havelock, Eric A. *Origins of Western Literacy.* Toronto: Ontario Institute for Studies in Education, 1976.

———. *Preface to Plato.* Cambridge: Harvard Univ. Press, 1963.

———. "The Preliteracy of the Greeks." *New Literary History* 8(1977):369-91.

Kroll, Barry M., and John C. Schafer. "Error-Analysis and the Teaching of Composition." *College Composition and Communication* 29(1978):242-49.

Lloyd-Jones, Richard. "Is Writing Worse Nowadays?" *Spectator* [Univ. of Iowa], April 1976, 2.

Lunsford, Andrea A. "Cognitive Development and the Basic Writer." *College English* 41(1979):38-46.

Luria, A. R. *Cognitive Development: Its Cultural and Social Foundations.* Trans. Martin Lopez-Morillas and Lynn Solstaroff. Ed. Michael Cole. Cambridge: Harvard Univ. Press, 1976.

Lyons, Gene. "The Higher Literacy." *Harper's,* Sept. 1976, 33-40.

Mellon, John C. *National Assessment and the Teaching of English.* Urbana, Ill.: NCTE, 1975.

———. "Round Two of the National Writing Assessment—Interpreting the Apparent Decline in Writing Ability: A Review." *Research in the Teaching of English* 10(1976):66-74.

National Assessment of Educational Progress: Writing Mechanics, 1969-1974. Denver: NAEP, 1975.

Ney, James W. "Error Analysis and the Teaching of Composition: A Misbegotten Marriage." Unpublished MS, 1980.

Ohmann, Richard. "Call for Articles: Literacy and 'Basics.' " *College English* 37(1976):819.

———. Editorial. *College English* 38(1977):441-42.

Ong, Walter J. "Literacy and Orality in Our Times." In *Profession 79.* Ed. Jasper P. Neil. New York: MLA, 1979, 1-7.

———. "Media Transformation: The Talked Book." *College English* 34(1971):405-40.

———. *The Presence of the Word.* New Haven: Yale Univ. Press, 1967.

———. *Rhetoric, Romance and Technology.* Ithaca, N.Y.: Cornell Univ. Press, 1971.

Piaget, Jean. "The Mental Development of the Child." In *Six Psychological Studies.* Ed. David Elkind. Trans. Anita Tenzer. New York: Vintage, 1968, 3-73.

"Report Urges Higher Level of Literacy in Britain." *Council-Grams* (National Council of Teachers of English) 36(1975):23.

Scully, Malcolm G. "Crisis in English Writing." *Chronicle of Higher Education,* 23 Sept. 1974, 1, 6.

Shaughnessy, Mina. *Errors and Expectations: A Guide for the Teacher of Basic Writing.* New York: Oxford Univ. Press, 1977.

Skels, Merrill. "Why Johnny Can't Write." *Newsweek,* 8 Dec. 1975, 58-62, 63.

Smith, Ron. "The Composition Requirement Today: A Report on a Nationwide Survey of Four-Year Colleges and Universities." *College Composition and Communication* 25(1974):138-48.

"Stone-Age Thinking." Guest Editorial. *Wall Street Journal.* Rpt. *Tempe Daily News,* 7 March 1975, 4.

Vygotsky, L. S. *Thought and Language.* Ed. and trans. Eugenia Hanfmann and Gertrude Vakar. Cambridge: MIT Press, 1962.

Werner, Heinz. *Comparative Psychology of Mental Development.* Rev. ed. New York: International Universities Press, 1948.

————. *Developmental Processes: Heinz Werner's Selected Writings.* Vol. 1. Ed. Sybil S. Barten and Margery B. Franklin. New York: International Universities Press, 1978.

Whitehead, Alfred North. *The Aims of Education and Other Essays.* New York: Macmillan, 1967.

"The Writing Gap." *Yale Alumni Magazine,* Jan 1976, 15.

Information Systems and Literacy

Paul A. Strassmann

In this essay, I discuss issues that are related to the interactive-computer medium and suggest how the spreading use of that medium may change some of our traditional concepts of literacy. I deal with four issues:

(1) How our ideas concerning the spoken and written language will be influenced as we move from the print medium toward the electronic medium;

(2) How the role of the English language may change as the role of electronic communications increases on a global scale;

(3) What kind of education we should give our young people now to prepare them for the careers they will follow between 1985 and 2040;

(4) What kind of education is needed by educators themselves to help students cope with the electronic culture.

Although literacy has many possible meanings, I prefer a definition that is broad in scope: "the ability of individuals to cope with communications within their civilization." This general definition implies that literacy is a cultural phenomenon dependent on the environment. To illustrate this important point, I will review what literacy has meant at various stages of human development.

Progress in Communication			
Period	Medium	Economic Organization	Civilization
1 million B.C.-10,000 B.C.	speech	tribal	hunting
10,000 B.C.-A.D. 1500	script	feudal	agriculture
A.D. 1500-A.D. 2000	print	national	industrial
A.D. 2000-	electronic message	universal	information

With the evolution of human society, the communications medium has changed, and, as a result, the focus of literacy has changed. We must understand that human society is now at the edge of a discontinuity, the end of the Gutenbergian era and the beginning of the "electronic display" era. As we enter this new stage of historical development, we can expect the form and content of our communications to change. Today's ideas are firmly rooted in an industrial civilization defined by national economic interests, and our concepts of literacy are shaped largely by our dependency on printing technology. With the increasing use of new technologies, our concepts of literacy are bound to change.

The likelihood of this impending transition is supported by an examination of trends in the historical patterns of employment. Observing the distribution of the U.S. work force over a period of one hundred years, we see radical changes in the way people earn their livelihood. Since the 1950s our country has become predominantly occupied with the creation, distribution, and administration of information. By 1990, only about fifty percent of the work force will be manufacturing objects and producing food. The rest will occupy most of the time just communicating. From an economic standpoint it is important to be concerned about the effectiveness with which all these people carry out their tasks. Literacy is therefore a special concern since it is one of the underlying capabilities that enable our economy to function effectively.

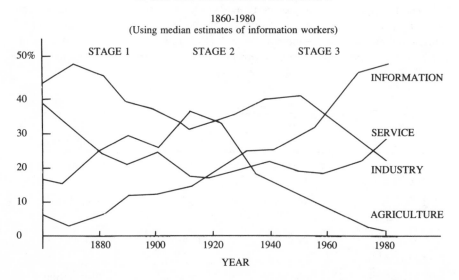

FOUR-SECTOR AGGREGATION
OF THE U.S. WORK FORCE BY PERCENT

1860-1980
(Using median estimates of information workers)

On a labor-time-weighted basis, we may estimate that in 1980, workplace communications were distributed approximately as follows:

Verbal communications	50%	(including telephone)
Written communications	35%	
Electronic communications	15%	(via computer)

These shares are bound to change. The workplace forecast for 1990 is based on fifty-five million people in "information employment" jobs. The salaries and benefits of these individuals may absorb sixty-five to seventy percent of the total labor value added. Because the labor cost per capita will be so high, there will be a great incentive to increase the output of employees by equipping them with communications-enhancing technology. I believe that about half of the information work force will be equipped with "electronic workstations," an electronic medium through which at least half of their communication will take place. The young people now in schools will have to operate in a work environment dominated by electronics. Will they be adequately equipped to perform well in this environment?

U.S. OFFICE AUTOMATION PROFILE

	1990
Information Employment	55 million
Labor Cost	$2,500 billion
Technology Cost	$480-600 billion
Labor Cost per Capita	$45,500
Technology Cost per Capita	$8,700-10,900
Technology/Labor Ratio	18-22%
Workstations	20-30 million

A few historical examples help to illustrate the problems of literacy at various stages of development.

Literacy in tribal cultures was dominated by the oral medium. Language was poor in form and in content, and communications were limited to tribal concerns. Although script did not exist, there were memory aids to assist in the telling of the tales that represented accumulated human experience, and only a few selected individuals were trusted with handing down oral traditions. This specialization meant that the only information that was retrievable—even to the most literate members of the culture—was that which dealt with the essence of tribal existence: law, tradition, and religion.

If you carefully examine artifacts representing tribal communications— totem poles, notched sticks, Inca quipu, Indian ceremonial robes, and the like— you will be impressed by their graphic richness. By themselves, these graphics are meaningless. They come alive only when supported by a narrator. The feats of memory shown by these narrators were prodigious, and the oral tradition of these storytellers preserved the equivalent of many books for centuries.

The creation of a stable agricultural civilization led to the destruction of tribal forms. Successful agricultural states were based on the oral medium but employed a standardized language aided by syllabic script. The content of messages became increasingly concerned with property and with religion as a means of preserving the stability of society. This change called for standardization of verbal sounds in a geographically bounded feudal domain by means of syllabic notation. Even after the invention of the alphabet, the meaning of written messages remained ambiguous because spelling and vocabulary were not standardized. Each group of scribes created, recorded, and distributed texts in direct support of their limited tasks. The notation and legibility of texts were unimportant since all texts were read aloud and literacy remained the preserve of a few privileged members of society.

The advent of the industrial age coincided with the rise of the nation-state. To communicate in this environment, a much higher level of standardization of language sounds and of written language became necessary. Alphabetic symbols are now restricted in usage even though the phonetic sounds generated from texts still remain imprecise. Schools and information industries continue to concentrate their efforts on standardizing vocabulary, grammar, and syntax, and the role of the commercial printer has been highly significant in establishing and promoting this standardization. Industrial literacy demands universal knowledge of text creation and sophisticated reading skills, while it places decreasing value upon oral skills. Oral language has become too ambiguous to be relied upon for preserving and communicating complex information. As a result, records of legal, legislative, and scientific matters are now stored in writing only.

To illustrate the problems of language representation in the industrial age, let me point to the ambiguity in translating phonetic sounds into a limited set of alphabetic codes. The sound *sh,* for instance, is represented in English by eleven different letters or letter combinations: *sh*oe, *su*gar, na*ti*on, o*ce*an, ma*ch*ine, mi*ss*ion, fa*ci*al, fa*sc*ism, lu*sci*ous, man*si*on, and lu*x*ury. The inability of the written language to represent adequately and unambiguously the spoken language limits its applicability to culturally unified national groups, and, consequently, literacy continues to be defined in a cultural context.

The cultural bias of written languages becomes ever more pronounced when we explore the meaning of words themselves. The ambiguity of words varies in different national languages. For instance, in English a simple sentence like the following can only be understood in a cultural context:

$$\text{Civilized}_{10} \; \text{man}_8 \; \text{can}_2 \; \text{not}_1 \; \text{live}_{14} \; \text{without}_3 \; \text{religion}_9$$

Individual words have a wide range of meaning as indicated by subscripts (e.g., the word "civilized" can be used in ten different meanings). Hence, industrial civilization continually struggles with the problems of meaning, content, ambiguity, and redundant communication. Vast bureaucracies and complex legal and procedural frameworks are constructed to eradicate or compensate for these inadequacies. At the same time, other members of society exploit ambiguity and redundancy in poetry and the arts.

As products of the industrial age enter global markets, there is an increasing need to organize communications on a global scale. Nationally based written languages fail to resolve the problem of ambiguity in meaning and content. Understanding messages without resorting to culture-specific contexts becomes a prerequisite for a global community where international division of labor is accepted. Now that commercial messages flow across national boundaries, we need to be able to understand them without the costly administrative burdens of export bureaucracies, translators, and flocks of lawyers.

The social and economic challenge of literacy in the future is to achieve global understanding and global communications. Therefore, the primary task of the electronic age is to standardize meaning and thus further our ability to deal with complexity in international relationships. The immediate, short-term task of the electronic age is to make possible communication among individuals in a peer group. Such a peer group would be initially defined by interests that include narrow areas of specialization (e.g., molecular biochemists), commercial interests (e.g., all international currency traders), or occupation (e.g., air-traffic controllers). Only after peer-group communications are improved can we hope to improve communication and enhance understanding among interdisciplinary specialists (e.g., product planners, health officers).

The principal means for achieving these objectives are already embedded in the electronic computer technologies that exist today. Voice recognition and speech synthesis permit translation between the digitally encoded medium and verbal expression. Artificial intelligence permits translation between the digitally encoded message and the language-specific context of the recipient.

The vehicle for establishing global literacy will very likely involve group authorship of text. The "group text" will be machine translated into a "carrier" language. The "carrier" language will represent an underlying message that will be machine translated in order to be understood by everyone, regardless of national or cultural context. The "group text" will be written in a language to which each member of the peer group will be able to contribute.

We already have several candidate "carrier" languages that have the attributes of clarity, lack of ambiguity, and simple representation. These languages operate on a scale far exceeding anything previously known and are most widely referred to by the generic name "software." Software, I believe, in its most general definition as an artificial language constructed for communications between human beings and computers, will become the "carrier" language of the future. The language itself—its content, syntax, and grammar—will also become the dominant intellectual asset and property of humankind. Thus, the understanding of software in its total context will be a primary component of literacy in the electronic age.

In what follows, I will explore the literacy requirements that apply to the world of commerce and to the language of the workplace. Private life will continue to use the rich heritage of the past, and the collective use of tribal, feudal, and national forms will continue to be essential. The new literacy should not be a substitute for the old; on the contrary, it should be a new layer on top of a solid understanding of the past.

Education for the electronic age will begin with the tools. Traditional forms of literacy require proficiency with technique—use of reeds for cuneiform script, brush calligraphy for Chinese ideograms, penmanship for script, and typing for printed text. The electronic age requires proficiency in dealing with computer terminals. Information networking is another tool of electronic literacy. In the same way that access to a library and the ability to locate information are essential for contemporary literacy, so familiarity with electronic networking is mandatory for anyone who wishes to participate in exchanging information on a global scale. Computer-aided graphics equipment is another tool of the electronic medium; charts, graphs, diagrams, and logical networks are essential elements in improved communication of messages.

The most important change arising from the electronic medium will be found in the messages it will convey. If we comprehend how the format and language of the older media influenced the vocabulary and the grammar of written messages, it should be easy for us to understand how a totally new medium can influence the language of the future.

The logic on which computer software is constructed can be found in the programming and systems coding that exist today. Almost all the dominant higher-level languages in the world are of English-language origin (e.g., FORTRAN, COBOL, APL). With minor exceptions, data-base definition languages are also of English origin. Most of the documentation in use throughout the world is available only in the original English versions.

Computer-coding languages have the unique attribute that their meaning, definition, and usage are precisely described. The software constructed by means of these codes can be checked for logical consistency and completeness. The procedural and logical message of software is therefore uniquely suited for conveying information that is culturally independent. As a result, computer languages meet the criterion of universality, but their structures are alien and incomprehensible in the traditional sense of literacy.

We need another discipline—presently known in computer science as artificial intelligence—as the intermediary between a culturally comprehending human being and the mathematically logical computer codes. There is now sufficient evidence that artificial intelligence has developed a capability to "understand" ambiguous language and generate intelligible human sentences from logical constructs based on mathematical notation. Great advances also have been made in "problem-definition languages." It is a uniquely human attribute to be able to structure a question and elicit a response. If electronic networks are to serve human needs on a global scale, they must be capable of acting as an intermediary between people who perceive problems in culturally different ways. I see this class of problem-definition languages as a major advance in facilitating computer-aided understanding.

The great power of graphic languages enriches communications. Except for the use of graphics to illustrate a text, existing research almost totally ignores graphics as a way of enhancing understanding of written messages. The new computer medium makes it easy to use graphic means to improve understanding. The electronic medium can also be used as an auxiliary extension of the human mind to scan large volumes of text, data, or pictures. Human beings can now be endowed with vastly enlarged capabilities to deal with massive amounts of data as a way of finding valuable information.

In summary, the future electronic message has completely different attributes from the messages we now routinely send and receive. The ability of our intellectuals to deal with these new experiences will determine whether or not they are literate. Completely new skills are needed to cope with an environment that is rich in electronic messages.

To prepare for the future, our educators must pioneer our understanding of the workplace in which students will operate when they enter careers. Therefore, educating the educators becomes a matter of highest priority. To be effective, educators of electronically literate students need to become proficient in handling text editors, in the use of personal microprocessors, in the ability to search data bases, in skills to address devices and services in complex networks, in the ability to select and connect to the global software marketplace, and in teleconferencing to permit interdisciplinary or international cooperation to create intellectual property on a cooperative basis.

I regard the following as the major challenges to teachers of electronic literacy:

- Recognizing that the electronic medium will be dominant in the workplace after year 2000.
- Equipping our young people to cope with the challenges of the new literacy.
- Teaching electronic medium and electronic message skills in the 1980s so that the class beginning in 1990 will not enter the work force electronically "illiterate."

The literacy of the future involves an augmentation of our past knowledge; it is not a rejection of essential oral, writing, and reading skills. The new electronic medium will most likely cause readjustment in the relative importance and usage of the existing media. What will ultimately matter will be the balanced capability of individuals to cope with the new world of global interdependence.

Literacy in the Marketplace

English and Science—
Symbiosis for Survival

Paul B. Weisz

In 1980 I had the pleasure of visiting China, where I gave some lectures at a chemical research institute. In writing as a scientist to an audience concerned with literacy, I face a situation that is nearly as foreign to me as that visit was, since the discipline I represent is very different from the professional work of most persons likely to read this book.

During my stay in China I spoke of my admiration for the written Chinese language and explained that I had told students at Princeton University about the rich content of the Chinese ideograms for "science" (shown in fig. 1). These characters incorporate the symbol for grain (A), representing the vital or essential; the symbol for cup or measure (B), conveying the idea of the quantitative; and the hand of the master (C) dispelling ignorance or, more literally, bringing light to darkness—the darkness being symbolized by the child (E) shaded from light by the roof above (D). I admire these characters because they are so rich in suggestive meanings and associations—far more so than our plain word "science." But even more important to my theme in writing here, I find them rich and strange, far removed from our own habits of thinking about writing. Even the Chinese students in my audience confessed that they had never looked beyond the surface of these characters for "science" to see their component meanings.

The ancient Greeks perceived strangers to be valuable because they were

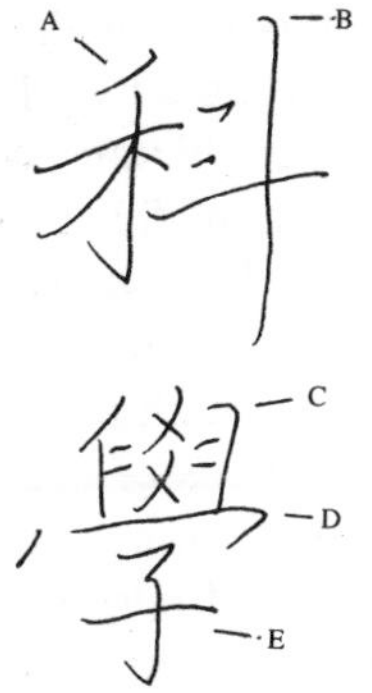

Figure 1

125

bearers of news. It seems to me that we do not welcome "strangers" today with the same expectation that they will bring us news to help us cope with society. Most of us perceive what seem to be unprecedented tensions: problems with resource supplies, worldwide inflation, revolts against institutions, rising crime rates, terrorism, and drug abuse. My message will suggest that another serious problem we often overlook is that even in our own culture we are strangers to each other. Having placed ourselves upon specialized islands, we have neglected lateral communication. We need to develop a more common language and to benefit from the knowledge that abounds around us if we are to maintain our society and ensure its survival.

Although the evolution of human society is complex, certain factors are more significant in its development than others. I propose to look at three such factors that strongly determine the health and condition of our society: (1) the availability of work energy; (2) the existence of nature's basic priorities, which are built into all living organisms by biological evolution; and (3) communication between individuals and groups within a society.

The concept of work is sometimes discussed in basic physics, although little time is spent on its far-reaching significance. Energy comes in many forms, and one form can be transformed into another. A battery, for instance, turns chemical energy into electrical energy, the energy of a fuel can be turned into heat, and with a motor or an engine, these energy forms can be turned into work energy.

Work is the most important energy form for shaping a society. While heat broadens the land area and light lengthens the hours of the day during which we can operate, we need work energy to push, pull, move, lift, turn, break, forge, and shape things, including ourselves. The amount and rate of availability of work determine the capabilities of a society.

Figure 2 shows an estimate of the amount of energy per capita that has been available to human beings since 10,000 B.C. (computed from data provided by Brown). In the beginning, work energy arose only from manual labor (A), but the discovery of fire and its uses increased human ability to take nourishment, withstand discomforts, and do more work (B). Being enterprising creatures, people soon discovered that other energy sources could be exploited to accomplish desired ends: they harnessed bullocks, elephants, and horses to extract work from animals; built sailing ships to extract work from the winds; discovered that water, caught at higher elevations, could transport itself under the force of gravity to where they wanted it for irrigation. Such inventions significantly increased the availability of work energy, and people were able to do more and more— construct what they wanted, harvest more food, provide for more safety, bear more children, and live longer lives. With more and more work energy available the population increased and conditions of life improved.

The availability of work took more dramatic leaps upward with the discovery that heat energy can be turned into work. Although initially wood and peat were the only known fuels (D), enormous stores of other fuel energy were

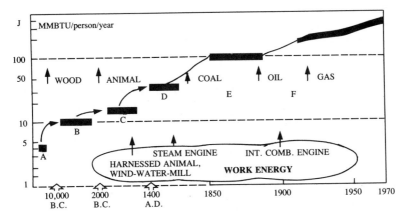

Figure 2

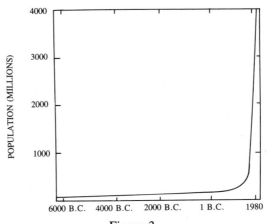

Figure 3

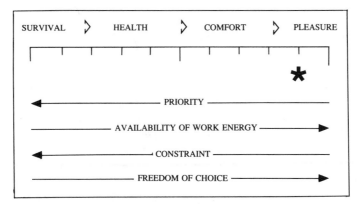

Figure 4

soon discovered: work was extracted from coal by the early 1800s to fire steam engines, locomotives, and ships (E); and the discovery of petroleum and natural gas as sources of work energy in the mid-1800s led to the invention of the internal combustion engine. From that point forward we have had access to a tremendous amount of work energy obtainable at a rapid rate (beyond F).

Today, as I note in "Population and Energy," every man, woman, and child has available an added work capability equivalent to twelve-hundred working slaves (131). In direct proportion to the increased work capacity, the human population with its essentially fixed land area began to explode (fig. 3). Many of us fail to realize that it was this enormous availability of work energy that created and now maintains our huge society. Most of us take it for granted; some of us cannot conceive of society any other way.

A second factor that strongly determines the health and condition of a society is the existence of biological priorities. The objectives to which an organism can and will turn its attention follow a strict order of basic priorities sketched at the top of figure 4. Society is able to satisfy more and more of the conditions (shown from left to right) in proportion to the work energy available and the drive and intelligence to use it. The current position of Western society on this scale is probably best characterized by the star, somewhere well in the pleasure area.

Although this scale of priorities may seem to be simply a matter of common sense, it is based on concrete demonstrations in biology: for example, the structural evolution of the brain. The most primitive assembly of neural cellular structures, as they evolved in the lowest life forms, controls the most vital functions needed for survival—the visceral functions (heart, lungs, digestion, and motor movements). As the brain evolved, other structures were added, the hindbrain and midbrain remaining the innermost and most protected structures. Structures that deal with deliberate behavior and basic emotions are located in a more outward and advanced part of the brain, as MacLean points out. These structures account for our efforts to establish societies that fulfill our drives and desires, clearly a lower priority than survival itself. The final and outermost structure added to the brain was the neocortex, which controls such advanced human functions as subtle perception and action. While these functions make possible our enjoyment of the "finer things in life," they are clearly least related to our survival.

Thus far I have discussed two factors that determine the possible state of society: the availability of work energy and the biological priorities that determine how the available work energy will be used. Each successive need on the scale requires not only greater intelligence of individuals but also an effective collective social intelligence (see my article "From Bits to Brains").

Lewis Thomas has aptly reminded us of the significance of collective social intelligence. He tells of watching an individual ant perform a random, meaningless bumping encounter with a morsel of food. When ten ants gather, they bump around with a suggestion of a specific aim—to move the morsel. A hundred ants gather and begin somehow to communicate as a team. Together the ants move the morsel to a predetermined destination. Thomas' story applies as well to people: the actions of single individuals often appear to have little sense, while a community forms plans and controls their execution.

The functioning of a social network is more complex, of course, in an advanced human society. The first human communities had a relatively simple structure of tasks. Some members hunted for food; others made simple clothing, cooked, and helped children grow up. The number of specializations was small, and the roles and purposes served by members of the community were clear. Every individual could recognize easily his or her relationship to the life and needs of family, village, and society. As the land had to nourish and support the lives of an exponentially growing population, it became an ever more complex task to produce, provide, store, and distribute food, work energy, clothing, housing, services, and recreation.

Unfortunately, as the population expands, effective communication between functions becomes simultaneously more complex and more crucial. We now have developed an enormous number of special tasks and many labels of specialization. In New York, I examined the index of listings in the Manhattan *Yellow Pages*. There are twenty thousand listings, and they didn't include corn farmers, anthracite miners, or beer tasters.

Specialization in modern human society has gone beyond the level that is essential for purposes of efficiency. As figure 5 suggests, the affluent society—having entered into an era where it can afford to divert work energy to comforts and pleasure—also develops intellectual affluence and its consequences. In other words, specialization proliferates simply because we can afford it and enjoy it. Mastering a "specialty" gives us gratification, bolsters our pride, and becomes a matter of status. When specialization becomes institutionalized, it is further anchored as a way of life. Specialists characteristically create their own language and their own media of communications, which reinforce the institutionalization and, in turn, ensure still greater isolation.

A striking example of this isolation exists in the institutional structure of education. The disciplines represented by the departments of our colleges and universities continue to generate more and more material, prescribe more exercises, and demand more sophistication; each "specialty" develops a special language, journals, societies, and departments. Communication is confined within each discipline and lateral communication hardly exists.

Integrative leadership is difficult to develop when common concepts and interests are cloaked in the special dialects and languages of the disciplines. In 1979, a conference on "the crisis in scientific research" was organized by prominent scientists and educators, including Nobel laureates from many fields. Among others expressing the same concern, Ashley Montague deplored "the present degree of specialization [that] has resulted in a condition of intellectual isolationism" and suggested that this "inbred scholastic isolationism" is "largely irrelevant to the content of contemporary science and the problems of modern

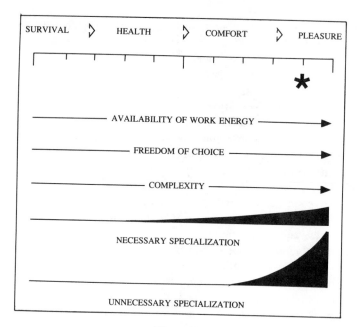

Figure 5

Figure 6

life." At the conference, some of the most respected scientific leaders expressed their concerns about the insularity of the disciplines and the resulting difficulties in developing a common and basic understanding of the way the social network functions. Such insularity can drive society back to more primitive states.

Our economic and intellectual affluence is reflected not only in the structure of institutional education but also in the changing psychology of society. Gertrud Höhler of Paderborn University has described some relatively recent social and psychological phenomena that may be attributed to our affluence. Since World War II, she notes, individuals and groups have made increasing demands on society without accepting proportionately more responsibility. Such demands have been accompanied by an increased expectation and drive for instant gratification. Increased drug use, the sexual revolution, and the idea that social and personal demands should be met immediately are only a few indications of this expectation. Further, recent times are characterized by what is called the "loss of self" syndrome and its consequences—increasing numbers of people who drop out of school, leave home, or seek divorces in the hope of "finding themselves."

The first two phenomena—personal demands and the search for instant gratification—are related to our failure to communicate an understanding of the role of work energy and effort in the achievement of any lasting and meaningful goal. While the first and second laws of thermodynamics speak to this issue—in describing the constraints governing the conservation and transformation of energy—they are usually taught only as part of physics or chemistry, and seldom are they recognized as relevant to everyday life in society. These laws are treated as part of a "specialty," not part of the general body of knowledge that human beings need. The "loss of self" syndrome is the necessary consequence of our failure to provide an overview of individual roles and their importance to the total functioning of the human community. The relationship in our society between division of knowledge and presence of social tension is clear. As knowledge and activity become more sophisticated, the bridges of understanding and interaction grow weaker and weaker. Now, more than ever before, such bridges are needed for both social and psychological survival.

What can we do? Clearly, we must find ways to build bridges of understanding. I am speaking not of emotional understanding, however important it may be, but of an interdisciplinary understanding involving knowledge. We need to transmit understanding across generations and provide institutions that will broaden rather than narrow the scope of knowledge.

I used to suffer from kidney stones, an affliction that can produce spells of pain said to be among the most severe that one can experience. During attacks, I would receive a quarter grain of morphine sulfate, and within about two minutes the pain would ease and then disappear. Once, during the minutes after I had taken the morphine, my mind turned to reliving and reexamining my current research problems in the laboratory. I experienced calm clarity and deep insights, and I brought forth elegant and simple solutions. This state was of relatively short duration before I progressed to fatigue and deep sleep, and by the next morning the details of my insights were gone—replaced, I might say, by a hangover.

It was obviously important that I write down my thoughts and insights as they occurred. For the first time, I found myself eagerly awaiting the next attack of pain, and I began to realize the traps by which one can get hooked on a drug. When—at last—agony set in, I progressed through the previous sequence of stages. But now I was armed with a pencil and a pad of paper. I saw and felt my solutions, the logic, the answers, and I struggled to put them down. I tried and tried but could not grasp and translate anything into coherent meaning. When I awoke to find that I had written nothing at all, I felt furious, depressed, and cheated by my own brain. I had experienced how language highlights the difference between emotional impression and intellectual understanding.

A happier experience involves my association with a fine and successful research team whose members represent many of the educational disciplines, including physics, chemistry, several engineering disciplines, economics, and others. This team has especially distinguished itself by developing new catalysts that can be placed in a chemical reactor to form new chemicals selectively. Other accomplishments of the team include the development of a solid catalyst used to form gasoline from petroleum and the innovation of another solid catalyst called ZSM-5, which is used in making polyester.

Once a month members of the team contribute to a newsletter, which reports new insights or findings encountered during the month. This kind of regular reporting can easily become a nuisance, but our effort has become one of the most important and creative parts of the research process itself. The newsletter emerged from our objective to reexamine our findings enough to convey their significance in plain English, which any scientist, engineer, or manager can understand. This exercise in writing has provided the most effective way to recognize clearly what we really know, as opposed to what we think or feel we know—as was the case with my clinical morphine experience. It has become a significant part of our research efforts and appears to give us a higher probability for tangible success. Equally important is that the newsletter is an example of a small "institutional" mechanism for building those bridges between disciplines that seem to me so important.

Most institutions do not encourage—in fact, they discourage—attempts to step outside of one's disciplinary bounds. Yet the courage to step across the boundary, when done with scholarly skill, results in pioneering accomplishments. Biochemistry provides an illuminating example of such success. Not long ago, the field of biochemistry did not exist; it was a no-man's-land lying between chemistry and physiology. Schools of biochemistry were first established in Austria-Hungary in the early part of this century, and the significant accomplishments of scientists working in biochemistry in Austria-Hungary (and its successor nations) were recognized by a rapid succession of Nobel prizes (see the discussion by Rollin D. Hotchkiss quoted in Chargaff [358]).

I began my career as a physicist, a very mathematical physical science.

Not long ago in a bookstore in London, I opened a book entitled *Linguistics at Large* and found myself getting an entirely new insight into the meaning of the Pythagorean theorem. For countless generations, we have learned that the square of the hypotenuse equals the sum of the squares of the other two sides. But Colin Cherry, the author of an essay in that book, "Language and Extra-Linguistic Communication," gave convincing evidence that there is really nothing special about squares. If we were to draw semicircles across the sides of the triangle instead, we would find that the area of the semicircle on the hypotenuse is also equal to the sum of the semicircles on the other two sides. In fact, as shown in figure 6, a cat on the hypotenuse equals the sum of the cats on the other two sides! In suggesting this point, Cherry demonstrates how teaching is constrained and affected by the social institutions and interests of the time. The ancient Greeks were not interested in cats, he says, or figures in general but were preoccupied with the straight line geometries useful in navigating by the stars.

When I returned from London, I told a class of graduate students in chemical engineering at Princeton University about Cherry's insight. In the bookstore, I had been persuaded by Cherry's prose argument, but with a class of mathematically sophisticated engineering students, I felt compelled to write the proof in terms of mathematical formulas containing integrals.

When I mention the need to bridge the disciplines, I have in mind the sort of creative research that would develop and add yet another discipline: interdisciplinary science. Such a discipline, established in its own right, would reexamine basic and elementary concepts contained in our current disciplines and outline the breadth of our wisdom and the implications that follow from it. To be effective, it would have to do so in a language more accessible than the languages of most existing sciences.

Let me illustrate why such a different perspective is so important. At one point in my career in catalytic chemistry, I was part of a group of several chemical engineers who worked out some relationships that describe how the effectiveness of solid catalyst granules depends on their size and on the speed with which molecules get in and out of the solid. Several years later, I discovered an article by A. V. Hill describing many similar analyses performed by physiologists in studies on red blood cells quite a long time ago. Some years after our work, a group of biochemists again derived the same principles, this time to show how the length of the tail of a spermatozoon depends on the concentration of a chemical called ATP (Nevo and Rikmenspoel). We all struggled independently with the same fundamental relationship, which could be described and taught as a simple general law (see my "Diffusion and Chemical Transformation") for any system where material or energy is transformed—whether in the physical, chemical, or biological world.

Another example of interdisciplinary truth is manifested in my observations of the squirrel-proof bird feeder we have in our yard—an ingeniously constructed device (fig. 7). The birds sit on a bar some twelve inches long in front of a slot that offers the food. The bar is mounted on a swivel, and if the weight of the

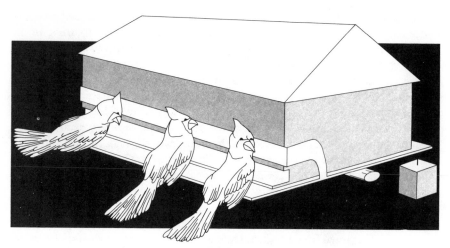

Figure 7

NUMBER OF BIRDS
ON FEEDER

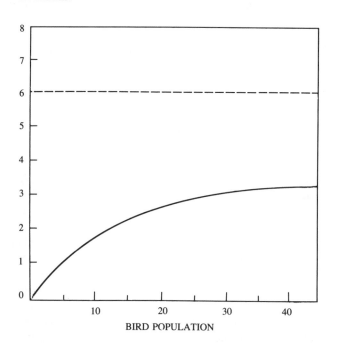

BIRD POPULATION

Figure 8

visitor on the bar is greater than a set maximum, the bar will depress and close the slot that provides access to the food. It is a hilarious sight to see a squirrel arrive on the bar and be puzzled and frustrated because the gate closes before its eyes.

After setting up this feeder, I realized that a twelve-inch-long bar can simultaneously accommodate six birds if they are each two inches wide. I wondered how often the gate would close when cold and hungry birds would come in great numbers. So I did some research, and figure 8 shows a sketch of my observations. The ordinate represents the approximate average number of birds that I observed sitting on the bar of the feeder; the abscissa shows the numbers of birds anxiously gathered on the lawn to await a turn at the feeder. As the figure shows, the number of birds sitting on the bar increases with feeding pressure. When the number of hungry birds in the area goes up, the curve approaches a maximum. The maximum average number on the feeder is closer to three than to the potential maximum of six. A bird has a very definite territorial demand for space around itself, and it will fight and chase off any other bird that gets too close. So, in essence, the effective space occupied by a bird sitting on the bar is nearly four inches. With no more than three to four birds on the feeder, the gate can easily be set to allow for a maximum weight of birds and to prevent even the lightest squirrel from robbing their food.

The previous paragraphs tell you about how the feeder works, but I have also exposed you to some rather sophisticated interdisciplinary concepts. The curve showing occupancy, against the pressure for wanting to be there, is called an adsorption isotherm by the physical chemist who uses this term to describe the behavior of molecules adsorbing on surfaces. The formalized knowledge about such curves "belongs" to physical chemistry, but it applies equally well to bird feeders, to communications science (where it describes the overloading of circuits), to inventory problems in marketing, and to a lot of other areas.

The relation of the number of hungry birds to the number that can feed at one time at our feeder is also encountered in nuclear and atomic physics, where it is called the effective collision cross-section. In physics, we are concerned with various force fields that extend from the atomic nuclei across a larger territory and repel approaching particles.

It may seem trivial to discuss the serious challenges in education, science, and communication in terms of cats and bird feeders. Nevertheless, it brings home the point that one can identify universal laws of behavior that reach across disciplines. It is more difficult to describe the bridges between thermodynamics, kinetics, and dynamics, and such fields as sociology, economics, and communications. Yet such bridges exist, and we can profit from building more of them.

Our institutions, the departmental systems of our universities, and the reporting and publication systems of our journals must accommodate the need for bridging between disciplines so that we can achieve coherence in understanding society and the world. As a starting point, we should encourage and provide the means for individuals to gain competence in two disciplines instead of one.

Doctoral theses that demand knowledge and advisers from two disciplines should be encouraged, and we should design institutional support for such activity so that students and faculty will work on problems that lie between fields.

Our major challenge is to do research and to create courses and programs of an interdisciplinary science. This effort requires pioneering work and special courage since the institutional system is not geared to reward it. The sponsorship and endowment of professorships dedicated to such interdisciplinary research and teaching objectives could be decisive in supporting breakthroughs.

In all these efforts, a key ingredient is language; we must learn to use it both to create and to convey understanding. We need to engage language and communication, English and science, to create a better coherence between knowledge and life. Such coherence is badly needed for the maintenance and the survival of our society.

Works Cited

Brown, Harrison. "Energy in Our Future." *Annual Review of Energy* 1(1976):1-36.

Chargaff, Erwin. "How Genetics Got a Chemical Education." *Annals of The New York Academy of Science* 325(1979):345-60.

Cherry, Colin. "Language and Extra-Linguistic Communication." In *Linguistics at Large*. Ed. Noel Minnis. London: Victor Gollancz, 1971, 269-93.

Hill, A. V. "The Diffusion of Oxygen and Lactic Acid through Tissues." *Proceedings of the Royal Society of London,* ser. B, 104(1929):39-96.

MacLean, P. D. *A Triune Concept of the Brain and Behavior.* Toronto: Univ. of Toronto Press, 1973.

Nevo, Abraham C., and Robert Rikmenspoel. "Diffusion of ATP in Spermflagella." *Journal of Theoretical Biology* 26.2(1970):11-18.

Thomas, Lewis. "On Societies as Organisms." In *The Lives of a Cell.* New York: Viking, 1974, 11-15.

Weisz, Paul B. "Diffusion and Chemical Transformation." *Science* 179(1973):433-40.

———. "From Bits to Brains." *Chemtech* 10(1980):589-90.

———. "Population and Energy." *Chemtech* 10(1980):131-32.

The Invisible Discourse of the Law: Reflections on Legal Literacy and General Education

James Boyd White

The subject of this essay is legal literacy, but to put it that way requires immediate clarification for that phrase has a wide range of possible meanings. At one end of its spectrum of significance, for example, legal literacy means full competence in legal discourse, both as reader and as writer. This kind of literacy is the object of a professional education, and it requires not only a period of formal schooling but years of practice as well. Indeed, as with other real languages, the ideal of perfect competence in legal language can never be attained: practitioners are always learning about their language and about the world, they are in a sense always remaking both, and these processes never come to an end. What this sort of professional literacy entails and how it is to be talked about are matters of interest to lawyers and law teachers, but this meaning of legal literacy will not be discussed here. At the other end of the spectrum of legal literacy are people who recognize legal words and locutions as foreign to themselves, as part of the world of the law. A person who is literate in this sense knows that there is a world of language and action called "law," but little more about it: certainly not enough to have any real access to it.

Between these extremes is another possible meaning of legal literacy: the degree of competence in legal discourse that is required for meaningful and active life in our increasingly legalistic and litigious culture. Citizens who are ideally literate in this sense are not expected to know how to draft deeds and wills or to try cases or to manage the bureaucratic maze, but they do know when and how to call upon the specialists who can do these things. More important, they are able to protect and advance their own interests: for example in dealing with a landlord or a tenant or in their interactions with the police, with the zoning commission, or with the Social Security Administration. People with this type of literacy are able not only to follow but to evaluate news reports and periodical literature dealing with legal matters—from Supreme Court decisions to House Committee reports. They know how to function effectively in positions of responsibility and leadership (say as an elected member of a school board or as chair of a neighborhood association or as a member of a zoning board or police commission). This sense of the term legal literacy embodies the ideal of a fully competent and engaged citizen, and that ideal is a wholly proper one to keep before us.

But this ideal is for our purposes far too inclusive, for however one defines "legal literacy," one who possesses such literacy also has a great deal in addition: a complete set of social, intellectual, and political relations and capacities. But perhaps we can meaningfully ask, What is the legal literacy that such an ideal figure would have? How could this sort of competence be taught? What seem to be the natural barriers to its acquisition? In the first part of this paper I deal with these questions, but in reverse order. I begin by identifying those features of legal discourse that make it peculiarly difficult for the nonlawyer to understand and use. I then suggest some ways in which those features might be made comprehensible and manageable, and how their value and function might be appreciated. This discussion in turn will constitute my answer to the first question, that is, what kind of legal literacy should an ordinary citizen have, and how can it contribute not only to the development of social competence but to a true education of the mind and self?

The Invisible Discourse of the Law

It is a common experience for a nonlawyer to feel that legal language is in a deep sense foreign: not only are its terms incomprehensible, but its speakers seem to have available to them a repertoire of moves denied to others. Nonlawyers neither understand the force of legal arguments nor know how to answer them. But the language is, if possible, worse than merely foreign. It is an unpredictable, exasperating, and shifting mixture of the foreign and the familiar. Much of what lawyers say and write is, after all, intelligible to the nonlawyer, and one can sometimes speak in legally competent ways. But at any moment things can change without notice: the language slides into the incomprehensible, and the nonlawyer has no idea how or why the shift occurred. This is powerfully frustrating, to say the least.

But legal illiteracy is more than frustrating, for it entails an increasingly important disability, almost a disenfranchisement. At one time in our history a citizen did not need to have any specialized knowledge of law, for our law was a common law that reflected the customs and expectations of the people to such a degree that ordinary social competence was normally enough for effectiveness in the enterprises of life. No special legal training was required. But in our increasingly bureaucratic and legalistic world, this assumption seems less and less realistic. Frustrated citizens are likely to feel that their lives are governed by language that they cannot understand—in leases, in form contracts, or in federal and state regulations. Who, for example, can read and understand an insurance contract or a pension plan? An OSHA or IRS regulation? Yet these documents govern our lives and are even said in some sense to have the standing of our own acts, either directly, as in the contracts we sign, or indirectly, as in the laws promulgated by officials who represent us. In a democracy this unintelligibility is doubly intolerable, for the people are supposed to be competent both as voters who elect the lawmakers and as jurors who apply the laws. They cannot do these things if they cannot understand the law.

What can explain this flickering pattern of intelligibility and unintelligibility, the stroboscopic alternation of the familiar with the strange? The most visible and frequently denounced culprits are the arcane vocabulary of the law and the complicated structure of its sentences and paragraphs. Thus, people ask why lawyers cannot be made to speak in words they recognize and in sentences they can understand. If lawyers would do so, the ordinary citizen could become competent as a reader of law and even as a legal speaker. Our political method of democracy and its moral premise of equality demand no less. It may be indeed that the only actual effect of this obfuscating legal jargon is to maintain the mystique of the legal profession, and if that mystique is destroyed so much the better.

Impulses such as these have given rise to what is known as the plain English movement, which aims at a translation of legal language into comprehensible English. This movement has had practical effects. At the federal level, for example, one of President Carter's first actions was to order that all regulations be cast in language intelligible to the ordinary citizen, and New York and other states have passed laws requiring that state regulations and certain form contracts meet a similar standard.

If such directives were seriously regarded, they might indeed reduce needless verbosity and obscurity and streamline unwieldy legal sentences. But even if they succeeded in these desirable goals, they would not solve the general problem they address, for, as I try to show, the most serious obstacles to comprehensibility are not the vocabulary and sentence structure employed in the law but the unstated conventions by which the language operates—what I call the "invisible discourse" of the law. Behind the words, that is, are expectations about the ways in which they will be used, expectations that do not find explicit expression anywhere but are part of the legal culture that the surface language simply assumes. These expectations are constantly at work, directing argument, shaping responses, determining the next move, and so on; their effects are everywhere but they themselves are invisible. These conventions, not the diction, primarily determine the mysterious character of legal speech and literature: not the "vocabulary" of the law but what might be called its "cultural syntax."

In what follows I identify those features of the cultural syntax of legal language that seem most radically to differentiate it from ordinary speech. I then outline some methods by which I think students can be taught to become at least somewhat literate in a language that works in these ways. Finally I suggest that this kind of literacy not only entails an important increase in social competence but itself contributes to the development of mind and attitude that is the proper object of a general education.

The Language of Rules

Many of the special difficulties of legal language derive from the fact that at the center of most legal conversations there is a form we call "the legal rule." Not so general as to be a mere maxim or platitude (though we have those in law, too) or so specific as to be a mere order or command (though there are legal versions of these), the legal rule is a directive of intermediate generality. It establishes relations among classes of objects, persons, and events: "All A are [or: shall be] B"; or, "If A, then B." Examples would include the following:

(1) Burglary consists of breaking and entering a dwelling house in the nighttime with intent to commit a felony therein. A person convicted of burglary shall be punished by imprisonment not to exceed 5 years.
(2) Unless otherwise ordered by the court or agreed by the parties, a former husband's obligation to pay alimony terminates upon the remarriage of his former wife.

Legal conversations about rules such as these have three major characteristics that tend to mystify and confuse nonlawyers.

The Invisible Shift from a Language of Description to a Language of Judgment

The form of the legal rule misleads ordinary readers into expecting that once it is understood, its applications will be very simple. The rules presented above, for example, have a plain and authoritative air and seem to contemplate no difficulty whatever in their application. (Notice that with the possible exception of the word "felony," there is nothing legalistic in their diction.) One will simply look to the facts and determine whether or not the specified conditions exist; if so, the consequence declared by the rule will follow; if not, it will not. "Did she remarry? Then the alimony stops." Nothing to it, the rule seems to say: just look at the world and do what we tell you. It calls for nothing more than a glance to check the name against the reality and obedience to a plain directive.

In practice, of course, the rule does not work so simply—or not always. Is it "breaking and entering" if the person pushes open a screen door but has not yet entered the premises? Is a garage with a loft used as an apartment a "dwelling house"? Is dusk "nighttime"? Is a remarriage that is later annulled a "remarriage" for the purpose of terminating prior alimony? What if there is no formal remarriage but the ex-wife has a live-in boyfriend? These questions do not answer themselves but require thought and conversation of a complex kind, of which no hint is expressed in the rule itself.

Of course there will be some cases so clear that no one could reasonably argue about the meaning of the words, and in these cases the rule will work in a fairly simple and direct fashion. Most of our experience with rules, in fact, works this way: we can find out what to do to get a passport or a driver's license, we know what the rules of the road require, we can figure out when we need a building permit, and so on. But these are occasions of rule obedience for which no special social or intellectual competence is involved.

One way to identify what is misleading about the form of a legal rule might be to say that it appears to be a language of description, which works by a simple process of comparison, but in cases of any difficulty it is actually a language of judgment, which works in ways that find no expression in the rule itself. In such cases the meaning of its terms is not obvious, as the rule seems to assume, but must be determined by a process of interpretation and judgment to which the rule gives no guidance whatever. The discourse by which it works is in this sense invisible.

The False Appearance of Deductive Rationality

If one does recognize that there may be difficulties in understanding and applying a rule, one may still be misled by its form into thinking that the kind of reasoning it requires (and makes possible) is deductive in character. A legal rule looks rather like a rule of geometry, and we naturally expect it to work like one. For example, when the meaning of a term in a rule is unclear—say "dwelling house" or "nighttime" in the burglary statute—we expect to find a stipulative definition elsewhere (perhaps in a special section of the statute) that will define it for us, just as Euclid tells us the meaning of his essential terms. Or if there is no explicit definition, we expect there to be some other rule, general in form, that when considered in connection with our rule will tell us what it must mean. But it is often in vain that we look for such definitions and rules, and when we do find them they often prove to be of little help.

Suppose, for example, the question is whether a person who is caught breaking into a garage that has a small apartment in the loft can be convicted of burglary: does a statutory definition of "dwelling house" as "any residential premises" solve the problem? Or suppose one finds in the law dealing with mortgages a definition of "dwelling house" that plainly does (or does not) cover the garage with the loft: does that help? Upon reflection about the purpose of the burglary statute, which is to punish a certain kind of wrongdoing, perhaps "dwelling house" will suddenly be seen to have a subjective or moral dimension, and properly mean "place where the actor knows that people are living" or, if that be thought too lenient, "place where he has reason to believe that people are living."

Or consider the annulment example. Suppose one finds a statutory statement that "an annulled marriage is a nullity at law." Does that mean that the alimony payment revives upon the annulment of the wife's second marriage? Even if the annulment takes place fifteen years after the date of that marriage? Or suppose that there is another statute, providing that "alimony may be awarded in an annulment proceeding to the same extent as in a divorce proceeding"? This would mean that the wife could get alimony from her second husband, and if the question is seen in terms of fairness among the parties, this opportunity would be highly relevant to whether or not her earlier right to alimony has expired.

The typical form of the legal rule thus seems to invite us to think that the important intellectual operations involved in our use of it will be those of deduction and entailment, as in geometry: that our main concern will be with the relations among propositions, as one rule is related to others by the logical rules of noncontradiction and the like, and that the end result of every intellectual operation will be determined by the rules of deduction.

In fact the situation could hardly be more different. Instead of each term in a legal rule having a meaning of the sort necessary for deductive operations to go on in the first place, each term has a range of possible meanings, among which choices will have to be made. There is no one right answer to the question whether this structure is a "dwelling house" or that relationship a "remarriage"; there are several linguistically and logically tolerable possibilities, and the intellectual process of law is one of arguing and reasoning about which of them is to be preferred. Of course the desirability of internal consistency is a factor (though we shall soon see that the law tolerates a remarkable degree of internal contradiction), and of course in some cases some issues will be too plain for argument. But the operations that lawyers and judges engage in with respect to legal rules are very different from what we might expect from the form of the rule itself. They derive their substance and their shape from the whole world of legal culture and draw upon the most diverse materials, ranging from general maxims to particular cases and regulations. The discourse of the law is far less technical, far more purposive and sensible, than the nonlawyer is likely to think. Argument about the meaning of words in the burglary statute, for example, would include argument about the reasons for having such a statute, about the kind of harm it is meant to prevent or redress, and about the degree and kind of blameworthiness it should therefore require. Legal discourse is continuous at some points with moral or philosophic discourse, at others with history or anthropology or sociology; and in its tension between the particular and the general, in its essentially metaphorical character, it has much in common with poetry itself. The substantive constitution of legal discourse is of course too complex a subject for us at present; what is important now is to see that this discourse is invisible to the ordinary reader of the legal rules.

These characteristics of legal language convert what looks like a discourse connected with the world by the easy process of naming, and rendered internally coherent by the process of deduction, into a much more complex linguistic and cultural system. The legal rule seems to foreclose certain questions of fact and value, and of course in the clear cases it does so. But in the uncertain cases, which are those that cause trouble, it can better be said to open than to close a set of questions: it gives them definition, connection with other questions, and a place in a rhetorical universe, thus permitting their elaboration and resolution in a far more rich and complex way than could otherwise be the case. Except in the plainest cases, the function of the ordinary meanings of terms used in legal rules is not to determine a necessary result but to establish the uncertain boundaries of permissible decision; the function of logic is not to require a particular result by deductive force but to limit the range of possibilities by prohibiting (or making difficult) contradictory uses of the same terms in the same sentences.

But you have perhaps noticed an odd evasion in that last sentence and may be wondering: Does not the law absolutely prohibit inconsistent uses of the same terms in the same rules? Indeed it does not, or not always, and this is the last of the three mystifying features of legal discourse about which I wish to speak.

The Systematic Character of Legal Discourse and the Dilemma of Consistency

I have thus far suggested that while the legal rule appears to operate by a simple process of looking at the world to see whether a named object can be found (the "dwelling house" or the "remarriage"), this appearance is highly misleading, for in fact the world does not often present events in packages that are plainly within the meaning of a legal label (or plainly outside of it). Behind the application of the label is a complex world of reasoning, which is in fact the real life of the law but to which the rule makes no overt allusion and for which it gives no guidance. To the extent that the form of the rule suggests that the controlling mode of reason will be deductive, it gives rise to expectations that are seriously misleading. The real discourse of the law is invisible.

This feature of the law may seem bad enough, but in practice things are even worse, and for two reasons. First, however sophisticated and complex one's reasoning may in fact be, at the end of the process the legal speaker is required after all to express his or her judgment in the most simple binary terms: either the label in the rule fits or it does not. No third possibility is admitted. All the richness and complexity of legal life seem to be denied by the kind of act in which the law requires it to be expressed. For example, while we do not know precisely how the "dwelling house" or "remarriage" questions would in fact be argued out, we can see that the process would be complex and challenging, with room both for uncertainty and for invention. But at the end of the process the judge or jury will have to make a choice between two alternatives and express it by the application (or nonapplication) of the label in question: this is or is not a "dwelling house." In this way the legal actors are required to act as if the legal world really were as simple as the rule misleadingly pretends it is. Everything is reduced to a binary choice after all.

Second, it seems that the force of this extreme reductionism cannot be evaded by giving the terms of legal rules slightly different meanings in different contexts, for the rudiments of logic and fairness alike require that the term be given the same meaning each time it is used, or the system collapses into incoherence and injustice. The most basic rule of logic (the rule of noncontradiction) and the most basic rule of justice (like results in like cases) both require consistency of meaning.

A familiar example demonstrating the requirement of internal consistency in systematic talk about the world is this: "However you define 'raining' the term must be used for the purposes of your system such that it is always true that it either is or is not 'raining.' " Any other principle would lead to internal incoherence and would destroy the regularity of the discourse as a way of talking about the world. To put the principle in terms of the legal example we have been using: however one defines "dwelling house" for purposes of the burglary statute, it must be used in such a manner that everything in the world either is or is not a "dwelling house"; and because the law is a system for organizing experience coherently across time and space, it must be given the same meaning every time it is used. Logic and fairness alike require no less.

The trouble is that these principles of discourse are very different from those employed in ordinary conversations. Who in real life would ever take the view that it must be the case that it either is or is not "raining"? Suppose it is just foggy and wet? If someone in ordinary life asked you whether it was raining out, you would not expect that person to insist upon an answer cast in categorical terms, let alone in categorical terms that were consistent over a set of conversations. The answer to the question would depend upon the reason it was asked: Does your questioner want to know whether to wear a raincoat? whether to water the garden? to call off a picnic? to take a sunbath? In each case the answer will be different, and the speaker will in no case feel required to limit the response to an affirmation or negation of the condition "raining." One will speak to the situation as a whole, employing all of one's resources. And one will not worry much about how the word "raining" has been used in other conversations, on other occasions, for the convention of ordinary speech is that critical terms are defined anew each time for the purposes of a particular conversation, not as part of a larger system.

What is distinctive about conversations concerning the meaning of rules is their systematic character. Terms are defined not for the purposes of a particular conversation but for a class of conversations, and the principle of consistency applies across the class. And this class of conversations has, as we have just seen, a peculiar form: in the operation of the rule, all experience is reduced to a single set of questions—say, whether the elements of burglary exist in this case—each of which must be answered "yes" or "no." We are denied what would be the most common response in our ordinary life, which would be to say that the label fits in this way and not in that or that it depends on why you ask. The complex process of argument and judgment that is involved in understanding a legal rule and relating it to the facts of a particular case is at the end forced into a simple statement of application or nonapplication of a label, under a requirement of noncontradiction over time.

But there is still another layer to the difficulty. We may talk about the requirement of consistency as a matter of logic or justice, but how is it to be achieved? Can we for example ensure that "dwelling house" will be used exactly the same way in every burglary case? Obviously we cannot, for a number of reasons. First, different triers of fact will resolve conflicts of testimony in different ways—one judge or jury would believe one side, a second the other—and this builds inconsistency into the process at the most basic level, that of descriptive fact. Second, while the judge may be required to give the same instruction to the jury in every case, the statement of that instruction will to some extent be cast in general terms and admit a fair variation of interpretation even where the historical facts are settled (e.g., a judicial definition of "dwelling house" as "premises employed as a regular residence by those entitled to possession thereof"). Third, if the instruction includes, as well it might, a subjective element (saying for example that the important question is whether the defendant *knew* he was breaking into a place where people were living), there will be an even larger variation in application of what is on the surface the same language.

In short, the very generality of legal language, which constitutes for us an important part of its character as rational and as fair, means that some real variation in application must be tolerated. As the language becomes more general, the delegation of authority to the applier of the language, and hence the toleration of inconsistency in result, becomes greater. As the language becomes more specific, this delegation is reduced, and with it the potential inconsistency. But increasing specificity has its costs, and they too can be stated in terms of consistency. Consider a sentencing statute, for example, that authorizes the punishment of burglars by sentences ranging from probation to five years in prison. This delegation of sentencing authority (usually to a judge) seems to be a toleration of wide variation in result. But it all depends upon how the variation is measured. For to insist that all burglars receive the same sentence, say, three years in jail, is to treat the hardened repeater and the inexperienced novice as if they were identical. That treatment is "consistent" on one measure (burglars are treated alike) but "inconsistent" on another (an obvious difference among offenders is not recognized).

For our purposes the point is this: the requirements (1) that terms be defined not for a single conversation but for the class of conversation established by the rule in question and (2) that the meaning given words be consistent through the system are seriously undercut in practice by a wide toleration of inconsistency in result and in meaning. I do not mean to suggest, however, that either the requirement of consistency or its qualifications are inappropriate—quite the reverse. It seems to me that we have here identified a dilemma central to the life of any discourse that purports to be systematic, rational, and just. My purpose has simply been to describe a structural tension in legal discourse that differentiates it sharply from most ordinary speech.

In addition to the foregoing I wish to mention one other quality of legal discourse that radically distinguishes it from ordinary language: its procedural character.

Procedural Character of Legal Speech

In working with a rule, one must not only articulate substantive questions of definition—is "dusk" "nighttime"? is a "bicycle" a "vehicle"? etc.—one must also ask a set of related procedural questions. Every question of interpretation involves these related questions: Who shall decide what this language means? under what conditions or circumstances, and subject to what limits or controls? Why? And in what body of discourse are these questions to be thought about, argued out, and decided? The answers to such questions are rarely found in the rule itself.

Suppose, for example, the question is what the word "nighttime" should mean in the burglary statute or, to begin not with a rule but with a difficulty in ordinary life, whether the development of a shopping center should be permitted on Brown's farm. It is the professional habit of lawyers to think not only about the substantive merits of the question and how they would argue it but also about (a) the person or agency who ought to decide it and (b) the procedure by which it ought to be decided. Is the shopping-center question a decision for the zoning commission, for the neighbors, for the city as a whole, for Brown, or for the county court? Is the "nighttime" question one for the judge to decide, for the jury, or—if you think what matters is the defendant's intent in that respect—in part for the defendant? Every legal rule, however purely substantive in form, is also by implication a procedural and institutional statement as well, and the lawyers who read it will realize this and start to argue about its meaning in this dimension too. The function of the rule is thus to define not only substantive topics but also procedures of argument and debate and questions about the definition and allocation of competencies to act. The rule does so either expressly or by implication, but in either event it calls upon discourse that is largely invisible to the reader not legally trained.

To sum up my point, what characterizes legal discourse is that it is in a double sense (both substantively and procedurally) constitutive in nature: it creates a set of questions that define a world of thought and action, a set of roles and voices by which experience will be ordered and meanings established and shared, a set of occasions and methods for public speech that constitute us as a community and as a polity. In all of this, legal discourse has its own ways of working, which are to be found not in the rules that are at its center of the structure but in the culture that determines how these rules are to be read and talked about.

I have identified some of the special ways of thinking and talking that characterize legal discourse. Far more than any technical vocabulary, it is these conventions that are responsible for the foreignness of legal speech. To put it slightly differently, there is a sense in which one creates technical vocabulary whenever one creates a rule of the legal kind, for the operation of the rule in a procedural system itself necessarily entails an artificial way of giving meaning both to words and to events. These characteristics of legal discourse mean that the success of any movement to translate legal speech into plain English will be severely limited. For if one replaces a legal word with an ordinary English word, the sense of increased normalcy will be momentary at best: the legal culture will go immediately to work, and the ordinary word will begin to lose its shape, its resiliency, and its familiarity and become, despite the efforts of the drafter, a legal word after all. The reason for this is that the word will work as part of the legal language, and it is the way this language works that determines the meaning of its terms. This is what I meant when I said that it is not the vocabulary of the legal language that is responsible for its obscurity and mysteriousness, but its cultural syntax, the invisible expectations governing the way the words are to be used.

Teaching Legal Literacy: The Method of a Possible Course

Thus far I have been writing as a lawyer to nonlawyers, describing those features of legal discourse that most mark it off from ordinary speech and make it difficult to understand. Now I wish to write differently, as one teacher to another, and ask what kind of knowledge of this language can best be the object of an advanced high school or college writing course. What kind of legal literacy can nonprofessionals be helped to attain? How can we best teach them?

As I have made clear, I start with the idea that literacy is not merely the capacity to understand the conceptual content of writings and utterances but the ability to participate fully in a set of social and intellectual practices. It is not passive but active, not imitative but creative, for participation in the speaking and writing of language includes participation in the activities language makes possible. Indeed, true literacy involves a perpetual remaking both of language and of practice.

To attain full legal literacy would accordingly require that one master both the resources by which topics are argued in the law and the set of procedural possibilities for argument that are established by the law, from the administrative agency to the jury, from the motion to strike to the writ of mandamus. Literacy of this sort is the object of a professional education and requires full-time immersion in the legal culture. It obviously cannot be attained in one high school or college course.

But we need not assume that nothing can be done to reduce the gap between the specialized language of the law and the ordinarily literate person. While one cannot make nonlawyers legally literate in the sense of full and active competence at law, one can do much to teach them about the kind of language law is and the kind of literature it produces. I think a student can come to understand, that is, something of what it means to speak a discourse that is constitutive and procedural in character and founded on the form we call the rule. The successful student will not be able to practice law or even to follow lawyers in all their moves, but he or she will have some knowledge, both tacit and explicit, of the kinds of expectations lawyers bring to conversations, the kinds of needs and resources they have, and the kinds of moves they are likely to make. If what is at first invisible can be seen and understood, legal discourse will lose some of its power to frighten and to mystify. One will, of course, still experience a lack of comprehension, but these experiences will more often occur at expected moments and be of expected kinds. And one will be more confident about what one does comprehend, more certain about the moments at which one is entitled to insist upon clarification or upon being heard. All this can come from understanding the legal system as a constitutive discourse based on the rule.

But how is such an understanding to be created? An explicit analysis of the sort I have sketched above will be of little assistance to most students, for it proceeds largely at the conceptual level, and literacy involves knowledge of a very different kind. (A student could learn to repeat sentences describing the rhetoric of law, for example, without ever having any real sense of what these sentences mean.) Of almost equally limited value for our purposes are most courses in the structure and nature of our government, for once again students often learn to repeat what they hear without any sense of what it means. (Think of the clichés about "checks and balances," e.g., or the "imperial presidency.") Courses that attempt to teach students legal substance are often not much better, for knowledge of the rules does little good unless the student understands something of what it means to read and write a discourse based on rules. Besides, it frequently happens that the topics chosen are those of current popular interest, like abortion or the death penalty, where legal discourse (at least at the Supreme Court level) is not sharply distinguished from ordinary political and journalistic talk.

More promising than such courses, or useful perhaps as a possible supplement to them, would be a course that asked students to write not about the law but about analogues to the law in their own lives. The idea would be that students would become more competent not at law itself but at lawlike writing, and they would learn not only about the law but about themselves and the world.

Suppose students were asked to write a series of assignments about an aspect of their own lives that was regulated by rules—say, their athletic team, or the school itself, or their apartment house, or their part-time jobs. These rules could be examined from several different perspectives. First, for example, students might be asked simply to reproduce the rules governing parts of their lives. Without overtly burdening the students with legal knowledge, this assignment would raise sophisticated and interesting questions about the nature of rules in their social context (e.g., about the relation between written and unwritten rules). One might ask the students, "In what form do these rules appear in the world? Are they written and published, and if so where? How do you know that these rules apply to you? Are they all the rules, and if so how do you know that? If the rules are not written and published, how do you even know what the rules are? Why do you suppose they are not written and published?" or, "What exceptions are there to these rules, and how do you know?" And so on. Similar questions could be raised about the relation between rules and authority: "Who promulgated these rules, and upon what authority? How do you know? What does it mean to have authority to promulgate rules of this kind?" And so on.

The students could then be asked to talk about the ways in which questions arising under their rules should be resolved. What problems of meaning do these rules present? How should they be resolved, and by whom, acting under what procedures? Perhaps here a teacher could reproduce one or two sets of rules the students had provided and think up imagined situations where the application of the rules would be problematic. (After one or two such assignments, the students could be asked to do it themselves.) This type of assignment would present students with the difficulty of thinking in terms of a system meant to operate with constant or consistent—or at least apparently consistent—definitions over time, for they can be led to see that the way they resolve the meaning of the rules in one case will have consequences for others. This involves an extension of imaginative and sympathetic capacities and a complication of the idea of fairness. It might also begin to teach them that in difficult cases the meaning of the rules cannot be seen in the rules themselves but must be found elsewhere, in the resources and equipment one brings to thought and argument about the questions. What is more, since these resources are partly of our own invention, it is right to ask how they can be improved. Finally, depending on the particular system of rules, this method may lead the students to think in terms of procedures and competences: why the judgment whether a particular player is "trying hard" (as required by a rule) is a matter for the coach, not for the players (or vice versa); why the umpire's decision that a pitch is a strike or a ball must (or must not) be final, and so on. Or one might consider rules governing life in a cooperative apartment and the procedures by which decisions should be made when there are real differences of opinion about the necessity of roof repair, the costs of heating, and so on.

Finally, students could be asked to draft rules of their own devising, whether regulations or contractual provisions, and submit them to collective criticism. Such a project could be a real lesson in the limits both of language and of the mind, as students realize how little power they actually have to determine what meaning words will have to others and how little they can imagine the future that their rules are intended to regulate. The assignment would draw on students' own experiences without using legal terms or technicalities. It need not even be done in Standard English: the students' writing (or talking, if these assignments were done orally) should indeed reflect the way people actually speak in their own world. And one important lesson for us all might be the discovery that it is not only in the law or only in the language of the white middle class that community is constituted or that argument about justice proceeds.

Such exercises, with material from the students' own lives, would tend to make the process seem natural and immediate, within their ordinary competence. But in the process they should be introduced to questions of extraordinary depth and sophistication: about the construction of social reality through language (as they define roles, voices, and characters in the dramas they report); about the definition of value (as they find themselves talking about privacy or integrity or truthfulness or cooperation); about the nature of reasoning (as they put forward one or another argument with the expectation that it cannot be answered, as they try to meet the argument of another, and so on); and about the necessarily cooperative nature of society (as they realize that whatever rules they promulgate can work only with the assistance of others and must work equally for all people and all cases); and so on. They might learn something of what it means that the law seeks always to limit the authority it creates. They might even come to see that the question "What is fair?" should often include the qualifications "under this set of rules, under these procedures, and under these particular circumstances." It might be a good thing toward the end of the course to read as well some actual legal materials: a statute, a judicial opinion, a piece of a brief. If I am right in my expectations, after working on rules in their own lives the students would find this material more complex, more interesting, and more comprehensible—also perhaps more difficult—than before. The result would itself be an important demonstration of legal literacy and a direct manifestation of the student's competence as an educated citizen.

The law itself can be seen as a method of individual and collective self-education, a discipline in the acknowledgment of limits, in the recognition of others, and in the necessity of cooperation. It is a way in which we teach ourselves, over and over again, how little we can foresee, how much we depend upon others, how sound and wise are the practices we have inherited from the past. It is a way of creating a world in part by imagining what can be said on the other side. In these ways it is a lesson in sympathy and humility. Of course a professional training is no guarantee of such an education—far from it—but it is not a prerequisite either. What I mean to suggest in this paper is that a training in the analogues of law that are found in ordinary life, if done in the right way, can be a stage in such a development: that this kind of legal literacy may be a true part of general education.

The Language of the Bureaucracy

Janice C. Redish

For many years, the media have poked fun at the pomposity and incomprehensibility of much of the writing that our government produces. Egregious examples of gobbledygook are easy to find; try, for instance, to make sense of these two passages:

> Example 1: From a Department of Agriculture regulation
> ¶928.310 Papaya Regulation 10.
> *Order*. (a) *No* handler shall ship any container of papayas (*except* immature papayas handled pursuant to ¶928.152 of this part):
> (1) During the period January 1 through April 15, 1980, to any destination within the production area *unless* said papayas grade at least Hawaii No. 1, *except* that allowable tolerances for defects may total 10 percent: *Provided,* That *not* more than 5 percent shall be for serious damage, *not* more than 1 percent for immature fruit, and *not* more than 1 percent for decay: *Provided further,* That such papayas shall individually weigh not less than 11 ounces each.

> Example 2: From an Immigration and Naturalization Service form.
> If you are the spouse or unmarried minor child of a person who has been granted preference classification by the Immigration and Naturalization Service or has applied for preference classification, and you are claiming the same preference classification, or if you are claiming special immigrant classification as the spouse or unmarried child of a minister of religion who has been accorded or is seeking classification as a special immigrant, submit the following. . . . (INS Form I-485)

You may find yourself shaking your head in dismay, as I did when I first read these sentences. Shaking our heads, however, won't improve bureaucratic writing.

For the language of bureaucracy to change, the system and the people in it must relinquish the pervasive philosophy and style of writing. In the 1970s, bureaucratic writing did begin to change. A small but growing body of well-written, direct, personal, and understandable bureaucratic documents has been

151

developed. Although these examples are less often quoted by the media, they exist. For instance:

>   Example 3: From a Federal Communications Commission regulation.
>   *CB Rule 5. How do I apply for a CB license?*
>   (a) You apply for a CB license by filling out an application (FCC Form 505) and sending it to the FCC, Gettysburg, Pa. 17326.
>   (b) You can get applications from the FCC, Washington, D.C. 20554 or from any FCC field office. (A list of FCC field offices is contained in CB Rule 45.) Many CB equipment dealers also have application forms.
>   (c) If you have questions about your application, you should write to the Personal Radio Division, Washington, D.C. 20554.
>   Example 4: From a Department of Education form.
>   You can use the form in this booklet to apply for a 1980-81 Basic Educational Opportunity Grant (Basic Grant). A Basic Grant is money to help you pay for your education after high school. It is not a loan, so you do not have to repay it. To get a Basic Grant, you have to meet certain requirements.

The FCC example was written by a lawyer and a program specialist (who has since become a lawyer). I helped write example 4 (and the document from which it was taken) as a consultant to the Department of Education. Both these documents went through the extensive reviews that are characteristic of the government, and both were eventually accepted. Many other examples exist, but most bureaucratic documents have not been rewritten into clear English. Why? And what can English teachers do to foster a change in the language of the bureaucracy?

In this paper, I want to explore the status and future of bureaucratic language by addressing four questions:

(1) What are the characteristics of bureaucratic writing?
(2) How did bureaucratic writing develop and what encourages it not to change?
(3) Where do the pressures for change come from?
(4) What can be done to foster greater literacy in bureaucratic writing among both writers and users of government documents?

Characteristics of Traditional Bureaucratic Language

What characterizes the traditional bureaucratic language that becomes a candidate for a column on gobbledygook? I am going to limit this discussion to prose (as distinct from forms). And I am going to look first at style (the sentences and words).

One of the points I want to make is that style is only part (and perhaps not the most important part) of the problem in bureaucratic language. Style, however, is the most obvious feature of any piece of writing. Most clear writing guidelines focus on style, and readability formulas (which purport to measure comprehensibility of documents) count only stylistic features.

Style

Bureaucratic writing that is difficult to understand has three major stylistic problems. It is nominal, full of jargon, and legalistic.

Bureaucratic writing overuses nouns. Nouns replace pronouns, verbs, and adjectives. Traditional bureaucratic style does not directly address the reader. If a human subject is mentioned at all, a generic or class term is used.

> Example 5: All employees shall submit to the Director of Personnel within 30 days after their entrance on duty. . . .
> Example 6: Interested persons may . . . submit . . . written comments regarding this proposal.

The effect is both formal and abstract. Readers have to make the connection between themselves and the generic class.

The nominal style of bureaucratic writing is also reflected in the way writers focus on the inanimate object of the action rather than on the actor. Things are more important than people. Thus, bureaucratic writers overuse the passive voice because passive sentences focus on the object.

> Example 7: Proposals must be received no later than 4:00 p.m. June 2, 1981.

The government doesn't care who is submitting the proposal; it only insists that the proposal arrive by a certain time. Most readers can understand a simple sentence, such as this one, even when it is in the passive. They have trouble, however, when they have to read entire passages that involve no human agents.

> Example 8: From a Small Business Administration regulation.
> ¶124.1-3 Advance payments.
> (a) *Definitions.* Advance payments are disbursements of money made by SBA to a section 8(a) business concern prior to the completion of performance of a specific section 8(a) subcontract for the purpose of assisting the said 8(a) business concern in meeting financial requirements pertinent to the performance of said subcontract. Advance payments must be liquidated from proceeds derived from the performance of the specific section 8(a) subcontract. However, this does not preclude repayment of such advance payments from other revenues of the business except from other advance payments.

Research shows that readers have great difficulty understanding this type of bureaucratic writing. In trying to make sense out of a passage such as this one, readers create actor-action scenarios. When they explain the passage, they put the pronouns in and make the sentences active (Flower, Hayes, and Swarts).

Another characteristic of bureaucratic writing is the overuse of nouns made out of verbs. The preceding sentence, in fact, is an example of this problem. I should have written: bureaucratic writing uses too many nouns that are made out of verbs. The first sentence has no human actor. The subject is the inanimate noun "characteristic." The sentence has no action verb, only the linking verb "is." The implied action ("use") is buried in a derived noun, "the overuse of."

The following example has two derived nouns:

Example 9: *Failure* to follow these directions will result in *disqualification* of the applicant.

Again the effect is both formal and abstract. Do applicants realize that they are being addressed?

When bureaucrats write in the nominal style they tend to use all the features of the style together. Look again at example 8. How many derived nouns do you find?

The three features of the nominal style that I have mentioned—nouns instead of pronouns, passive sentences focusing on inanimate nouns, and nouns instead of verbs—characterize both bureaucratic and legal writing. The fourth feature of the nominal style is characteristic of both bureaucratic and academic writing but is less often found in nonbureaucratic legal writing. Government writers frequently use nouns to modify nouns. (We call these "noun strings.")

Example 10:
consumer information service
health maintenance organization
host area crisis shelter production planning workbook

Noun strings can become acronyms, which can then be used in other noun strings.

Example 11: Nonbusiness FWREI expenses incurred by the taxpayer are limited to $5,000 per year.
(Author's note: FWREI stands for Federal Welfare Recipient Employment Incentive.)

Acronyms serve to separate "in" people, who know what they mean (or, at least, what they refer to) from "out" people, who do not have that information.

Noun strings are a shorthand; they take less space to write, but they are difficult for laypeople to understand. A reader who is not familiar with the material must figure out how the nouns relate to each other in order to understand the concepts being discussed. Take this sentence as an example:

Example 12: Four major characteristics influence *consumer information seeking and utilization behavior.*

The italicized words are a string of nouns. Two of the nouns ("seeking," "utilization") are derived from verbs. The phrase means: "the *behavior* of *consumers* as they *seek* and *use information*."

Noun strings obscure connections, make concrete actions into abstract nouns, and move the human actors into subordinate positions. Because noun strings often become frozen units, they are like jargon—meaningful to certain people, obscure to others.

Bureaucratic writing is full of jargon.   A specialized vocabulary serves a dual purpose for any professional group. It permits clear communication within the group, and it indicates to both insiders and outsiders who belongs to the group and who does not.

Some jargon is both useful and necessary. For example, the government promulgates laws and regulations. "Promulgate" is a word that is not used in everyday English; it has a meaning understood by legislators and bureaucrats; we cannot easily find an everyday English equivalent for it. "Promulgate" is bureaucratic jargon in a nonpejorative sense of the word "jargon."

But problems arise with bureaucratic jargon in at least three situations. The first is when bureaucratic writers use words that serve only one of the two purposes. These are words that don't have clear and special meanings; they only say, "I know the 'in' terms." Examples include "prioritize," "finalize," "impact" (as a verb), and "implement" (as a verb). Clear everyday English equivalents exist for each of these words. They mark a piece of writing as bureaucratic and as fair game for ridicule in the media.

The second situation in which bureaucratic jargon becomes a problem is when it is combined with the jargon of another professional discipline. Most bureaucratic writers must, in fact, address at least two audiences who do not share jargons (agency contract specialists and engineers, e.g., or lawyers and nursing-home operators). Bureaucratic writers in this situation must control several jargons; many don't, and they misuse words frequently.

In the third place, bureaucratic jargon becomes a problem when government writers have to communicate with a general audience. The general audience, by definition, doesn't share the jargon. (If everyone knew what all the special terms meant, there wouldn't be any "in" language.) The writer may be caught in a bind. The internal audience (peers and supervisors) may demand an internally acceptable style and jargon. The external audience (the general public) may demand a clear and direct writing style. Academic and business writers share this dilemma, but perhaps it is less of a problem to them than to the bureaucratic writer, who is now supposed to be responsible and responsive to the people.

Bureaucratic language is highly legalistic.   Jargon is supposed to facilitate communication within the group that shares a specialized vocabulary, but aspects of traditional bureaucratic writing hinder communication even within the "in" group. Because many government documents are also legal documents, bureaucratic writing often includes archaisms and long, overly inclusive, and convoluted sentences that are typical of legalese.

> Example 13: (a) *General*. (1) Every application for Federal financial assistance to carry out a program to which this part applies, except a program to which paragraph (b) of this section applies, and every application for Federal financial assistance to provide a facility shall, as a condition to its approval and the extension of any Federal financial assistance pursuant to the application, contain or be accompanied by an assurance that the program will be conducted or the facility operated in compliance with all requirements imposed by or pursuant to this part.

Furthermore, many of these documents must be read and followed by nonlawyers. Local police officials may be the primary audience for this sentence from the pre-1978 version of the Citizens Band radio rules:

> Example 14: Applications, amendments, and related statements of fact filed on behalf of eligible government entities, such as states and territories of the United States and political subdivisions thereof, the District of Columbia, and units of local government, including incorporated municipalities, shall be signed by such duly elected or appointed officials as may be competent to do so under the laws of the applicable jurisdiction.

This is not an extreme example. Sentences of 120-150 words are common in bureaucratic documents. Research in psychology and linguistics shows that long convoluted sentences overtax people's capacity to process information.

Bureaucratic documents written in a highly legalistic style are not necessarily comprehensible to lawyers. When our team at the Document Design Center sits down with a group of government lawyers to rewrite a bureaucratic document, we often find that they disagree on what the document is saying; often, they cannot explain what the bureaucratic language means.

Legal language is the subject of the essay by James Boyd White in this volume and already has a literature of its own (see, e.g., Mellinkoff and Charrow, Crandall, and Charrow). Therefore, I will not dwell here on the stylistic characteristics of legal language except to note that many of the features that are thought of as bureaucratic are the legacies of the intertwined history of legal and bureaucratic language.

Pragmatics

In discussing the language of the bureaucracy so far, I have quoted only short passages from bureaucratic documents. I have used these sentences to illustrate features of traditional bureaucratic style. The solution to stylistic problems is fairly easy. We could recommend a clear writing guideline to remedy each of these problems, and, if the guidelines were applied appropriately, the result would be likely to be a much more readable document.

But that's not the whole picture. Understanding a document requires more than just being able to read the separate sentences. The document as a whole must make sense. The organization must be useful, the purpose clear. If there are procedures to be followed, they must be laid out logically.

A major problem with bureaucratic documents is the lack of attention paid to pragmatics—to the context in which the document will be used, to the audience, and to the rhetorical situation. Perhaps because bureaucratic language derives in large measure from legal language, many bureaucratic documents have traditionally served a denotative rather than a communicative function. The existence of the document and the statement of the facts in writing are of primary importance. Comprehensibility is secondary, if it is considered at all.

H. P. Grice, a philosopher of language, has pointed out that successful communication is based on a principle of cooperation between the parties involved. Each person must be trying to communicate and must believe that the other is also trying to communicate. Readers of a document written in traditional bureaucratic language may be frustrated because they believe the document is trying to communicate when, in fact, the writer had no such intention. Bureaucratic writers have told me that the purpose of their documents—usually regulations and notices—is to set down the rules, not to tell people what to do (even though people outside the agency have to perform according to the rules).

The lack of attention to pragmatics in bureaucratic writing can be seen in poor organization, uninformative headings and tables of contents, a lack of concern for what the audience needs to know, and lack of coordination along the chain from writer to final product.

Bureaucratic documents are poorly organized.   Much of what the government has to tell people is procedural information—how to go about doing something. Even documents that seem to be about rights and obligations are often procedural. They describe events and actions that occur in a certain order. Government writers are sometimes more concerned with getting down all the nuances of the law (the exceptions and the special cases) than with explaining logically, step by step, what to do. They tend to focus on and to write section by section instead of first outlining the entire document and organizing the sections in a way that makes sense to the person who has to use the document to perform some action.

In addition to being procedural, many bureaucratic documents are primarily used for reference. Although the users may read a regulation from start to finish once to become familiar with it, after that they are likely to need the regulation only when a specific problem arises. At that point, the reader has a question and wants an answer to it as quickly and easily as possible. The same is true for contracts, manuals, and even requests for proposals. Reference documents require a different organization from narratives, persuasive memos, or committee reports.

Bureaucratic headings and tables of contents are uninformative.   For a document to serve well as a reference, it is not enough for the writer to organize it well. It is also necessary to give the reader clues to the organization. A characteristic trait of difficult bureaucratic documents is that the table of contents and the section headings are often useless to the reader. Example 15 is the table of contents of one agency's rules governing a set of grants programs. The writer could not possibly have developed this table of contents with the readers in mind.

Recent research by Swarts, Flower, and Hayes on a different set of regulations shows that poorly conceived headings are often misleading. Given the heading of a section, participants in the study could not accurately predict the content of that section, nor could they accurately match sentences taken from the regulations with the headings used in the regulation.

Useful headings and tables of contents can be written for bureaucratic documents. Compare this table of contents from another agency's grants program with example 15.

Example 16:
Part 161e—Financial Assistance for Consumers' Education Projects
Subpart A—General
Sec.
161e.1   What is the Consumers' Education Program?
161e.2   Who is eligible to receive an award?
161e.3   What regulations apply to the Consumers' Education Program?
161e.4   What definitions apply specifically to this program?
Subpart B—What Kinds of Projects Does the Office of Education Assist
             under This Program?
161e.10 What are the purposes of the projects?
161e.11 What categories of activities are supported?
161e.12 What subject matter may be included?
161e.13 Will particular program subject matter be emphasized?
Subpart C—How Does One Apply for a Grant?

When bureaucratic writers are concerned with helping their audience through a document, they can begin by stating what the document is for and what the document covers.

Example 17: Federal Communications Commission Rules for Recreational Boaters.
Subpart CC—How to Use Your VHF Marine Radio
General
VHF Marine Rule 1. Who are these rules for?
These rules are for recreational boaters who have put VHF (Very High Frequency) marine radios on their boats. A VHF marine radio is a two-way radio for boaters. VHF marine radios operate on channels in the very high frequency band between 156 and 162 MHz.
VHF Marine Rule 2. What do these rules tell me?
Rules 3 through 9 tell you how to get a license for your radio. Rules 10 through 20 tell you how to operate your radio.

Table of Contents

Example 15

Poor organization and lack of useful headings are not unique to the language of the bureaucracy. They are common failings of weak or untrained writers in every sector. But the tradition of noncommunicative documents in law and in the bureaucracy has meant that until recently government writers have had few well-organized and well-presented models to follow.

Bureaucratic documents lack concern for what the audience needs to know. Bureaucratic documents are traditionally written from the writer's perspective, not from the reader's perspective. In legal-bureaucratic documents, the lawyer's concern that all contingencies be covered often takes precedence over selecting appropriate and necessary content for the readers.

Even when a bureaucratic writer wants to focus on an audience, the task is difficult. In many government agencies, information brochures are written by trained writers who know about the importance of keeping the reader in mind, but the writer can only imagine who the reader is. Time and funds are rarely available for interviewing a sample of prospective readers. The bureaucracy often isolates writers from their audiences, and there is seldom feedback to tell a writer that the information in a booklet is at the wrong level or answers the wrong questions. If there is feedback, it may be routed to the wrong department and never reach the writer at all.

Bureaucratic documents lack coordination.   The division of responsibility in the bureaucracy discourages people from using writing as a means of communication. For example, my colleagues and I at the Document Design Center recently agreed to help the information services division of an agency evaluate how well readers understood one of its brochures. Our first discovery was that no one at the field offices we had selected as research sites had read the booklet. In fact, no one had seen it. The distribution system had somehow failed. Imagine the devastating effect on the agency's writers when they learned that their brochure had never even reached the clients. Many such experiences lead writers to the belief that "no one will read it anyway."

Complexified, Complex, and Simple Language

In the past five years, an effort to simplify the language of bureaucratic documents (and of consumer contracts in the private sector) has gained significant momentum. The purpose of this effort is to make the language of the bureaucracy communicative and comprehensible—but not necessarily super simple. The term most commonly associated with the effort has been "plain English." New York's Sullivan Act and the similar statutes in Connecticut, Hawaii, New Jersey, and Maine are called "plain language laws."[1] The Practising Law Institute has twice run courses "Plain Language in Public Documents." The Document Design Center publishes a monthly newsletter with the title *Simply Stated.*[2]

Perhaps "plain English" and "simply stated" are misleading terms. Bureaucratic writers (and lawyers in the private sector) are concerned that they are being asked to oversimplify—to write in all cases to a hypothetical "person on the street," to reduce everything to a "Dick and Jane" style of writing. Some early versions of the "plain language" bills specified that all consumer contracts had to be written at the eighth- or ninth-grade reading level. (Not one of these bills has become law.)

The notion that simplifying the language of bureaucracy must necessarily result in simple language is mistaken. The bureaucratic language that is being attacked is a highly complexified language with features of style and pragmatics that set it apart from mature, complex writing that college composition teachers expect of their students. The purpose of the "plain language" movement is not so much to simplify as to "decomplexify" bureaucratic documents.

President Carter's executive order requiring a change in the language of the bureaucracy did speak of both simple and "plain English," but it also emphasized the level necessary to reach the reader.[3] It said that "Regulations shall be as simple and clear as possible" and that "The official [approving regulations] should determine that . . . the regulation is written in plain English and is understandable to those who must comply with it." We can take this last statement to be the most critical one. The order required that writers pay attention to the full rhetorical situation, to the purpose and the audience, of what they were writing.

Sometimes a highly simplified vocabulary and style are appropriate and necessary in the new language of bureaucracy. The Citizens Band radio regulations, addressed to 15 million CB owners, must reach many people who do not read on a college level. But other bureaucratic documents do not have such broad or general audiences and do not need so simple a vocabulary.

If you look again at the features of bureaucratic language that I have described, you will see that the language of the bureaucracy (and the language of the law) is not just ordinary English with hard words and long sentences. As Charrow suggests, even highly educated people who can control the formal registers of written and spoken English do not understand bureaucratic and legal language.

Distinguishing complexified language from complex language and both from simple language is important for two reasons. It helps us deal with the fears (and correspondingly the attitudes and motivations) of writers in the bureaucracy. It helps us to understand the origins of (at least some of) the worst gobbledygook in bureaucratic documents.

I would like to hypothesize that poor writers who do not control the mature style of formal written English do even more poorly when they try to write in the complexified language of bureaucracy. They follow the models without understanding and produce what Joseph Williams calls the "perplexed style," a hypercorrected bureaucratese. For example, the following sentence, the opening statement in a request for proposal, shows a writer trying to sound "bureaucratic" without understanding how to write.

Example 18: The purpose of this project is to create an awareness on the behalf of the consumer as to how one must proceed to effectively impact upon regulatory agency policymaking processes.

The three-tiered characterization of bureaucratic language and the distinction between control of complex versus complexified styles have implications for how we train (or retrain) bureaucratic writers. I will return to that topic, but before we get there, I want to add to my characterization some thoughts on why bureaucratic documents are written the way they are.

How Did the Language of Bureaucracy Become So Complexified?

From a historical perspective, there seem to be two major explanations for the features of bureaucratic language. One is the legal tradition. The other is an earlier attitude that government should represent itself as formal and impersonal.

The Legal Tradition

The domain of the language of bureaucracy overlaps significantly the domain of legal language. Legal language retains its frozen forms of medieval English for a number of reasons. Lawyers believe the rigidity of language is necessary for accuracy. Mellinkoff effectively destroys this argument, but in trying to change the language of bureaucracy, we must deal directly with the lawyer's perception that clear language and legal accuracy are incompatible concepts. Danet and Charrow, Crandall, and Charrow have described the ritualistic and "magical" aspects of complexified legal language. Many lawyers feel that if lay readers were to understand legal language, it would lose some of its magic; and the resistance to changing legal language rubs off onto bureaucratic language as well.

The Government as Impersonal Guardian of the Public Welfare

In a workshop I gave to a group of government writers in 1980, one of the lawyers expressed dismay at my suggestion that he use personal pronouns and active sentences in his bureaucratic documents. "But we were taught to write in the passive," he said. Whether or not he was explicitly taught the impersonal passive (not just passive sentences, but passive sentences with no agents), the models he was given to follow were certainly written that way. The traditional bureaucratic style is called "the public passive" and is meant to indicate a strong, impersonal, and therefore impartial, institution.

The change to plain English represents a radical philosophical departure from the tradition of the bureaucracy. The call for a new style rests on a belief that the impersonal government has not been impartial and has not been responsive to the people. The demand for a new style is also a demand for a government that is open to public inspection and to public participation. In part, a resistance to the new style of plain English may be an unwillingness to accept this philosophical shift.

In addition to the two historical traditions that I have just discussed, there are many other forces that work against change in the language of the bureaucracy. Let me briefly mention six: institutional inertia, the models that writers have to follow, the social prestige of a special language, time pressures, the review process, and the lack of training to understand and therefore change the style.

Institutional Inertia

The federal bureaucracy is a gigantic institution, and even a small agency is inextricably part of this large organization. In the government, people move from agency to agency following paths of specialization (contract officer, personnel specialist, program analyst, legal counsel). Although personnel changes across agencies can be a vehicle for the spread of new ideas, they can also be a leveling force. If you want to expand your possibilities for promotion to include agencies beyond the one you are in, you have to play the game as it is defined in the overall organization, not just in your own agency.

In any institution it is easier and safer to do things as they have always been done. Change requires taking risks, and if there are no rewards for risk-taking, there are no incentives to do so. The bureaucracy as an institution probably offers less incentive for taking risks than do other large institutions such as private industry or academia. Look at what happened to people who "blew the whistle" on budget overruns.

Higher-ranking people in an institution, however, have more control over the way things are done and consequently are freer to take risks. In the government, in particular, top-level executives move frequently among the business, academic, and public sectors. They have options beyond the institution they are currently in and therefore are not as constrained to play it safe as lower-echelon people might be. This fact suggests that the best path to change is to convince top-level people, who would then reduce the level of risk that change would entail for lower-level people.

Traditional Models

We don't yet know much about how writers acquire institutional literacy—how they learn to write job-related documents. A few process studies are now under way, by Odell and Goswami: ("Nature and Functions"), Scribner and Jacobs, and Mikulecky, but more work needs to be done in this area. We do know that few courses are available to prospective government employees on how to write in the language of bureaucracy. We can assume that writers learn by imitating the style of existing documents, and it is clear that more models are available in the traditional language of the bureaucracy than in a communicative, comprehensible style.

Social Prestige

The specialized features of any complexified language emerge at least in part from a desire among members of a group to be seen as separate. Group members and outsiders can tell who belongs by the way they write and speak. Despite the fact that we laugh at examples of bureaucratic writing, the bureaucracy is a prestigious place to work. The language of the bureaucracy, however infelicitous it may be, is adopted by news commentators and the public when they want to sound as if they too are "in the know." For months, we all discussed the "hostage crisis situation."

Time Pressures

It takes longer to do things a new way, and, in any institution, time is money. Although you may believe that the government is an extremely inefficient and costly institution and that government documents take forever to appear, bureaucratic writers usually feel that they are under unreasonable time pressures. Congress sometimes mandates that a law be turned into regulations in a few months. The OSHA (Occupational Safety and Health Administration) rules that were published under very quick deadlines are an example of how time pressures help produce gobbledygook.

We may argue that communicative, comprehensible English is easier and faster to write than is gobbledygook (and I think that is true), but changing styles and creating new models take time. Instead of being instructed to revise and rethink a form or a regulation when Congress changes the law, writers are only given the time to amend an existing document to account for the changes. The result over time is often to add to the disorganization, inconsistency, and incomprehensibility of the original document.

The Review Process

An institutional review process can benefit both writers and users of documents. Problems arise, however, when the review process becomes as cumbersome as it is in many government agencies.

A federal regulation may require as many as ten or twenty levels of review for one document. Although the staff of a program will write it, the agency's general counsel must approve it; OMB (the Office of Management and Budget) may review it; and people at all levels in the organization—from the program supervisors to the secretary—must sign off on it. The effect can be devastating. Compromises in policy and language may obscure rather than clarify. The writer may get fed up with trying to keep the style clear. We do not teach our students how to write by committee, how to deal with reviewers, or even to expect to have to revise what they write.

Institutions, particularly ones as hierarchically arranged as government agencies are, tend to isolate writers from their real (final, external) audience. Mechanisms for feedback from the people who use bureaucratic documents are weak. Direct feedback comes haphazardly (e.g., letters and calls of complaint); types of indirect feedback (such as error rates on forms) are, in theory, available but are seldom used.

Without feedback from the audience, writers do not know when they have fallen into the trap of being too familiar with the vocabulary and style of their profession. The vocabulary and concepts of any field become commonplace to those who use them repeatedly. The shared jargon and style serve an important communicative function within the profession, but it is easy to forget that others may not immediately understand what you are saying. Over time as I work with government regulations, I become more and more used to bureaucratese. Material that shocked me three years ago seems ordinary now. Staying attuned to an audience one does not regularly meet requires an extraordinary expenditure of time and energy.

In a system with many layers of review, writers may also lose a sense of responsibility for the documents. By the time a federal regulation appears in print, the author may well have a different job and other concerns. Of course there are some very stable offices in the government, where a cadre of people have remained for several years building strong programs. There are offices that take public testimony seriously and try to communicate effectively with an external audience despite the inconveniences and counterpressures of a cumbersome review process. But when the chain that joins writer and user has as many links as it does for most bureaucratic documents, the writer may not even know that it is knotted or broken somewhere along its length.

Research on writing in work settings shows that writers are highly attuned to their immediate audiences (Odell and Goswami, "Writing in a Non-Academic Setting," and Goswami). For writers in the bureaucracy, the immediate audience is the internal one—the reviewers. Government writers perceive that their supervisors want to see the traditional language of the bureaucracy. This perception is a major deterrent to change. We have tried to combat both the perception and the reality it may reflect. Whenever we train a group of writers, we give a half-day workshop for their supervisors. We foster communication between writers and reviewers at the beginning of a project.

The issue of the writer's perception versus the reviewer's reality, however, raises some interesting questions about how any systematic change occurs in institutions (not just changes in acceptable style). Is change most effective when it comes down from the top? What signals of change are most likely to be taken seriously? Are the perceptions of staff writers accurate reflections of institutional reality? Do perceptions of what is acceptable lag behind changes in the attitudes

of upper-echelon reviewers? How does the bureaucracy, where policy at the top
is highly political and may shift drastically every four years, differ in its writer-
reviewer relationships from other institutions? It seems to me that if we want to
change the language of bureaucracy, we have to have a better understanding of
the process of institutional change.

Lack of Training

The final reason I want to offer for why bureaucratic documents are so
difficult to understand is that few people who write the language of bureaucracy
were ever trained to be writers. Regulations are written by lawyers, engineers,
and policy analysts. Requests for proposals are written by program specialists.
IRS forms, instructions, and publications are developed by tax-law specialists.
Writers and editors, employed by the agencies to help have far less prestige and
clout than do the experts in the subject matter.

When we examine university-level curricula in this country, we still find
few courses that might prepare future bureaucrats to understand the principles
of clear document design and the realities and possibilities for writing in institutional settings. The programs at the University of Michigan and the University
of Maryland are unusual. Technical writing courses for engineers are an appropriate model, but the content is not applicable to most bureaucratic documents.
The effect of a lack of training is that even professionals who write well in other
contexts are too easily co-opted into using the poor models of the institution,
while poor writers do even more poorly with the complex demands of institutional
writing.

I have tried to answer the question "How did the language of bureaucracy
become so complexified?" by pointing to the forces that shaped that language
and that pressure it to remain uncommunicative and incomprehensible. I have
suggested these eight factors:

- the legal tradition
- a philosophy that government should be impersonal
- institutional inertia
- traditional models
- social prestige
- time pressures
- the review process
- lack of training

I have ended each of these first two sections with a point that has direct
implications for educators. Let us, however, again postpone that discussion until
we have reviewed our third major topic. Let us look now at pressures for changes
in bureaucratic language.

Why Should We Change the Language of the Bureaucracy?

In the 1970s Americans began to realize that the bureaucracy had grown to enormous size and was influencing the lives of more people in more ways than ever before. Pressures came from many sources for the government to reduce the burden of its paperwork both for institutions and for the public.

Although it has never been more than a minor issue, the clear-language movement received support from both industry and consumers. On the one hand, it became part of Carter's deregulation package—which was what industry wanted. On the other hand, it was part of the general rise of consumerism—of the effort to make government open, responsive, and communicative.

What reasons can we cite for the need to change the language of bureaucracy? For the sake of brevity, I will keep this discussion to four critical reasons:

- The growth of government does place a paperwork burden on us all.
- Reorganizing and rewriting bureaucratic documents can significantly reduce that burden.
- Reorganizing and rewriting bureaucratic documents can increase compliance with government rules and save the government money.
- Bureaucratic documents can be improved and still be legally accurate and sufficient.

The Paperwork Burden

The expansion of government and the burden of its paperwork requirements often present serious problems. In its report on rulemaking, the Commission on Federal Paperwork wrote (54) that in the mid-1970s the number of pages in the *Federal Register,* where notices and regulations are presented to the public, was growing by more than ten percent a year—45,422 pages in 1974, 57,072 pages in 1976. The Commission on Federal Paperwork began its final summary report (3 Oct. 1977) by estimating that government paperwork costs $100 billion a year or about $500 for each person in this country (5). *U.S. News and World Report* in 1978 reported that Americans spend 785 million hours each year filling out 4,987 different federal forms.

Poorly written and poorly designed documents cost us time and money both as individuals and as taxpayers. A few years ago, thirty-four percent of the students applying for federal financial aid had to go through the process at least twice (sometimes three or four times) because they did not understand how to complete the form accurately. The students paid in time and frustration—and sometimes in not getting money they were entitled to. The taxpayers paid in processing costs, paper and mailing for extra forms, maintaining toll-free telephone lines, and hiring people to answer questions.

Making Documents Easier Can Significantly Reduce the Burden on the User

Bureaucratic documents can be changed so that readers find them easier to understand and use. In one year, with minor changes on the form and major changes in the information and instructions, we reduced the error rate on the financial aid applications by about seven percent.

Take as another example the recently revised marine radio regulations for recreational boaters (47 CFR 83). Before the Federal Communications Commission revised these rules, recreational boaters who have two-way radios on their boats had to buy a copy of a regulation that was several hundred pages long, find the rules and parts of rules that applied to them, and understand long and complex explanations in legal language in order to comply with the law. The same rules also regulated use of two-way radios on ocean liners and merchant ships.

By selecting only the rules that apply to recreational boaters, the FCC was able to reduce the relevant information to just four pages in the *Federal Register* (which the FCC now publishes as an eleven-page question-and-answer booklet). In an empirical evaluation of the old and new versions of these rules made by Felker and Rose, both experienced boaters and people interested in boating who had never seen the rules before performed significantly better with the new rules than with the old ones. They answered more questions correctly, found the information more quickly, could more often identify the correct section, and considered the new rules much easier to use.

We *can* write clear and useful bureaucratic documents.

Making Documents Clearer Can Significantly Ease the Government's Job and Save the Government Money

Writing clear and useful bureaucratic documents helps the agencies that produce them as well as the citizens that use them. Many poorly written bureaucratic documents are rewritten in other forms in an attempt to make them clearer. Thus, from regulations we get guidelines, manuals, explanatory memos, letters of interpretation, and so on. All these restatements take time and money (for people, paper, and printing). Moreover, something is liable to get lost in the translation, and discrepancies between, for example, the regulation and the manual can be the cause of time-consuming and costly further work.

Multiple documents are not necessary. The Department of Education, for example, has rewritten the regulations for some of its grants programs in a well-organized question-and-answer format with clear language. The regulations are so straightforward that they are now used as the guidelines that go directly to people who want to apply for a grant.

Bureaucratic agencies are charged not only with deciding on the policies and rules for carrying out the law but also with monitoring and enforcing compliance with their rules. Monitoring and enforcement are costly, so the agency must seek ways to increase voluntary compliance. (Obviously, industry and individuals have many reasons for not complying with government rules. Ignorance or misunderstanding may not be the most significant cause of noncompliance.)

When the number of CB radio owners in the United States increased dramatically in the mid-1970s, the Federal Communications Commission decided that the most cost-effective way to increase compliance with the rules was to rewrite them so that CB users could understand them. The revised CB rules (47 CFR 95) are well organized, clearly written, and available as an attractive booklet. Before the new rules went into effect, the FCC had an office of five people who spent all day answering telephone questions about the CB radio rules from people who were trying to comply with them. After the clear-English version of the rules was distributed, the calls stopped. All five employees were transferred to other jobs.

Bureaucratic Documents Can Be Improved and Still Be Legally Accurate and Sufficient

The bureaucratic writer worries about the tension between clarity of language and legal accuracy and sufficiency. It is an important concern. But, for all the reasons given earlier in this paper, the growing body of clear-English legal documents attests to the possibility that a document can meet both the lawyer's and the writer's criteria.

All the clear-English documents I have referred to in this section are legal documents. The agencies' legal counsels have accepted them. Litigation has not ensued. Furthermore, activity on the state level and in the private sector supports the change from traditional bureaucratic language to clear, communicative English. As of August 1979, Pressman writes, twenty-five states had laws or regulations requiring readability in at least some types of insurance policies. By 1980, five states had plain language laws requiring comprehensible consumer contracts. As banks, insurance companies, realtors, and department stores rewrite their documents, the exempted federal notices stand out as outdated monuments to the uncommunicative bureaucratic tradition.[4] They look and sound like what they are—legalese that few consumers understand. But the necessity of writing in the traditional bureaucratic style is belied by the surrounding clear-English text.

Similarly, the irony of writing incomprehensible laws and regulations that require others to write clearly may someday catch up with federal writers. Warrantors regulated by the Magnuson-Moss Act (which requires comprehensible product warranties) and bankers governed by the Federal Reserve Board's Regulation Z (which requires truth in lending and therefore sets standards for many credit documents) are quick to point out that the legislative drafters and regulation writers do not follow their own requirements.

Implications for Educators

What can we do to foster change to a clearer, more communicative language of the bureaucracy? The problem obviously needs to be attacked on several levels at the same time. Each factor contributing to the maintenance of traditional, noncommunicative language must be addressed. We must:

- increase on-the-job training in document design for writers, forms designers, and supervisors;
- develop more models of clear legal and bureaucratic documents; influence decision makers, supervisors, and reviewers to reduce the time pressure on writers, to support efforts within their agencies to write well, to appreciate the need for clear communication, the benefits of clear communication, and the fact that it can be done;
- support research on job-related reading and writing skills and on translating that knowledge into educational practice; and
- develop college courses that are directed toward the skills and knowledge students will need in their professions.

Clearly, the development of more focused advanced composition courses is only one of many strands in the fabric that must be woven to improve legal and bureaucratic writing, but such courses are appropriate to discuss in this book.[5]

What can instructors do in advanced composition courses to better prepare students for professional schools (in law or management) and for the professional writing they will do on the job? First of all, to attract these students, we must offer advanced composition courses that reflect the situations for which they are preparing themselves. Courses in technical writing and business writing do not fill this need. The topics, rhetorical situations, and document types are not relevant.

Within an advanced composition course on document design, an important early goal is to give students both an appreciation for the amount of time that professionals spend in writing, whether they are lawyers, administrators, policy analysts, or technical specialists, and an appreciation of how important writing skills are in getting promotions and in succeeding in managerial roles. We can accomplish this goal by presenting case studies of people at work or, even better, by having the students go out of the classroom to do the case studies themselves. Furthermore, training in an advanced composition class should include discussion of the problems of writing in an organizational setting such as a bureaucracy so that students are equipped to deal with the social context of their work as well as with the basic skills of composing clear sentences.

Another important aspect of training is to make the writing tasks resemble those in the workplace. Writing in college classes is usually an individual endeavor, while writing in organizations is often collaborative. We can make some of the longer writing assignments in an advanced course collaborative and discuss the interactions that facilitate and that hinder arriving at a well-organized, well-

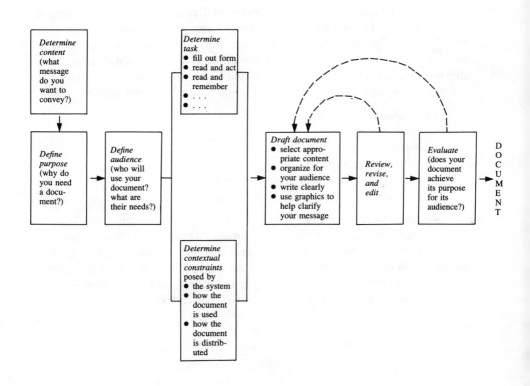

written product. College writing is seldom reviewed by many people with different perspectives, and even less often must it be revised to meet the criticisms of multiple reviewers. We can make review and revision part of each assignment, and again we can discuss how different interactions with reviewers hinder or facilitate a good final product.

Although composition teachers and texts speak of different audiences and different purposes, exercises in most classrooms reflect neither the types of documents nor the range of rhetorical situations that students will meet in institutional settings like the federal bureaucracy. Advanced composition courses should include writing and rewriting real documents for different, real audiences. And the students should take their writing to members of the audience to find out if it meets their needs, if they understand it, if they can use it.

All these things can be done in an advanced composition course. For example, my colleagues and I at the Document Design Center are developing a junior-senior level course in document design based on the model on page 171. In a tryout at Carnegie-Mellon University, students working in small groups selected documents that they thought would be difficult, and, following each step in the model, they interviewed responsible officials and users, analyzed the document, and then reorganized, revised, and retested it. They worked with

- the student government rules,
- a student loan form,
- consent forms,
- credit card agreements,
- descriptions of graduate programs, and
- instructions for using equipment.

All these were documents in use on campus or in the community. In most cases, students on campus were an appropriate audience, and other students or administrators were reviewers representing the official point of view on the document. In the process of this course, the students learned a great deal about different audiences and purposes as they honed their writing skills. They learned about themselves as writers, and they enjoyed the course.

Notes

[1] New York: General Obligations Law S5-702, effective 1 Nov. 1978; Connecticut: Pub. Act. No. 79-532, Laws 1979, effective 1 Oct. 1979; Hawaii: Act 36, Hawaii Legislature 1980, effective 1 July 1981; New Jersey: Ch. 125, Laws 1980, effective 16 Oct. 1980; Maine: Title 10, Ch. 202, effective 15 Sept. 1979.

²*Simply Stated,* newsletter available from Document Design Center, American Institutes for Research, 1055 Thomas Jefferson St., N.W., Washington, DC 20007.

³EO12044, March 1978, revoked by President Reagan in EO12291, Feb. 1981.

⁴For example, the Federal Trade Commission requires that this notice be printed in this manner on the front of consumer credit contracts:

NOTICE: ANY HOLDER OF THIS CONSUMER CREDIT CONTRACT IS SUBJECT TO ALL CLAIMS AND DEFENSES WHICH THE DEBTOR COULD ASSERT AGAINST THE SELLER OF GOODS OR SERVICES OBTAINED PURSUANT HERETO OR WITH THE PROCEEDS HEREOF. RECOVERY HEREUNDER BY THE DEBTOR SHALL NOT EXCEED AMOUNTS PAID BY THE DEBTOR HEREUNDER.

⁵In this section, as in the rest of the paper, I concentrate on those who write the language of the bureaucracy. In developing instruction in the 1980s, we must also be concerned with literacy for consumers of bureaucratic documents. No matter how much we decomplexify the language of the bureaucracy, government documents (especially forms) will require literacy skills that are different from reading novels or textbooks, as Holland and I point out.

Works Cited

Charrow, Veda R. "Linguistic Theory and Legal or Bureaucratic Language." In *Linguistic Theory and Exceptional Languages*. Ed. L. Obler and L. Menn. New York: Academic Press, 1982, 81-102.

————, JoAnn Crandall, and Robert P. Charrow. "Characteristics and Functions of Legal Language." In *Sublanguage: Studies of Language in Restricted Semantic Domains*. Ed. R. Kittredge and J. Lehrberger. Berlin: Walter de Gruyter, 1982, 175-90.

Commission on Federal Paperwork. *Final Summary Report*. 3 Oct. 1977.

————. *Report on Rulemaking*. 15 July 1977.

Danet, Brenda. "Language in the Legal Process." *Law and Society Review* 14.3(1980):445-564.

Felker, Daniel, and Andrew M. Rose. *The Evaluation of a Public Document: The Case of FCC's Marine Radio Rules for Recreational Boaters*. Washington, D.C.: American Institutes for Research, 1981. ED 213 026.

Flower, Linda, John R. Hayes, and Heidi Swarts. *Revising Functional Documents: The Scenario Principle*. Pittsburgh: Carnegie-Mellon Univ., 1980. ED 192 345.

Givens, R. A. *Drafting Documents in Plain Language 1981*. New York: Practising Law Institute, 1981. A4-3093.

Goswami, Dixie. "Naturalistic Studies of Nonacademic Writing." In *Moving between Practice and Research in Writing: Proceedings of the NIE-FIPSE Grantee Workshop*. Los Alamitos, Calif.: SWRL Educational Research and Development, 1981.

Grice, H. Paul. "Logic and Conversation." In vol. 3 of *Syntax and Semantics*. Ed. Peter Cole and Jerry L. Morgan. New York: Academic Press, 1975, 41-58.

Harley, James, Mark Trueman, and Peter Burnhill. "Some Observations on Producing and Measuring Readable Writing." *PLET* 17(1980):164-74.

Holland, V. Melissa. *Psycholinguistic Alternatives to Readability Formulas*. Washington,
    D.C.: American Institutes for Research, 1981. ED 214 370.
————, and Janice C. Redish. "Strategies for Understanding Forms—and other Public
    Documents." In *Analyzing Discourse: Text and Talk*. Ed. Deborah Tannen. Wash-
    ington, D.C.: Georgetown Univ. Press, 1982, 205-18.
MacDonald, D. A., ed. *Drafting Documents in Plain Language*. New York: Practising
    Law Institute, 1979. A4-3034.
Mellinkoff, David. *The Language of the Law*. Boston: Little, Brown, 1963.
Mikulecky, L. Indiana Univ. "Literacy Requirements in Industry." Paper presented at
    NIE Conference on Basic Skills, Washington, D.C., May 1978.
Odell, Lee, and Dixie Goswami. "The Nature and Functions of Writing." Unpublished
    MS.
————. "Writing in a Non-Academic Setting." *Research in the Teaching of English*
    16(Oct. 1982): 201-24.
Pressman, Rebecca. *Legislative and Regulatory Progress on the Readability of Insurance
    Policies*. Washington, D.C.: American Institutes for Research, 1979.
Redish, Janice C. "How to Draft More Understandable Legal Documents." In *Drafting
    Documents in Plain Language*. Ed. Duncan A. MacDonald. New York: Practising
    Law Institute, 1979, 121-56.
————. "Readability." In *Document Design: A Review of the Relevant Literature*. Ed.
    D. Felker. Washington, D.C.: American Institutes for Research, 1980, 69-94.
————. "Understanding the Limitations of Readability Formulas." *IEEE Transactions
    on Professional Communication* PC-24 (March 1981):46-48.
Scribner, S., and E. Jacobs. Center for Applied Linguistics. "Naturalistic Study of Literacy
    in the Workplace." Paper presented at NIE Conference on Basic Skills, Washington,
    D.C., May 1978.
Swarts, Heidi, Linda S. Flower, and John R. Hayes. *How Headings in Documents Can
    Mislead Readers*. Pittsburgh: Carnegie-Mellon Univ., 1980. ED 192 344.
"Ways Federal Forms Eat Away Your Time." *U.S. News and World Report*, 26 June
    1978, 58.
Williams, Joseph. *Style: Ten Lessons in Clarity and Grace*. Glenview, Ill.: Scott Foresman,
    1981.

Writing outside the English Composition Class: Implications for Teaching and for Learning

Lee Odell, Dixie Goswami, and Doris Quick

For composition teachers and researchers, the current interest in literacy has been accompanied by three sets of questions that take us well beyond our traditional concerns as teachers of English. Some of these questions have to do with possible relations between writing and learning. For some scholars the question is this: How does the act of writing contribute to our understanding of the subject we are writing about? For others who have become interested in what classical rhetoricians called Invention, the question is: Can we identify some of the conscious intellectual activity that enables writers to explore a topic systematically and sensitively?

A second set of questions has to do with writing in disciplines other than English. What must one know or be able to do in order to write well in, say, biology or sociology? What analytical skills will one need in order to write a well-thought-out case study or laboratory report? What qualities of style and organization are important for a given discipline? Do different disciplines vary in the demands they make of writers? Do lab reports entail conceptual, stylistic, or organizational skills that differ from those skills required for a case study? A third set of questions has to do with writing in nonacademic settings—writing, for instance, that people do as a normal part of their day-to-day work. In a given work setting, how many different types of writing must people be able to do? How do these writers conceive of their audience and purpose? What tacit knowledge guides their performance of routine writing tasks?

Widespread interest in these three sets of questions is relatively new in our profession. For much of this century, the teaching of composition has been dominated by practical stylist rhetoric, a rhetoric that emphasizes Arrangement and Style and pays virtually no attention to Invention. It was only in the mid-1960s that many of us became interested in the rhetorical tradition, which assumes that the process of discovery is, in part, systematic, conscious, teachable. It was perhaps five or ten years after this reawakening of interest in Invention that many of us became concerned about the teaching of writing in disciplines other than English, and, except for those of us who teach courses in business or technical writing, interest in nonacademic writing is more recent still. Perhaps because each field of inquiry is relatively new, perhaps because each is so inherently interesting, we have tended to treat them as entirely separate matters. That is, we have not tried to see whether answers to one set of questions might relate to answers to the other sets of questions.[1] Our purpose in this article is to explore this relationship, to try to see whether our understanding of writing in nonacademic settings might give us a useful perspective on writing that goes on in colleges and universities. In undertaking this task, we assumed that in order to understand, say, writing in the social sciences, we would need to investigate not only the writing students do in history, political science, or economics courses but also the writing students do when they take jobs related to their major fields of academic study. This assumption invites a number of questions, if only because we know that many undergraduates take jobs that are not directly related to their undergraduate majors. We shall address this issue in the final section of this article.

To examine some of the relationships between academic and nonacademic writing, we worked with two groups of writers: five university undergraduates who had taken extensive course work in economics and political science and five legislative analysts employed by a state legislature. We chose the legislative analysts because they held positions that entailed a good bit of responsibility and yet did not require formal training beyond the bachelor's degree. That is, these analysts held interesting positions that undergraduates might aspire to when they had completed their undergraduate training. Further, these analysts did some of the kinds of work that might be required in many government offices. They did research, analyzed legislation, wrote various types of memos and reports, and drafted letters (usually signed by a superior) to constituents or to persons in other government agencies. We selected undergraduates in economics and political science since it is not uncommon for students in these fields to plan to work in state or federal government. All these undergraduates had received good grades in their history, economics, or political science courses and were identified by their professors as being good writers. On the basis of interviews, analyses of writing samples, and a review of instructors' comments on the undergraduates' papers, we will answer these questions: How do the two groups of writers (undergraduates and legislative analysts) describe the contexts in which their writing exists? What inferences can we make about the conceptual skills or strategies they employ? How do the two groups differ with respect to conceptual strategies and descriptions of context?

Contexts for Writing

In order to find out what writers understood about the contexts for their writing, we first asked each writer for a sample of the writing he or she typically performed. Then we identified features that appeared in all the writing done by each participant. Although the writing varied in form (ranging from papers and "take home" examinations for the undergraduates to letters, reports, and memos for the legislative analysts), all the writers regularly attempted to provide information and/or to justify a conclusion. Modifying a procedure we have discussed elsewhere (Odell and Goswami, and Odell, Goswami, and Herrington), we identified a number of instances in which each writer had asserted a conclusion, had provided a rationale for a conclusion, and had provided additional information through a parenthetical expression, a nonrestrictive clause, a passage beginning "that is" or "for example," or a sentence in which a writer commented in more specific detail about an idea mentioned in the preceding sentence. At each of these instances, we asked writers whether they would be willing to delete the phrase in which they had provided elaboration or had asserted or defended a conclusion. We assured writers that we felt that the passage in question did not necessarily need to be deleted, and we repeatedly emphasized that we were primarily interested in their reasons for deleting or refusing to delete a given statement. As had been the case in our previous work, this procedure allowed writers to talk in some detail about context. More specifically, the procedure elicited information about the audiences they were addressing and the circumstances in which their writing had been done.

Audience

Both the legislative analysts and the undergraduates repeatedly referred to their audience as they explained why they were—or, more typically, were not—willing to delete a given statement. Furthermore, both groups of writers frequently expressed their interest in providing their audience with information or with helping their readers see the implications of a given statement. The interviews made it clear, however, that the students and the legislative analysts had radically different conceptions of the audiences they were addressing.

Students invariably spoke of their audience in impersonal terms: they would refer to "a reader" or "whoever happens to read this." They almost never referred to the primary audience for their writing, the professor who had assigned, graded, and commented on their writing. When students did refer to their professor, they indicated only a limited awareness of the professor's personality or values. They mentioned only those characteristics that would figure in the professor's evaluation of student writing. Furthermore, students' statements about their audience seemed self-contradictory. All the undergraduates indicated, explicitly or implicitly, that their writing must be detailed enough to be comprehensible to a reader who knew nothing about the subject at hand. Yet students either stated or implied that their reader was very knowledgeable. One student declined to omit a particular statement because, he said, one of the two "sacred sins" was "to leave out something [the instructor] thought was important." Another student was unwilling to delete a parenthetical expression in which she defined a specialized term from economics: "[that] is a word I don't think anyone ever heard of."

Yet in the next breath, she mentioned that the term appeared in the text for the course and in the notes she had taken from the professor's lecture. For her professed purpose of informing the person who would read her paper, the term needed no definition.

The analysts' perceptions of their audiences differ from those of the undergraduates in almost every respect. They rarely referred to "a reader" or "whoever happens to read this." Instead they usually referred to a specific audience, the person or group who would actually read a given piece of their writing. Furthermore, they expressed a very clear sense of their audience's values, of the audience's interests and concerns that went beyond the topic at hand. For example, in writing an argument in opposition to a piece of legislation, one analyst refused to omit a particular piece of information about the legislation: "That's the kind of thing that would immediately . . . stand out in a legislator's mind. . . . That's the kind of argument legislators like because that's gonna affect people in their district." Another analyst, again writing an argument in opposition to a particular bill, refused to delete her conclusion that the bill would place an "unnecessary burden" on taxpayers. "I think the words 'unnecessary burden' are what would be really noticeable to the [legislative committee] members. Anything that would be an unnecessary burden to their constituents is . . . most important to them," if only because, as the same analyst remarked in another context, it's "something that they get a lot of telephone calls on."

Analysts attributed different characteristics to various audiences. But all the analysts indicated that their audiences were likely to be similar in several ways. For one thing, all the analysts indicated that their readers could usually make an immediate personal response to what the analyst had written. This was particularly true for "bill memos," in which analysts assess the pros and cons of a given piece of legislation. Analysts not only must write these memos but also must read them aloud at meetings of the legislative committee considering a particular piece of legislation. At these meetings, the analyst's audience is free to challenge or raise questions about anything the analyst has said. Moreover, the audience (i.e., members of the committee) is rarely satisfied merely to raise a particular issue; instead the audience expects the analyst to be able to answer questions or respond to challenges on the spot. A similar situation holds true for interoffice memos. The writer might not be physically present while the audience reads a memo, but two analysts noted that if they were to omit certain statements from memos to superiors, they could expect to be called to the superior's office and asked to provide the needed information. As in the case of the bill memo, the writers' task would not be completed until the readers' questions were answered, their curiosity satisfied.

Apparently this inquiry is often prompted by another characteristic analysts attributed to their audience. Almost invariably, analysts asserted that their audience knew far less about a given subject than did the analysts and, consequently, that the audience frequently had to rely on the analysts' knowledge and judgment. Analysts repeatedly said that their readers expected them to investigate issues thoroughly, going beyond their present knowledge to anticipate consequences that the audience might not even have considered. For example, in a background memo to a legislator, one analyst insisted on listing examples of specific types of farmlands that would be affected by a recent piece of legislation. His reasoning: Even though he was a specialist on agricultural legislation, he had discovered that the legislation affected more types of farmland than he had previously realized. He reasoned that if the information were unfamiliar to him, it might very well be unfamiliar to his reader, who was engaged in a legislative election campaign. He anticipated that the bill would probably be mentioned in debates or press interviews and, further, that knowledge of the specifics of this bill would almost certainly impress farmers in the legislator's district: ". . . the more aware she was about the specifics of this bill, the more apt farmers were to buddy up with her."

Circumstances

In explaining their willingness or unwillingness to delete a given statement, analysts would frequently locate that statement (or, indeed, an entire piece of writing) in a sequence of ideas and events that preceded or ensued from the statement. For example, one analyst felt it was essential to include a parenthetical element that provided details about an opponent's argument. Since he felt that this argument "didn't hold water," he wanted the argument fully explained so that he could refute it completely. In discussing other pieces of writing, both the analysts and the undergraduates frequently observed that inclusion of a particular statement emphasized the point they were trying to make or that the absence of a particular statement would weaken their argument, making it more vulnerable. Implicitly, all participants in our study, undergraduates and legislative analysts alike, agreed with one analyst (and, of course, thousands of composition teachers) that "an argument has two parts," an assertion and a "follow through," a passage that illustrates, explains, or justifies the assertion.

As this analyst's comment suggests, all the legislative analysts were fairly conscious of the way a given statement related to a sequence of ideas within the text they had written. It was very unusual, however, for analysts to refer to only this type of sequence. Quite frequently, references to an intratext sequence were accompanied by comments about some other type of sequence.[2] On a few occasions, analysts would justify including a particular statement by referring to events that took place prior to their writing.[3] For instance, when we asked one analyst whether she would consider deleting a list of examples, she replied: "Never. Not in a million years. Because that was exactly what the Governor's office was opposed to. . . . [These facts had been the crux] of an enormous argument over the past years." In other words, her statement existed for her in the context of an ongoing argument about the subject of her memo.

On at least one occasion, awareness of prior experience helped an analyst justify his unwillingness to elaborate upon one of his assertions. In writing his argument in opposition to a particular bill, the analyst contended that the proposed legislation would have a "chilling effect" on the operation of certain state agencies. When asked if he were willing to delete this conclusion, he refused. Indeed, he mentioned that he might even have elaborated on that conclusion but then remarked, "I know the history of the committee, and I know that we have had similar bills to this, and we have had that argument previously. . . . I can say 'the bill will have a chilling effect' to my committee and that will click in their heads. . . . They will think of past bills we've dealt with and [know] exactly what a *chilling effect* that will mean." The analyst notes that he assumes, given their prior experience, that committee members "will formulate more detailed arguments in opposition than the one I wrote here."

In addition to commenting on prior events, analysts occasionally mentioned events that were likely to transpire subsequent to a given piece of writing.[4] More specifically, when we asked if they would be willing to delete a particular statement, analysts commented on the ways a reader might think or act if the statement were not in the text. Frequently they anticipated only a single action: A reader might not understand the implications, might become confused, or might raise a particular question. But occasionally analysts developed a comparatively lengthy scenario. Some of these scenarios entailed such personal consequences as a reduction in their credibility as analysts. For example, one analyst refused to delete one bit of elaboration because he felt the statement brought his argument to a logical conclusion and that its omission made this particular argument more vulnerable to being "struck down" by a member of the legislative committee he was addressing. The analyst felt rather strongly about this point: "If the argument is weak, [if] it's not brought to its conclusion, they're gonna have less faith in your analytic ability, less trust in your comments. And once that happens, even when you do have a good argument, they're gonna be leery about it."

Another analyst was concerned about the political consequences of one of his statements. In a personal memo to a legislator, the analyst noted parenthetically that the legislator's opponent probably did not understand a particular issue. He was unwilling to delete that statement for this reason: "Although the issue I raised might be confusing to some, I just don't think her opponent had looked into it seriously enough. . . . [Since the opponent] doesn't know this stuff [she might be] more apt to carefully look this over and try to understand it herself." A more Machiavellian scenario was projected by another analyst. In a letter he had written, he claimed that a particular point of view was the only "responsible" position on an issue before the legislature. He was unwilling to delete his claim: "That's a political strategy. If people we're addressing this to do not take this position, we can come back four weeks from now and call them irresponsible. . . . We go on record as saying [that only] this position is responsible; any other position they take, we can come down and blast as highly irresponsible, because we've gone on record as saying [that only] this is responsible."

One analyst managed to anticipate both political and personal consequences.

She was unwilling to delete a passage that she felt explained a relatively esoteric argument in opposition to a particular bill: "I don't think I'd leave that out, because to me it would be embarrassing to have committee members say, 'Well, wait a minute. Why is this [argument] in the memo?' " She was particularly eager to avoid this embarrassment since "the people who would probably ask [that question] are the people who are more relaxed with me, which are [members of Party A]. And I don't want [members of Party A] to look bad [by allowing members of Party B to] start saying 'Well, you guys don't realize it, but this is actually what happens.' "

In at least two respects, the undergraduates' comments seem similar to those of the analysts. As did the analysts, students indicated a given statement was important because it helped develop the point they were making in their writing. Also, the undergraduates frequently imagined ways a reader might react to the presence or absence of a given statement. Yet these similarities are less significant than they might seem. For one thing, the undergraduates' scenarios tended to be tentative; undergraduates were most likely to project what "a reader" *might* do or think. Occasionally the analysts speculated about what a reader might do. But typically they drew on their knowledge of their readers to predict what the reader *would* do. The analysts made tentative statements only about half as frequently as did the undergraduates. Further, the undergraduates projected brief scenarios; they anticipated only a single action as a result of their inclusion or omission of a given statement. Although they anticipated that, for example, a reader might raise a question at a given point, they never speculated about further consequences of the reader's having asked that question. Moreover, they did not relate their individual statements—or, indeed, their essays—to a larger sequence of events; most notably, the undergraduates never commented on the experiences that were part of the course for which the paper had been written and that preceded or ensued from the writing of their paper.

Conceptual Strategies

In discussing writers' perceptions of the audience and circumstances for their writing, we have drawn on interviews in which we asked writers to explain their reasons for being willing (or unwilling) to delete specific statements. By combining this source of information with two others, analyses of written texts and legislative analysts' and university professors' evaluative comments, we can make inferences about writers' conceptual strategies, in effect sets of questions that can help guide writers' efforts to explore information, formulate ideas, and evaluate their writing. Our interest in these strategies is based on several assumptions:

  • that writing well entails the ability to explore a topic and generate ideas;
  • that parts of the process of exploring data and formulating ideas are

mysterious but that parts of this process involve conscious intellectual activities, conceptual strategies that can be described and taught (see Young);
- that these strategies may be expressed as sets of questions that writers may ask themselves in order to guide their exploration of a topic (see Larson).

Our analysis of interviews, written texts, and evaluative comments on written texts indicates that both undergraduates and legislative analysts occasionally used some of the same conceptual strategies. As a rule, however, the two groups of writers appeared to be using different strategies, answering different types of questions. In describing these differences, we do not mean to suggest that writers should always use one particular set of conceptual strategies. Indeed, we assume that different writing tasks may make different demands of a writer and may require a writer to consider different types of questions (see Larson, Maimon et al., and Odell). Nevertheless, the differences between the two groups seem important. The analysts were concerned with questions that lead one to think critically about the texts one is writing about. Further, these questions seem useful both for generating ideas and for evaluating a draft of one's writing. The undergraduates, by contrast, seemed concerned with questions that do not lead one to think critically about the subject matter one is discussing and that are more useful for evaluating a draft of one's writing than for generating ideas.

Information from Legislative Analysts

Interviews.   We have already pointed out that the analysts were very aware of the contexts for their writing; they frequently referred to the audience they were addressing and to the circumstances that preceded or seemed likely to follow from what they had written. This concern for context was also apparent in their comments about the subject matter of their writing. In our interviews with them, analysts appeared to be concerned with this question for more than half the passages we discussed: What events preceded or followed from the text (usually a piece of proposed legislation) I am writing about? Especially in discussing their bill memos, analysts would occasionally comment on events that occurred prior to the drafting of the legislation they were discussing. They referred to prior legislation on the same topic or to the circumstances a legislator hoped to rectify by drafting a particular piece of legislation. Somewhat more frequently, analysts noted that a bill either duplicated or contradicted existing law or that the bill established procedures that were incompatible with currently accepted governmental procedures. Still more frequently, the analysts described the events that were likely to ensue from a given piece of legislation, especially the events that the sponsor of the bill might not have anticipated. For example, one analyst objected to a reasonable-sounding bill that would have required all restaurants to post the detailed results of an inspection by a state agency. In the interview, the analyst pointed out that these inspections are conducted only once every two years and that the inspections often revealed problems that could be corrected promptly. Consequently, this analyst noted, the proposed legislation could require a restaurant to post a sign indicating that it was deficient in one or more respects when, in fact, the deficiency might have been eliminated as soon as the restaurant owner had been made aware of the problem.

Implicit in the analysts' comments about context is a set of questions that one might ask about any piece of proposed legislation: What events preceded the drafting of the bill? How does the bill relate to existing law or procedure? What are the likely consequences of the bill? These questions, along with several others, are reflected in two other sources of information: bill memos written by the analysts and analysts' evaluation of the researchers' attempts to write bill memos.

Bill Memos.   Although bill memos are only one of the several types of writing done by legislative analysts, they are the type of writing that analysts do most frequently. All bill memos contain the same types of information—information about the legislative history of the bill, arguments in support of the bill, arguments in opposition to the bill, and so on. Much of this information is reported rather tersely. For example, a report of the legislative history of the bill simply requires an analyst to determine whether the bill has been introduced in previous years and, if it has been introduced previously, merely to list the actions taken on the bill and the dates on which those actions were taken. The arguments in support are usually taken directly from a memo prepared by the bill's sponsor. Consequently, it is usually the "arguments in opposition" section of the bill memo that requires analysts to develop their own arguments.

As we read arguments in opposition, we realized that all of them could be categorized as answering one or more sets of questions. Two of these types of questions, also apparent in the interviews, appear quite frequently. Thirty percent of the arguments in opposition provide answers to this sort of question: How does a given piece of legislation relate to existing legislation or to existing procedures? Does the legislation violate, duplicate, or repeal this other legislation or these other procedures? Another type of question that appears even more frequently (in 48% of the arguments in opposition) is this: What are the consequences of a particular piece of legislation? Will it have a negative effect on some person or institution? Is it too inclusive? Is it not inclusive enough—that is, does the legislation fail to apply to persons or institutions that it should apply to?

In addition to these two basic sets of questions, the bill memos occasionally answered three other questions: Is the legislation needed? Will the legislation achieve the sponsor's intent? Can the provisions of the legislation be implemented? These three additional questions appear much less frequently than do those cited in the previous paragraph. Issues of need are mentioned in only five percent of the arguments in opposition; references to sponsor's intent appear in eight percent of the arguments in opposition, as do references to implementation.

Evaluations of Researchers' Writing.   To complement our initial interviews and our analysis of arguments found in bill memos, we asked legislative analysts to evaluate our attempts to write one part of a bill memo, the part containing the arguments in opposition to a given piece of legislation. We wrote about bills for which analysts had previously written their own arguments in opposition. We interviewed the analysts separately, posing this request: "Assume that I am an intern or an assistant analyst whom you have asked to write arguments in opposition to X bill. Would you be willing to include my arguments in your bill memo?" We asked analysts to read our arguments aloud and to pause and comment on any statement that seemed particularly acceptable or unacceptable.

In general, analysts were concerned with the same issues we have already identified. That is, they were likely to praise (or criticize) our arguments insofar as we had considered (or failed to consider) such matters as the feasibility of the bill and the consequences that might ensue if the bill were to become law. Further, their evaluations of our work indicated some additional questions one might consider in analyzing a bill: Are the provisions of the bill clear? Does the bill stipulate exactly what procedures are to be followed and who shall follow those procedures? Who might be affected by the bill? What are the characteristics of people or organizations who might be affected? How might they react to the bill?

While evaluating the arguments we had written, analysts expressed their concern for these and other questions we have mentioned. But their comments made it clear that they did not evaluate our work simply by determining whether we had considered all the questions one might raise concerning a given bill. Instead they expected us to consider this question: How will our audience (members of a legislative committee) respond to the criticisms we have made? For example, when we criticized a bill's feasibility by saying that it attempted to address a problem of worker safety that appeared to be unsolvable, the analyst objected: "I think if a committee member saw that, he would immediately cause an uproar. They would look at it and start worrying about workers' safety. And if people [other than legislators] saw this—that we might be saying, 'We've got a problem on our hands that could cause lung cancer . . . [and that] we might not be able to solve [it]'—we'd have labor unions coming down on us. I would be very careful about doing something like that in a memo." Another analyst reminded us of the need for diplomacy in raising arguments in opposition to a bill that might have been sponsored by a member of the committee for whom we were writing.

In addition to expecting us to anticipate our audience's reaction, analysts made it clear that we must consider ways our answer to one question might lead us to revise or discard altogether our answer to another question. Thus one analyst rejected our argument that a particular bill would have undesirable consequences in that it would be burdensome to one group of citizens since it required them to take a very active role in carrying out the legislation. As the analyst pointed out: "If they were known to be an apathetic group it might put a burden on them and they might not want to participate. But [group X is] politically active. [Group X has] one of the strongest lobbyist organizations in the state, and in that way they are very politically conscious. I think they want to stay on top of things." In short, we had not carefully considered the characteristics of people who would be affected by the legislation, and therefore our assessment of the consequences of the bill was invalid.

In at least one instance, an analyst's evaluation of our writing seemed self-contradictory. In analyzing a bill that sought to regulate working conditions for a group of state workers, we were concerned with this question: How clear and specific are the provisions of this legislation? In our bill memo, we pointed out that the bill was weak because it was not specific; it failed to explain precisely which working conditions would be improved. The analyst approved of this argument, noting, "What I've found from my dealings with state agencies is that . . . if we don't specify what we want and [if] we give them too much leeway, they tend to slack off." But for another argument on the same bill, the analyst was unwilling to accept the argument that the bill was weak because it failed to specify the health standards which workers should be able to expect. The analyst pointed out that even the proponents of the bill had not identified these standards "either because they didn't know of any safe standards or because they were afraid that if they put them into law, [the standards] might be too strict and people might object to them on that basis. Or they might be too lenient, in which case they wouldn't be good enough [to suit the workers who would be affected by the legislation]." In this case, the lack of specificity was a strong point of the bill since it enabled the sponsor to avoid "a lot of negotiations with the people involved."

These last comments, of course, make it clear that the analyst's evaluation was not self-contradictory. In both instances, she was aware of events that had preceded the bill in question and of events that might transpire if the bill were (or were not) made more specific. In one instance, this awareness told her that the bill's lack of specificity was a weakness of the bill; in another instance, the same awareness told her that a lack of specificity might be one of the bill's strong points.

From these sources of information—interviews, analyses of bill memos, and analysts' evaluation of our writing—we get a sense of some of the questions one might consider in analyzing a piece of legislation:

- What are the likely consequences of this legislation?
- How does it relate to other laws or procedures?
- Is this legislation needed?
- Will this legislation achieve the sponsor's intent?
- Can this legislation be implemented?

- Whom will the legislation affect?
- Does the legislation stipulate what procedures are to be followed?

In answering these questions, it also seems important to keep in mind two additional questions: How does the answer to any one of these questions influence the way an analyst answers the other questions? How is an analyst's audience likely to react to the analyst's answer to any of these questions?

Taken together, these questions constitute a heuristic procedure for analyzing legislation. They represent a set of conscious strategies one might use in determining what bases there might be for opposing a piece of legislation. We cannot, of course, claim that these questions embody all the conscious intellectual activity a legislative analyst must engage in. On the other hand, we do argue that these questions have some epistemological significance. They can help guide one's analysis of a particular type of text. They can help a writer formulate the arguments he or she will present in a bill memo. Further, these questions can be useful in evaluating a draft of a bill memo. That is, before presenting a bill memo to a legislative committee an analyst might ask himself or herself such questions as these: Have I determined whether this legislation is needed? Have I identified the individuals or groups it might affect? Have I considered ways committee members might respond to my answers to the preceding questions?

Information from Undergraduates

Interviews.   As we noted earlier, undergraduates were rarely concerned with the same kinds of questions as were the legislative analysts. The undergraduates, for example, almost never dealt with this sort of question: What is the context for the materials I am discussing? In all our interviews with the five students, we found no instances in which a student mentioned events that preceded the writing of a text (usually a book or article) he or she was discussing. We found relatively few instances in which students noted a relationship between a particular text and other texts or ideas that had existed concurrently with the text under discussion. In all but one of these instances, the student was talking about a paper in which the instructor had specifically asked students to comment on this sort of relationship. Finally, we found only two instances in which students mentioned a consequence of the texts they had read and were writing about. Unlike the analysts, when the undergraduates commented on texts they wrote about, they gave little indication that they were concerned with such questions as these: What events led up to the text I am writing about? How did this text relate to concurrent ideas or texts? What were the consequences of this text?

Instead of asking these questions, students seemed more concerned with a different set of questions, which they seemed to be using to evaluate their own writing rather than to analyze what someone else had written:

- Have I justified my conclusions? Have I backed up my assertions with evidence?

- Have I defined specialized terms or familiar terms that have an unusual meaning in a particular context?
- Have I made my ideas "flow" smoothly? Does each conclusion follow logically from the previous conclusion?
- Have I answered the question the professor asked?
- Have I avoided oversimplifying complex issues?

Undergraduate Essays. To obtain a sample of undergraduates' writing, we asked that each provide us with at least three formal papers (as opposed to journals or in-class examinations) that had received a grade of A or B and that represented writing they felt was typical of the writing they had been asked to do in college. We wanted to have a reasonable basis for comparing this undergraduate writing with that of the legislative analysts. Since, in the materials we examined, analysts were writing about specific texts (i.e., drafts of specific pieces of legislation), we identified all the points at which each undergraduate made some comment about another text (e.g., a book or a magazine article). At each of these points we considered this question: In discussing this text, does the student comment on any of the issues (e.g., consequences, feasibility) that appeared so frequently in the legislative analysts' writing?

Comments about these issues did appear in undergraduates' writing, but they appeared relatively infrequently. As with the legislative analysts, students were most likely to consider the consequences of a given text or to consider its relation to other texts. But neither of these concerns appeared in more than fifteen percent of the paragraphs in students' essays. Other matters (e.g., can the ideas in this text be implemented?) appeared even less frequently. Indeed, students seemed relatively uncritical of the texts they were writing about. Most frequently, they simply paraphrased or quoted these texts as documentation for the points they wanted to make. They were very unlikely to make statements that implied they were aware of limitations of or problems with the texts they were citing in their own essays.

Professors' Evaluative Comments. When we examined professors' marginal and summary comments on students' papers, we found that students were occasionally encouraged to think about the kinds of questions that legislative analysts so frequently considered. Seven percent of the professors' comments encouraged students to consider the way one text related to another; another seven percent of these comments raised questions as to whether the ideas in a text could actually be implemented. Fifteen percent of the professors' comments focused on the likely consequences of texts students were analyzing. Professors were much more concerned, however, with matters of grammar and style (about 30% of their comments fell into this category) and about students' knowledge of the material they were discussing (about 20% of their comments fell into this category). Unlike the legislative analysts who evaluated our writing, the professors never wrote comments that indicated that answers to one question might influence one's answer to another question.

As was the case with the legislative analysts, we can draw on our three sources of data to represent at least some of the undergraduates' conceptual strategies as a list of questions:

- Have I justified my conclusions?
- Have I defined key terms?
- Do my ideas relate logically to each other?
- Have I answered the question the professor posed?
- Have I avoided oversimplifying complex issues?
- Have I summarized my sources accurately?
- Is my information correct?
- Have I ignored information the professor thinks is important?

All these are questions that writers might do well to ask, especially once writers have a draft that needs to be evaluated and revised. But these questions do not seem likely to lead one to think critically about the text one is writing about. These questions might lead a writer to gather additional information. But, with one exception (Is my information correct?), they do not prompt a writer to assess the validity of that information. Moreover, these questions seem less helpful when writers are in the early stages of the composing process, trying to explore information and formulate their ideas, feelings, attitudes. On the other hand, questions used by the legislative analysts seem useful throughout the composing process. When one begins to consider a topic, one might ask: What are the consequences of this? Who will be affected by it? In answering such questions as these, one can begin to formulate the conclusions that, as part of a draft, one will evaluate and revise. Another problem with the undergraduates' questions is that they seem far more general than do those posed by the legislative analysts. Indeed, the analysts' questions might help one see how to go about answering the undergraduates' questions. For example, in order to determine whether one's conclusion is justified, one might ask: Have I fully considered the consequences of the material I am discussing? Have I considered the consequences of the assertions I am making in my writing?

In other words, it seems to us that the legislative analysts are using a set of conceptual strategies that are more focused, more analytic, and more useful throughout the composing process than are the conceptual strategies used by the undergraduates.

Implications for Teaching

Early in this article, we raised the possibility that the study of writing in nonacademic settings might help us think more clearly about the writing that college and university students must do. When we began our study, we had expected to find substantial differences between writers in academic settings and writers in nonacademic settings. Since the nonacademic writers held jobs comparable to positions sought by some undergraduate students of history, political science, and economics, we had anticipated that our study might have implications for the teaching of writing in these academic disciplines. We now feel that results of our study have implications for the teaching of writing in any academic discipline. Further, we think that these results suggest ways writing relates to students' understanding of a given body of subject matter. That is, when we contrast the work of the undergraduates with that of the legislative analysts, we see writing not merely as a process of organizing and expressing ideas but also as a process of formulating ideas, as a process of learning. To suggest the implications of our work, we shall review what we found to be the major distinctions between writers in an academic setting and writers in a nonacademic setting. With each distinction, we shall also raise a series of questions that can help one rethink the relations between writing and learning in various academic disciplines.

Perhaps the most important distinction is the last one we described. Unlike the undergraduates, the legislative analysts in our study displayed a set of conceptual strategies that were relatively well focused and that were useful throughout the composing process—that is, useful in analyzing data and formulating assertions as well as in evaluating those assertions once they appeared in a draft. Given the importance of these strategies for at least one group of nonacademic writers, a college or university professor might want to consider these questions: How can I show students how to make conscious use of these strategies? How can I teach them, for example, to think critically about texts they read by considering the consequences that might logically flow from ideas expressed in those texts? These are useful questions. As one teaches students to use a particular set of cognitive strategies, one works toward two goals: helping students understand more fully the texts they read and increasing their chances of writing essays that are well thought out. But we think these questions are unnecessarily limiting, for we believe that different disciplines, even different subjects within a single discipline, require writers to use different conceptual strategies (see Maimon et al.). Perhaps a more widely useful set of questions is this: What kinds of data do I want students to write about? What kinds of questions should they consider in order to think and write well about these data? What kind of intellectual work do I want them to do?

At least initially, answers to this latter question come readily to mind. We want students to think critically, imaginatively, logically. . . . The problem is that these goals are difficult to define in ways that are useful to students. Indeed, it is quite easy to mislead ourselves about the kind of intellectual work we are asking student writers to do. For example, one colleague informed us that he was particularly eager for his students to "think critically" about a book he had asked them to write about. This instructor did not define the term "think critically," but we imagined several operations it might entail: considering the implications of the text; determining whether the text contained evidence that actually supported the author's claims; testing the author's conclusions against one's own experience or one's knowledge of related areas; trying to determine whether the circumstances in which the text was written might bias the author's presentation of information. When we read students' papers, however, we realized that none of this was important for the assignment at hand. The instructor had given As to those students who had summarized accurately and fully the complex argument found in the book they had read. Bs went to students who had mentioned all the main points and most of the more subtle points in the argument. Cs went to students who had missed the more subtle points, and so on. Of course it is perfectly reasonable to ask students to summarize a complex argument. But when we evaluate students on the basis of their ability to summarize, we mislead ourselves and our students by claiming that we are expecting students to think critically.

As one might expect, it is not easy to assess the intellectual demands of the writing assignments we give students, but there are two procedures that will help us identify some of these demands. If we have given an assignment in previous semesters, we can analyze student papers, asking this question: Do we find in the best papers answers to questions that rarely or never appear in the poorer papers? A more demanding but more rewarding procedure is for us to do our own assignments, paying attention to the kinds of questions we have to answer in analyzing information and formulating our ideas. Difficult as these procedures are, they will let us help students see more clearly how they might approach a particular task. Moreover, as we understand the conceptual demands our writing tasks make, we can solve some problems that arise when we try to change the audiences and circumstances for student writing.

When legislative analysts referred to the audience for their correspondence and bill memos, they talked of an audience that was relatively uninformed about the topic at hand, an audience that relied on the writer to provide information and to identify implications of a given set of facts, an audience that would make an immediate response to a writer's work and would not consider the writer's task complete until the writer had answered all the audience's questions. For at least two reasons, it is difficult to establish this writer-audience relationship between students and teachers. First, there are many situations in which we may reasonably expect students to write about subjects with which we are thoroughly familiar. Further, it is difficult to respond immediately to students' writing. Many of us feel we are doing well if we can return papers within a few days of the time students turn them in, and we feel very conscientious indeed if those papers bear comments as well as grades.

Despite these difficulties, it would still be worth our while to try to establish the sort of writer-audience relationship that the legislative analysts describe. As writers and as readers, we must acknowledge that the most stimulating topics are those that are open to serious debate, the most interesting questions are those to which we (as writer or as reader) do not already know the answer. Moreover, there is something inherently inefficient about the way we usually respond to student writing. Our response usually comes too late to be of any use to students.

Unless we are among the comparatively few teachers who have established an elaborate system of conferences or who require students to revise their work, students are unlikely to do anything about our questions. Consequently, our questions cannot influence the writing of the paper we are commenting on, and there is at least a good chance that our questions will not influence the next paper students do—especially if the next paper is written in a subsequent semester and read by someone who wants students to consider a set of questions that may be quite different from those we have asked.

One way to change the relationship between student-writer and teacher-audience is to ask students to do a number of short writing tasks, which they might read aloud in class and which we might respond to orally. We might, for example, stop at some point during a lecture or a discussion and ask students to write for a few minutes, speculating on the implications of a point that has just been made. Although we might want to collect these writings, we would not have to do so. We could simply call on individual students to read what they have written and, without seeming like inquisitors, ask students to respond to our questions about what they had written. If we were to do this fairly often and if we were to pose the sort of questions we expected students to answer in their longer, out-of-class essays, we would help students gain a clearer sense of the demands of the tasks we assign.

Another way to change the writer-audience relationship is to ask ourselves these questions as we plan the work of a given course: Does the course raise issues about which I am genuinely curious? Are there topics that are accessible to students and that are also complex enough to allow me to respond to students' writing as someone who wants to find out something? Are there topics that allow students to observe data that I have not had a chance to observe?

One ready response to these questions is simply to assign a library research paper, perhaps suggesting some possible topics or perhaps simply telling students to write on any topic that interests them and that is related to the subject matter of the course. This sort of response increases the chance that students may write about subjects with which we are not familiar. But it also raises some problems. Our interviews and our analyses of students' essays suggest that when undergraduates refer to other people's writing, especially secondary sources, they are more likely to paraphrase and synthesize than to analyze and evaluate the materials they read. Thus simply assigning a term paper or a research paper may not help students develop their ability to analyze the texts they read. Another problem is that, left entirely to their own devices, students often choose topics that are simply inappropriate: the scope is much too grand or too limited; the topics presuppose knowledge or conceptual skills that students may not possess.

In proposing that we change the writer-audience relationship between students and teachers, we are, quite obviously, also suggesting that teachers may need to change their conception of writing, expanding that term to include short, informal tasks as well as essays and term papers. Further, we are suggesting that teachers may need to identify new kinds of topics for students to write about.

All these suggestions presuppose that teachers have identified the important conceptual demands of the writing tasks they assign. If teachers have some sense of these demands, they can frame their questions so that they have some unity, so that teachers do not ask dozens of different questions but rather ask related questions that help students understand the basic cognitive skills the teacher wants students to work with. Another benefit of having assessed the conceptual demands of one's writing assignments is that a teacher will have a good way of evaluating students' writing. If teachers ask students to write on topics about which teachers are not well informed, it will be impossible to evaluate students' writing by the criterion implicit in this professor's comment: "I hear myself here—you seem to have understood perfectly what I tried to show in class. It's nice to know that at least one person is listening. A + ." Instead of basing grades on students' ability to remember conclusions the teacher has drawn, instructors can base their grades on students' ability to articulate their own conclusions that reflect students' use of basic processes that are central to the course.

In identifying these processes and making them central to a particular course, we begin to minimize one final distinction between the writing of the undergraduates and the legislative analysts in our study. As we have pointed out, the analysts occasionally located their writing in a sequence of events that were part of their experience in working at the job for which they were writing. The undergraduates did not locate their writing in comparable sequences of events. None of them referred to experiences that were part of the course for which they were writing and that led up to or followed from the essays about which we interviewed them. They gave us no indication that a particular piece of writing was part of a progression that led them from Point A, the knowledge and skills with which they entered the course, to Point B, the knowledge and skills the teacher hoped they would have by the end of the course. This finding seems incongruous, for all these undergraduates were bright, articulate young people who had evidently done a great deal of work in writing their papers. Yet they gave no indication that they saw their writing as part of the overall plan for the course for which they were writing. We think this problem is a serious one in part because we think writing should not be merely an added burden that teachers impose on students; we think that doing a writing task should be central to "doing" an academic subject. Certainly, the legislative analysts reported no disjunction between doing their writing and doing their job. Indeed, one type of writing—the bill memos—entailed a set of conceptual strategies that were central to the analysts' jobs. These analysts had access to a specific set of strategies that helped them formulate their ideas and that were—perhaps more important— recurrent; analysts were obliged to employ these strategies time and again.

As we have already indicated, we do not believe that all undergraduates in all courses should be asked to use any one particular set of strategies. But we do believe that teachers need to ask themselves these questions: What conceptual strategies constitute the core of my course? What kind of intellectual work do I want students to do throughout my course? As teachers answer these questions, they will increase their ability to help students see how a particular writing assignment fits into a particular course, to help students see the connection between writing and learning.

In the last assertion, we hope we make clear our understanding of the value of studying writing in nonacademic settings. We are not suggesting that we use our knowledge of this writing to reduce academic writing (or, indeed, academic course work) to a form of vocational training. As we acknowledged early in this article, many students do take jobs that are not closely related to their undergraduate major. Consequently, it seems difficult to justify training students to meet the highly specialized demands of a particular job. What we are suggesting is that when we look outside our classrooms, we gain new information that helps us reconsider our practices as teachers of writing and as teachers of a particular subject matter. That information leads us to encounter a series of new and troublesome questions, questions that cause us to rethink our assumptions and teaching practices, questions that lead us to see how we can help students become truly literate, in our own discipline, in other academic disciplines, and in the world outside our classroom.

Notes

[1] One notable exception is the work of David Lauerman, Mel Schroeder, and Kenneth Sroka at Canisius College in Buffalo, New York. Charged with the responsibility of designing advanced composition courses specifically appropriate for students in different academic disciplines (e.g., business, natural sciences, humanities), Lauerman and his colleagues interviewed Canisius College graduates who held the kinds of jobs that students in, say, business might aspire to. Using interview procedures similar to the procedure we shall describe later in this article, Lauerman and his colleagues devised assignments and classroom activities that introduced students to some of the conceptual, organizational, and stylistic problems they were likely to encounter when they took positions related to their major field of undergraduate training.

[2] Our interviews contained 42 instances in which legislative analysts referred to the sequence of ideas within their texts. In 36 of these instances, comments about intratext sequence were accompanied by comments about some other type of sequence.

[3] In our interviews, the five analysts commented on a total of 123 passages; i.e., each analyst commented on approximately 25 passages in his or her own writing. In all our interviews, there was a total of 14 instances in which analysts referred to events that took place prior to the time they did the piece of writing about which we were interviewing them.

[4] The five analysts mentioned subsequent events in commenting on 31 of the 123 passages about which we interviewed them.

Works Cited

Larson, Richard L. "Discovery through Questioning: A Plan for Teaching Rhetorical Invention." In *Contemporary Rhetoric*. Ed. W. Ross Winterowd. New York: Harcourt Brace Jovanovich, 1975, 145-155.

Maimon, Elaine, Gerald L. Belcher, Gail W. Hearn, Barbara F. Nodine, and Finbarr W. O'Connor. *Writing in the Arts and Sciences*. Cambridge, Mass.: Winthrop, 1981.

Odell, Lee. "The Process of Writing and the Process of Learning." *College Composition and Communication* 31(1980):42-50.

———, and Dixie Goswami. "Writing in a Non-Academic Setting." *Research in the Teaching of English* 16(Oct. 1982):201-24.

———, Dixie Goswami, and Anne Herrington. "Procedures for Assessing Writers' Background Knowledge." In *Writing Research: Methods and Procedures*. Ed. Peter Mosenthal, Lynn Tamor, and Sean Walmsley. London: Longman, in press.

Young, Richard. "Invention: A Topographical Survey." In *Teaching Composition: Ten Bibliographical Essays*. Ed. Gary Tate. Forth Worth: Texas Christian Univ. Press, 1976.

Literacy and Education

Testing Writing:
Procedures Vary with Purposes

Ralph W. Tyler

When America drafted two million men for military service during World War I, organizing and training persons who had had no previous military experience suddenly became an overwhelming problem. Who should be selected for officer training and who for the variety of technical tasks—construction battalions, signal corps, quartermaster corps, and the like? To help deal with these decisions, psychological advisers developed the Army Alpha Test and other classification tests to provide a basis for selecting and classifying this diverse group of young men. The tests proved successful, and after the war the same methodology was used to construct and develop tests of intelligence and achievement for school use.

Such tests are designed to place test takers on a continuum from those who score highest to those who score lowest. This method of testing enables one to identify the position of any individual in relation to the total group or to identify the people who compose any fraction of the group, for example, those in the top quarter or those in the lowest third. By administering the tests to a representative sample of a defined population (for instance, seventh-grade students in U.S. schools), the continuum reveals the distribution of that population (e.g., the distribution of all American seventh graders). Thus large-scale comparisons are made possible by such standardized tests: a seventh grader's performance, for example, can be compared to the scores of seventh graders nationwide, as opposed to the scores of only those students within the same classroom.

Until recently, the purpose of educational and psychological appraisal was to sort students from excellent to poor. Such an approach seemed necessary in earlier times: since most jobs were unskilled, and professional and managerial positions made up a small sector of the labor force, only the best and the brightest were encouraged to complete secondary school and aspire to those positions. In political and social spheres, the same pyramid prevailed: not more than five to ten percent of the population were expected to be well educated.

In 1800, about sixty percent of the U.S. labor force were engaged in agriculture; in 1900, thirty-eight percent were employed in agriculture (a shift of 22% in 100 years), and in 1981, less than five percent—a shift of thirty-three

percent in eighty-one years. Similarly, in 1800, the unskilled in all categories
constituted more than eighty percent of the labor force; in 1900 they made up
sixty percent; and in 1980, about six percent. It was only after World War II
that rapid changes in the occupational and social structure created sharp new
demands for education and many more opportunities for employment in such
fields as education, health, recreation, social services, administration, accounting,
and engineering. Now jobs requiring no schooling are few in number, while
tasks requiring at least a high school education make up nearly two thirds of
employment opportunities. Consequently, schools are now expected to educate
all (or nearly all) children rather than to sort out high performers and proficient
test takers and to encourage members of that group alone to go on with their
education.

Noting the shift in American policy from rationing education to helping
all students learn, educational leaders began to employ the same achievement
tests for a new purpose: to assess the learning progress of students. They failed,
however, to recognize the limitations of sorting tests when used to assess progress
in learning. Good tests of human progress provide a representative sample of
the behavior that is being appraised. An effective test of how well students have
learned a certain vocabulary, for example, will include a representative sample
of the words or kinds of words that the students are expected to know. Ideally,
most students should do well on such tests, since the material is supposed to be
familiar to them. But in a sorting test of vocabulary, words that all or almost
all students answer correctly will not help much to separate the students and to
place them on a continuum. The same is true for words that few can answer
correctly. Words or questions that help most to discriminate among students are
those that half of the students can define or answer correctly and half cannot.
This method of selecting items produces a test that sorts persons efficiently,
although it does not efficiently measure students' progress toward a specific goal
(e.g., the goal of learning specific new vocabulary items). Thus scores on sorting
tests do not reflect the extent to which students have learned what the schools
have to teach or what society expects them to learn, although many lay persons
interpret the scores this way.

A second problem with many sorting tests is that they give misleading
clues to students who seek guidance for their studies. Objective tests in the area
of writing are a prime illustration, but not the only one. A valid and objective
evaluation of written compositions requires professional agreement on criteria,
careful training of judges, and much time for reading and evaluating the essays.
Because such a process is expensive in time and money, test constructors have
commonly substituted tests of editing or other multiple-response or short-answer
tests. Although much less expensive to evaluate, these are not tests of composition. The correlation between the scores students get on such tests and the
ratings given their written compositions usually ranges from .40 to .60. Cor-
relations of this magnitude indicate that students' skills in writing cannot safely

be inferred from their objective test scores. Thus students who do well on such tests may be misled into thinking that they need not work on their writing skills.

Furthermore, tests that do not directly require students to write give them and their teachers the view that writing is not considered important and that little effort need be expended in the practice of writing. In 1936, the state of New York conducted a study of high school students in fifty-one cities to determine to what extent academic achievement reflected curriculum requirements and to what extent it reflected state examination requirements (see Gulick). The achievement of students corresponded much more closely to the examination emphasis than to the emphasis given in the curriculum. It seems fair to conclude that if students get clues from major testing programs that editing, knowledge of the mechanics of writing, and an extensive sight vocabulary are the primary objectives of composition—and little or no emphasis is placed on actual writing—they will focus their learning efforts on those skills. If writing is to be given strong emphasis, students should be tested in writing.

Finally, a serious limitation of sorting tests (when used for nonsorting purposes) is the requirement that a student's performance on all the exercises be summarized into a single score that can place the student on a linear continuum. The way students approach and respond to various exercises is an indication of their learning. For instance, a particular choice made among multiple alternatives might suggest kinds of partial learning. The pace at which they answer questions can also be indicative of their learning. A student may, for example, rapidly complete one section of a test and barely get through another. This kind of information can be useful in understanding student difficulties and improving instruction, but it is lost when the student's responses are all translated into a single score.

The use of sorting tests in American schools continues to diminish as educators become more aware of their limitations and as efforts increase to educate all students, not just high performers. New kinds of tests have been developed to replace the sorting variety and to serve a wider range of educational purposes. For instance, tests are now available to classroom teachers that help assess the needs of students in order to individualize instruction or place them at appropriate levels of educational programs. Other tests have been designed to monitor the progress of students, to diagnose learning problems, and to determine how well students have mastered specific units of instruction. Curriculum builders are using newly developed tests for the assessment of group needs. Administrators are finding that they can monitor the progress of classes and schools, assess student achievement at certain age or grade levels, and evaluate the effectiveness of instructional equipment and materials with appropriately constructed tests. Tests have also been developed for guidance counselors to use in helping students plan for the future, and legislators and other officials at various levels of government are now able to obtain information about the progress and problems of education in their jurisdiction with the help of certain tests.

These varied uses of tests were never anticipated when the early principles and theory of test construction and interpretation were being developed. Most of psychometric theory is based on the notion that educational tests are primarily to be used for sorting.

Although new tests are constantly being constructed, few have been developed for the testing of writing. To construct writing tests and use them appropriately for different purposes requires an understanding of some basic concepts of testing. To test any aspect of human behavior, one must obtain a representative sample of that behavior and identify its important characteristics. This simple statement embodies both the directions for constructing tests and faint clues as to the troublesome problems one will encounter while doing so. The remainder of this essay will be devoted to discussing strategies for constructing and evaluating tests of writing.

Several questions must be answered before teachers of writing set out to test their students. For example: What kind of writing is being taught and should be sampled? expository? narrative? persuasive? What characteristics of writing are emphasized in the course with the expectation that students will learn them? Answers to such questions clarify educational objectives and suggest the kinds of writing exercises that should be included in the test. But another question must be answered before proceeding: Should the test indicate what students can do under certain conditions or what they actually do? If the appraisal is to ascertain the way a student usually writes expository papers in science, social studies, and literature, for example, a representative sample of the papers the student has submitted in these classes must be collected. If, however, the appraisal is to see what students are able do, other questions must be answered: What exercises will elicit the type of writing teachers want to appraise? How can the test conditions best approximate those under which the student is or will be expected to produce the same kind of writing? Will subject material need to be provided to students to form a basis for their writing? Will the particular purpose of each writing exercise need to be explained or are the writing requirements so clearly understood that the students know the purpose, the intended audience, and the expected standards that are applied to the written work?

One sometimes overlooked question in developing writing tests is this: Does the proposed writing exercise really evoke the desired behavior? If a student's experience is that teachers of certain subjects accept mediocre writing and if the test exercises appear to the student similar to assignments given in those subjects, then the test results will likely be mediocre and not reflect what the student is capable of writing. Some exploration is usually required in developing tests to find out how students can be stimulated to do their best.

Answers to all the foregoing questions help educators construct valid tests—that is, tests that provide evidence about the behavior one intends to evaluate. As pointed out earlier, editing tests are not tests of writing; that is, the score on an editing test is not a good indicator of a student's writing skill. By developing test exercises that approximate as closely as possible the conditions under which students are usually expected to write expository prose, for example, validity is ensured. Such factors as the following should be considered in setting those conditions: complexity of the subject, number of words or pages required, opportunity to revise drafts, and time limits.

Another important feature of any test is its relative objectivity. Extensive use of multiple-response tests has led to the notion that only tests of this kind are objective, while essay tests and other forms of obtaining student reactions are subjective. This view is simplistic and mistaken. The appraisal of any human reaction requires human judgment in selecting and applying criteria as well as in reporting results. Human judgments are not eliminated by devising a multiple-response form, and this point is well illustrated by recent publicity that questions on the quantitative portion of the College Board Scholastic Aptitude Test have been presented to test takers with more than a single correct answer among the options offered.

Although human judgment is a necessary part of any evaluation process, what can be eliminated are idiosyncratic judgments and what is sought is agreement among competent judges. When a test result is reported in significantly different terms by different individuals, its usefulness is limited. In writing, such characteristics as comprehensibility, organization, and appropriateness of vocabulary could conceivably be defined in different terms by different English teachers. But in schools where instruction focuses on improving these characteristics of student writing, a common understanding is needed to guide the instruction. Once teachers reach agreement on what constitutes comprehensibility, for example, or good organization, they need to agree on how to measure and judge those features in a student's paper. One strategy that can be used to develop compatible ideas on how to measure such features is the following. Each paper in a collection should be rated by teachers on some hypothetical scale ranging from one to seven or one to five. As the teachers independently rate the papers, they will likely discover marked differences in the scores they assign to certain papers. These papers should be read again and discussed to seek an explanation for the varied ratings. Such discussions will usually resolve differences in judgment and reduce variations in the ratings of different judges.

Once a scale is agreed on and used in actual tests of writing, there are still likely to be a few judges who assign ratings that are much lower or higher than those assigned by others. These judges most likely have the same conception of comprehensibility or organization as the rest, but the numbers on the scale may have different meanings for them. A "one," for instance, may be perceived as unattainable by such judges, while the others assign "ones" to the top ten percent of the essays. For such cases, objectivity of rating is improved by establishing samples of written papers that are typically assigned each of the points on the scale so that the judges may compare the paper they are rating with the sample and when necessary adjust the level of rating accordingly. This holistic rating procedure, of course, is not necessarily appropriate for all aspects of writing. Appropriateness of vocabulary, for example, could be appraised by counting the number of times inappropriate terms are used and the cases in which a more appropriate term could have been used. This example is suggested not as an ideal way of appraising appropriateness of vocabulary but rather to indicate that one should consider how to best record and report a particular characteristic in terms that reflect the essentials of that characteristic.

The pursuit of objectivity is not an attempt to eliminate human judgments but to ensure agreement among judges as to the meaning of evaluative terms. One measure of the degree of objectivity of a test is the correlation between the ratings, scores, or descriptions assigned a set of papers by two or more judges appraising the papers independently. Difficulty in obtaining the desired degree of objectivity should not become a reason for failing to appraise important characteristics of student writing. It is far better to evaluate an important characteristic roughly than an unimportant one precisely. But above all, in testing writing as part of instruction, it is important not to lose information regarding the students' writing behavior that could help in understanding their progress and problems in learning to write. These clues often suggest ways of helping the student improve.

Another important feature of a test is its reliability. Tests are designed to appraise some aspect of human behavior (e.g., writing) by evaluating a sample of that behavior. When a test provides more than one sample of a student's writing, the rating of one sample may differ somewhat from that of another. Such differences occur for any number of reasons: for instance, the student may feel nervous while writing one sample (thus performing with less skill) and more at ease while writing another; the rater of the essays may be offended by one topic and not by another and score them accordingly; or the test questions may elicit inconsistent writing samples. The degree of agreement between the ratings of two or more samples is referred to as "test reliability." If two writing samples differ markedly in the scores they receive, the test is unreliable—that is, it gives inconsistent indications of the student's writing ability. One way to improve the reliability of a test is to include more exercises. A more practical way to increase reliability is to give a series of tests instead of expanding one. Either way, the results are likely to be more indicative of the student's ability (and thus more reliable) because they are based on a larger sample size.

Tests that are used for sorting purposes require a level of precision that is not possible to attain if every student is to be treated fairly. The use of derived scores frequently gives a false impression of a test's precision. For example, each raw score on the College Board Scholastic Aptitude Test is translated into a derived score based on a mean reference distribution of 500 and a standard deviation of 100. When it was reported that verbal test scores declined an average of 30 points over ten years, people failed to recognize that this figure was based on derived scores. Hence, the extent of the decline appeared much greater than if a decline of 2.4 in the average of the raw scores had been reported. In a single faulty question on a College Board Scholastic Aptitude Test (as has occurred at least twice since 1981), the difference of one point in raw score was equivalent to a derived score of more than ten points, and this difference shifted hundreds of test takers from their earlier relative positions on the continuum. This kind of instrument with its appearance of great precision is not needed for most educational purposes. Teachers are in a position to verify or reject the interpretations made from the tests they use as they work with students and find added evidence for verifying or raising doubts about earlier interpretations.

Decisions that are largely based on tests should not be irrevocable. Even when students demonstrate by a test that they have mastered the particular skills and knowledge emphasized in a unit of instruction, their progress on the next unit should be taken as a basis for verifying or rejecting the results of the unit mastery test. In general, if an important educational decision has to be based on a test, greater precision can be obtained by expanding the sample of exercises selected for each objective, by obtaining evidence from another relevant test or other source of information, or by both techniques.

Summary of Steps in Testing Writing

(1) Defining the Purposes for a Particular Test

Is the purpose of this test to guide instruction? Is it to furnish evidence of the type of progress a student or a class has made? Is it to evaluate a student's mastery of the basic concepts and skills presented in a unit of instruction?

The purpose of a test determines, among other things, what behavior should be sampled; what degree of objectivity will be necessary; whether every student will be tested with the same exercises or whether matrix sampling can be used; how detailed the analysis of the results should be; whether a comparison of results with the results from other groups of students will be useful; and whether school-related writing or other writing or both should be sampled.

(2) Specifying and Defining the Learning Objectives to Be Assessed

To learn to write well, one must develop a variety of skills, concepts, and attitudes. Curricula and programs of instruction in most schools and colleges are designed to give attention to particular objectives at different times and to help students develop all the essential skills and concepts by the conclusion of their schooling. Before constructing a test, one must decide what skills and concepts the test will appraise.

(3) Identifying Situations Where Objectives Are Utilized

One who has really learned something has internalized it and can be expected to use it whenever it is appropriate. Hence, if we wish to find out whether a student has learned certain writing skills, we should identify those

situations where the skills can be used and simulate them on the test. A variety
of contexts, tasks, and purposes define what kinds of writing skills are needed
and hence what types of situations should be simulated.

(4) Devising Ways of Presenting Situations

Once the situations have been identified, we need to simulate them in such
a way that they will evoke the reactions that the real-life situations would evoke.
It is often difficult to devise artificial situations that seem so real as to enure the
student's motivation to respond. Some students, particularly those from middle-
class homes, take formal test situations seriously and try to respond. Students
from lower-class homes, on the other hand, usually come from backgrounds
where tests are rare and seem irrelevant to their lives. Tests that use artificial
situations need to be reviewed carefully and tried out to ascertain whether they
evoke an appropriate response from the several kinds of students tested. When
it is possible to obtain representative samples of the students' reactions in real
situations, these should be used as tests. Trained observers and judges can obtain
a wealth of information about the learning of students from observations of their
daily activities and from an appraisal of their written work. These real situations
should not be overlooked in constructing tests in the field of writing.

(5) Selecting a Technique for Recording Responses

Test constructors must also decide how students should record their responses to the exercises. Most tests require students to respond by checking one
or more of a given array of answers or by writing a short response. The popularity
of multiple-choice tests is due in part to the ease with which students can record
their responses and in part to the apparent simplicity of appraising them. When
one's skill or ability is accurately indicated by a product—for instance, a composition, a piece of craft, or a work of art—the product itself becomes the record
that can be preserved for careful appraisal. Observation check lists, anecdotal
records, videotapes, and photographs can furnish records of reactions that cannot
otherwise be retrieved, as in speaking, social interaction, skills in using laboratory
equipment, and the like.

New technologies have provided new means for recording behavior. Slow-
motion movies, for example, highlight movements normally too rapid for observation and greatly improve diagnosis in physical education. Tape recorders
are a great asset in appraising oral performance, musical skills, and group problem
solving. Computers have tremendously extended the practicable ways of recording arithmetic skills, decision processes, and many forms of choices from
multiple lists. Computers are also likely to be used more and more in the testing
of writing. Students can type their compositions into the computer, easily revise
them, and store each draft (or just the final product if that alone is of interest)
for the teacher's appraisal. Quite clearly, there are many more possibilities
available today for recording aspects of human behavior than there were even

fifty years ago, and every possibility deserves our consideration as test constructors. In testing writing, however, it is crucial to get a record of the students' writing, whatever the means for doing so.

(6) Deciding on the Terms to Use in Appraisal

The age-old tradition of scoring or grading tests in terms of the number of correct responses has often prevailed even when the sum of correct responses does not furnish a useful or reasonably accurate appraisal of the student's attainment of the objectives. It is important to use terms or units that properly reflect both the desirable characteristics of the student's reactions and the undesirable or less desirable. Thus a plan for rating the organization of a student's paper should provide a description or a rating that distinguishes a well-organized paper from a loosely organized or disorganized one.

In appraising a student's selection of major emphases for a persuasive writing, the number of relevant major factors could be the units of desirable characteristics, while the failure to work out their interrelation could be a descriptive term of an undesirable characteristic. In some cases, as in diagnosis, the terms may need to indicate syndromes, or types of difficulties. Two appraisal schemes are often used in tandem to evaluate products (e.g., compositions). One indicates the level of quality of the total product (the total composition) and the other furnishes a report on the number of different desirable or undesirable features, like compound sentences and misspelled words.

Terms used to describe or rate human behavior usually are not defined very precisely. Hence, when such terms are used, it is important to gain agreement among competent teachers regarding their definitions and then to provide sufficient training in the application of the terms to samples of students' performance. Keeping examples of each term and rating level is a useful way of ensuring common standards in comparing a student's performance from one time to another or of comparing the performance of one group of students with other groups.

(7) Devising Means for Getting a Representative Sample

We all know that human behavior varies under different conditions, even when those conditions are clearly defined. For instance, one may read newspaper articles easily but find it hard to read directions for assembling an appliance; write clearly a critical review of a television program but write turgid prose in explaining an electronic phenomenon; use a large vocabulary in speaking of art and be limited in the words used to discuss social issues. For a test to furnish reliable information about what the student has learned, it must be based on a representative and adequate sample of the situations in which the learning can be exhibited.

To obtain a representative sample of something, it is necessary to define the universe of that "something" and then to draw random or stratified samples from the universe. For example, to obtain a representative sample of the situations in which seventh-grade students are expected to write, it is necessary to define the universe of things that seventh graders are expected to write—for example, kinds of personal letters, letters to vendors, written assignments in several classes, and expressive writing not assigned in school courses. It is from this universe that samples can be drawn for testing.

There are at least two ways to get a representative sample: by drawing samples from the universe by a random procedure or by dividing the universe into strata, randomly drawing samples from each strata, and then combining the samples by their appropriate weights. The adequacy of the sample—that is, its required size—depends both on the precision demanded for the purpose of the test and upon the variability of the student's reactions in the different situations. The greater the precision required and the more variable the student reactions, the larger the sample required for reliability.

Some of the new technologies help to solve the problem of obtaining an adequate sample of the student's reactions. A computer can keep in its memory the results of a student's performance on tests given periodically until a relatively large number of results have been recorded. Thus, for example, storing the results of weekly papers written over the course of a quarter or a semester will allow for a much more reliable appraisal than that obtained from a single paper.

The foregoing seven steps briefly summarize procedures to follow in constructing tests for use in the field of writing. They not only represent questions to be answered by teachers of writing and ways of thinking about testing but also indicate a systematic process for constructing needed tests. My main purposes, however, have been to distinguish testing for teaching and learning from testing for sorting students and to suggest how it is possible to test writing validly and to use the results in an instructional program for the improvement of writing.

Work Cited

Gulick, Luther Halsey. *Education for American Life: A New Program for the State of New York*. New York: McGraw-Hill, 1938.

Functional Literacy for
Community College Students

Arthur M. Cohen and Florence B. Brawer

Numerous critics have complained that schools teach people to read and write but fail to teach them to think. As long ago as 1869, Parkman noted that the schools produced an immense number of readers but what thinkers were to be found existed in spite of the schools. One hundred years later Ciardi complained that ". . . the American School System has dedicated itself to universal subliteracy. It has encouraged the assumption that a clod trained to lip-read a sports page is able to read anything. It has become the whole point of the School System to keep the ignorant from realizing their own ignorance. . . . An illiterate must at least know that he cannot read and that the world of books is closed to him" (48). And Mencken commented that "the great majority of American high school pupils, when they put their thoughts on paper, produce only a mass of confused puerile nonsense. . . . They express themselves so clumsily that it is often quite impossible to understand them at all" (quoted in Lyons 33).

More recently critics have claimed that students not only fail to become intelligent but fail even to learn the rudiments of reading, writing, and arithmetic. In *The Literacy Hoax: The Decline of Reading, Writing, and Learning in the Public Schools and What We Can Do about It*, Copperman reports that over 20 million American adults, one in every five, are functionally illiterate—that is, incapable of understanding basic written communication and arithmetic to a degree that they can manage satisfactorily in contemporary society. Many commentators, Copperman included, do not blame the schools alone, but each generation's cohort of criers has had a favorite target, and most of them eventually disparage the public schools.

Broad-scale denunciations are one thing, accurate data quite another. Although data on the number of people completing years of schooling have been collected by the Bureau of the Census for well over one hundred years, information on the literacy of the American population over the decades is difficult to compile. One reason that intergenerational comparisons are imprecise is that different percentages of the population have gone to school at different periods in the nation's history; a century ago, for instance, only the upper socioeconomic classes completed secondary school or enrolled in higher education. Difficulties in comparing are compounded because the United States does not have a uniform system of educational evaluation.

Nonetheless, available evidence suggests that the academic achievement of students in schools and colleges registered a gradual improvement between 1900 and the mid-1950s, an accelerated improvement between the mid-1950s and the mid-1960s, and a precipitous, widespread decline between the 1960s and the late 1970s. Results of the Scholastic Aptitude Tests taken by high school seniors showed mathematical ability at 494 in 1952, 502 in 1963, and 470 in 1977; verbal ability went from 476 in 1952 to 478 in 1963 and dropped to 429 in 1977 (Copperman). American College Testing Program and Graduate Record Examination scores also declined notably between the mid-1960s and the late 1970s, and the National Assessment of Educational Progress reported that seventeen-year-olds' command of the mechanics of writing declined between 1970 and 1974 (Bishop).

Reports emanating from the colleges confirm this slide. Surveys by Ladd and Lipset, Brawer and Friedlander, and the Center for the Study of Community Colleges suggest that faculty are disappointed with their students' lack of preparation. The Educational Testing Service (ETS) notes:

> At the University of California at Berkeley, where students come from the top eighth of California high school graduates, nearly half the freshmen in recent years have been so deficient in writing ability that they needed a remedial course they themselves call "bonehead English." (Bishop 2)

And although most of the freshmen at the City University of New York had at least an 80 average in high school, one third of them lacked even basic literacy, and ninety percent took some form of remedial writing instruction. The ETS list of institutions where entering freshmen were found to be seriously deficient in basic communication skills includes some of the most prestigious universities in the country. Harvard, Yale, Cornell, Brown, and Stanford are among the countless other institutions that have found the need to introduce some form of basic writing instruction.

It is not the purpose of this paper to recount the social and educational forces leading to the decline in student abilities that apparently began in the mid-1950s and accelerated throughout the 1970s. Suffice it to say that numerous events coalesced: the coming of age of the first generation reared on television, a breakdown in respect for authority and the professions, a pervasive attitude that the written word is not as important as it once was, the imposition of various nonacademic expectations on the public schools, and a decline in academic requirements and expectations at all levels of schooling. This last variable is worthy of elaboration because it is the only one that schools have the power to change directly.

Several premises underlie schooling: for example, students tend to learn what is taught; the more time spent on a task, the more one learns; students will take the courses required for completion of their programs. If these premises are, in fact, correct, then it follows that student achievement, however measured, will drop when expectations, time in school, and number of academic requirements are reduced. ETS reports:

> the nub of the matter is that writing is a complex skill mastered only through lengthy, arduous effort. It is a participatory endeavor, not a spectator sport. And most high school students do not get enough practice to become competent writers. (Bishop 4)

Since the 1960s the schools have put less emphasis on composition, and even in the composition courses, "creative expression" is treated at a higher level than are grammar and other tools of writing.

Criticism of the schools' ability to teach students to read and write extends to higher education, with specialization being a favorite target. Because each academic discipline has its own jargon, the argument goes, students learn to be literate only within the confines of the courses they take and rarely learn to read and write on a broader basis. College departments are criticized for attempting to produce majors and graduate students in their own disciplines without being concerned with literacy in general. English departments come in for their share of the attack, the claim being that too many professors concern themselves with literary criticism and esoterica while demeaning the teaching of composition and those who teach it.

The Community College

Community colleges developed during the twentieth century as a distinctly American educational form combining several missions. They were designed to fit into the educational mainstream reaching from kindergarten through graduate school by offering four types of educational experiences: capstone education for those who do not progress much beyond secondary school; the first two years of college for those who go on to baccalaureate and graduate studies; occupational training for those who seek employment; and casual, community-based education for those who want to pick up an occasional course. As community colleges evolved, they assumed the role of expanding access for everyone who might otherwise be excluded from higher education: women, the poor, minorities, and the ignorant.

By 1980 there were 1,230 public and private two-year colleges in the United States, and the enrollment figures point to their success in expanding opportunity. More than four million people (one third of all U.S. students in higher education) were enrolled in community colleges, including half of all the freshmen beginning college, half of all the minorities in higher education, older students, part-time students, and students from families who, in an earlier era, would not have entertained the idea of sending their children to college. Community colleges offer transfer or college-parallel lower-division studies, including remedial work in the same types of courses that are offered in senior institutions; occupational programs that prepare students for immediate employment; and community service offerings dedicated to short courses and programs of current interest for people who are not interested in pursuing academic degrees.

Of all postsecondary educational institutions in America, public community colleges admit the greatest number of poorly prepared students. Few maintain admissions standards; hardly any demand a minimum high school grade-point average; fewer than one in five imposes an entrance test; one third of them do not even require a high school diploma. Most community colleges allow students to matriculate while living at home and/or being employed. Through this general appeal they tend to enroll older students and part-time students, as well as recent secondary school graduates. Several studies have shown that both professional educators and the general public feel that the main contribution of two-year colleges is to provide equal opportunity for all to engage in postsecondary studies without regard to ethnicity, sex, age, family income, or physical or developmental handicaps.

The success of community colleges in expanding opportunity for people who might otherwise be excluded from postsecondary studies has been notable. Their success in educating all students, however, is variable. Attrition levels in most community college programs are high. Well over half the students who declare their intent to transfer to senior institutions either do not complete their community college studies or complete them and fail to transfer. In fact, the reverse phenomenon is more common, with many students entering the two-year college from undergraduate university programs, concurrently attending classes at both institutions, or enrolling in courses even though they already have the baccalaureate or advanced degrees.

Many students in nonselective occupational programs also drop out before concluding their training. In general, attrition in two-year colleges is the highest of all postsecondary education. Many of the multiple variables associated with attrition are beyond the college's purview. Yet numerous special programs have been established to combat the problem and enhance the probability of students completing occupational programs or programs that will enable them to transfer to baccalaureate degree-granting institutions. Learning laboratories, tutorial assistance, bilingual programs, and programs to teach reading, writing, and computational skills are found in most large institutions and in a sizable number of smaller colleges.

In the 1950s and 1960s community colleges received a large share of well-prepared students who were clamoring for higher education. But when the college-age group declined and universities became more competitive for students, the proportion of academically well-prepared students attending community colleges shrank, and community colleges experienced an increased enrollment of students who were illiterate in many areas. Literacy is certainly related to success in nearly all community college programs: transfer courses demand proficiency in reading, writing, and mathematics, and licensure examinations admitting students to practice after completing technological programs typically demand the same. Many community college programs are closed to students who cannot pass an entrance examination that is based on literacy. Literacy demands are placed on students through such administrative tasks as applications, the transmission of information regarding deadlines, requests for assistance, and other noninstructional but nonetheless important tasks that relate to a student's success in the institution. Thus although the colleges admit all students, some level of literacy is a requisite for entry to—and success in—most institutional operations.

Community colleges attempt to accommodate all types of students and, to some extent, to guide students to programs that fit their aspirations and abilities. Students who qualify for transfer programs are offered courses similar to those found in the lower division of four-year colleges and universities. For technical and occupational aspirants there are programs that teach the trades. Internal selectivity has been the norm in this area particularly; failing certain prerequisites, applicants have been barred from the health professions and technology programs. Students who want a course or two for their own personal interest find them both in the departments of continuing education and the transfer programs. Thus most students are easily accommodated by community colleges.

The poorly prepared students, however, have been a concern. What to do with marginally literate people who want to be in college but do not know why? How to deal with someone who aspires to be an attorney but who is reading at a fifth-grade level? Shunting these students to the trades programs was a favored ploy, giving rise to Burton Clark's cooling-out thesis. Offering a smattering of remedial courses where such students would be prepared more or less successfully to enter the transfer courses—or entertained until they drifted away—was another. But the decline in achievement exhibited by both secondary school graduates and dropouts in the 1970s hit the colleges with full force and, by most accounts, was increasing in intensity as the 1980s began. The issue of the marginal student has become central to instructional planning.

Guiding and teaching students who are unprepared for traditional college-level studies is the single thorniest problem for community colleges. Some institutions seem to have given up, as evidenced by their tendencies to award students certificates and degrees for any combination of courses, units, or credits— in effect, sending them away with the illusion of having had a successful college career. Others have established special instructional and counseling services for students with lower abilities, stratagems designed to puncture the balloon of prior school failure. But in most programs in most institutions, expectations for student achievement have declined.

Compensatory Education

Compensatory education is not new to community colleges. These colleges formerly offered, almost exclusively, disparate courses designed to prepare students to enter the college transfer program, and students were placed in the courses on the basis of entrance tests or prior school achievement. The courses were usually not accepted for credit toward an academic degree. Morrison and Ferrante estimated that in 1970 most of the public two-year colleges had developmental, preparatory, or remedial programs. Extrapolating from the sample of schools used in the American Council of Education's Cooperative Institutional Research Program, they concluded that all the colleges had some sort of special services for academically disadvantaged students—either special programs (39%), special courses (99%), or both.

"Remedial," "compensatory," and "developmental" are the most widespread euphemisms for courses designed to teach the basics of reading, writing, and arithmetic. Enrollments are high but few reliable surveys have been done to determine how high. It is difficult to compare courses across colleges because course titles, content, and numbering varies; Remedial Writing in one college is English Composition in another. Some estimates can be made, however, by counting the number of class sections offered. Using the 1977 catalogs and class schedules from a national sample of 175 public and private colleges, staff at the Center for the Study of Community Colleges tallied the sections in all the academic areas and found that nearly one third of all the mathematics offered was at a level below algebra and that around two fifths of all English (excluding literature) was remedial reading or composition (Cohen and Brawer, *American Community College*).

Clearly the colleges were devoting a major portion of their instructional effort to poorly prepared students. But several questions remain, ranging from program effect to institutional purpose: Do such programs really teach people to read and write? Should poorly qualified students be segregated in special programs or should they be allowed to enter regular classes? How does compensatory education affect the college staff? Can a college devote such a great proportion of its effort to remedial studies without jeopardizing its standards and its place in higher education? How many times should the public pay the schools to try to teach the same competencies to the same people?

Some of these questions can be answered with data; others are a matter of opinion. Numerous researchers and commentators have grappled with the issues presented by compensatory education in community colleges, and their reports abound both in published literature and in the files of the Educational Resources Information Center (ERIC).

Community colleges have little trouble identifying poor students, and compensatory courses and programs appear to have been effective where they have been established. Cohen's study of remedial English classes in fourteen community colleges found student writing ability at the end of the courses to be on the average equivalent to the writing ability of students who were beginning the regular college English classes. Several studies indicate that instructors of compensatory courses tend to pay closer attention to their students, integrate teaching with counseling, and provide a greater variety of learning materials than ordinary students receive. Although the results of compensatory courses are rarely documented, our observations suggest that students tend to improve when they are given supplemental counseling, tutoring, and learning aids and when they are singled out for additional work. Such an observation is not surprising, of course; special treatment of any sort usually yields special results. What is surprising is that reliable data on consistent program effects are not readily available.

Some compensatory education programs have been designed, often in conjunction with other agencies, for people who were not regularly enrolled at the college. These range from programs for special populations—such as the one for Navaho Indians described by Smith and for inner-city adult construction workers studied by Howard—to programs that include both academic and vocational skills and personalized educational placement and counseling for anyone with a minimal income, low reading level, erratic employment pattern, or arrest record (Conti et al.).

Compensatory education thus involves colleges not only with students who come to the campus seeking academic programs, degrees, and certificates but with adult basic education. Adult studies are often funded and organized separately, and sometimes, especially when colleges are responsible for adult education in their district, they lead to entirely separate structures. The Urban Skills Institute operated by the City Colleges of Chicago enrolled forty-five percent of the district's students in 1980. The College Centers maintained under the aegis of the San Francisco Community College District provide another case in point. Such structures take some of the pressure for compensatory education away from the colleges' regular programs.

How do faculty members feel about the massive compensatory education efforts and the poorly prepared students in their classes? The students' abilities exert the single most powerful influence on the level, quality, type, and standard of curriculum and instruction offered in every program in every school. Other influences—instructors' tendencies, externally administered examinations and licensure requirements, the entry levels imposed by succeeding courses in the same and other institutions—pale in comparison. Nothing can be taught successfully that is too distant from the students' comprehension. All questions of academic standards, college-level and remedial courses, textbook readability and coverage, course-pacing and sequence come to that.

Students are part of an instructor's working conditions, and except for the faculty recruited especially for compensatory programs, most feel their environment would improve if their students were more able. In response to the question "What would it take to make your course better?" fifty-three percent of the respondents to a 1977 national survey of two-year college science instructors replied, "Students better prepared to handle course requirements" (Brawer and Friedlander 32). That choice far outranked all others in a list of sixteen.

If students cannot be more able, instructors often feel it would be helpful if they were more alike so that instruction could be more precisely focused. Teaching groups of students whose reading or computational abilities range from the third to the thirteenth grade is discouraging; everything is more difficult, from writing examinations to showing group progress. Hence the unremitting pressure for ability grouping, remedial courses, and learning laboratories that serve to remove the poorer students from the classrooms.

Compensatory education affects instructors in several other ways. Veteran faculty remember when they had well-prepared students in the 1950s and early 1960s. They may feel nostalgic, perhaps even betrayed, because the conditions under which they entered the colleges have changed so. At the same time they may be pleased that the segregated compensatory education programs remove the poorest students from their own classes; over one fourth of the instructors teaching the traditional academic courses (humanities, sciences, social sciences, and technologies) would prefer "stricter prerequisites for admission to class" (Brawer and Friedlander). Nonetheless, the teachers in the compensatory education programs run the risk of becoming pariahs, similar in that regard to the occupational education instructors in the pre-1960s era.

The question of legitimacy is one of image in the eyes of the public, potential students, funding agents, and other sectors of education. Like any other public agency, an educational institution must maintain its legitimacy. Through numerous stratagems, community colleges have striven to maintain their claim to a position in the postsecondary sector. In the 1950s and 1960s, for example, they sought people with doctoral degrees to serve as staff members and rewarded current staff members who obtained higher degrees, even though the possession of a doctorate bears little or no relationship to a faculty member's professional activities, as we show in *The Two-Year College*. Having people with doctoral degrees on the staff was a way of saying, "We are as good as the senior institutions." One of the reasons for the move toward segregated compensatory programs has been an attempt to regain the legitimacy lost when the colleges accepted adult basic studies and job training programs that could in no measure be considered "college level." The unintended consequence of this latest attempt to gain legitimacy as a collegiate institution has been that students are held away from the liberal arts just at a time when they should be exposed to them. And extreme care must be taken lest it have the additional consequence of leading to ethnic separation within the institutions.

A school's legitimacy rests on its academic standards and the definition of its guiding principles. Academic standards certify that a student holding a certificate or degree has met the requirement for employment or for further study at another college; they are the basis for the reputation of institutions and the people who work within them. Even though community colleges typically maintain open admissions policies, they must still attend to these concerns. Their students must be certified; their instructional programs, testing and counseling services, course content, and course requirements must all relate to a shared vision of desired competencies and outcomes. Their certificates or degrees must evidence some set of proficiencies achieved at some minimum level.

What are the standards in compensatory education? In this area the special programs have several problems in common with the traditional. One of the main problems is the difficulty in setting fixed exit criteria for courses and programs that have no set entry requirements. A wide range of students will be attracted when people are allowed to enroll regardless of ability. Thus the exit criteria must be fluid, with a different standard for each student, or the type and duration of instruction must be greatly varied, or expectations must be maintained at an exceedingly modest level. All three options are implemented to some degree in practically all programs.

Standardized expectations of accomplishment—or exit criteria—suggest that social norms are in play, and social norms require that people act in accordance with certain standards in order to function adequately in particular social settings. On the other hand, when expectations of accomplishment are tailored to the desires or entering abilities of individuals, any accomplishment becomes satisfactory, and an institution succeeds if any gain in individual ability is shown. The difference between social and individual standards is, of course, an issue of absolute versus relative standards, and it strikes at the heart of compensatory education.

Different groups take different positions on this issue, but community college faculty tend to argue in favor of absolute standards. The Academic Senate for California Community Colleges (ASCCC) has studied extensively both approaches, and it deplores some of the pressures to lower standards: students entering college with inadequate basic skills but with expectations of passing the courses as they have done throughout their prior school careers; ill-prepared students who insist on enrolling in transfer courses rather than in remedial courses; and the cult of growth-oriented community colleges as evidenced by the aggressive student recruiting drives. The ASCCC Academic Standards Committee recommended that standards should be maintained through the use of diagnostic and placement testing, directive counseling, academic prerequisites for courses, and proficiency testing prior to awarding academic degrees.

Advocates of lifelong learning often provide an opposing view, claiming that institutions should be a resource to individuals for a wide variety of purposes. Cross defends that position well, arguing that substantial changes in school forms are needed so that anyone may learn anything at any time. Others assert that functional literacy is related to the milieu in which people find themselves. A functionally literate person in some school settings may be functionally illiterate in certain jobs. And a person who is quite able to communicate within the confines of certain jobs may be functionally illiterate for purposes of a college transfer program no matter how that program is defined.

Institutional legitimacy and faculty predilections rest on standards, defined outcomes, certifiable results. But the definitions guiding staff efforts and the precepts of continuing education or lifelong learning are relative; each person brings idiosyncratic backgrounds and aspirations to the institution, each finds a separate set of experiences. How can the two be reconciled in an open admissions institution? The question is not limited to compensatory education, but the influx of students with low academic ability has brought it to the fore. While the primary function of compensatory education programs is to provide more useful learning experiences for poorly prepared students, a secondary and less noticeable function is to protect, at least temporarily, the standards and expectations of the other portions of the college by segregating such students into separate enclaves. Issues of minority student segregation and tracking are not as easily submerged.

Compensatory education is designed to do what its name suggests: to compensate for deficiencies. Morrison and Ferrante suggest that these deficiencies are not merely those occasioned by failures of the lower schools but that they relate to cultural differences. For example, in lower class families, procurement of food, clothing, and shelter is a matter of daily concern, and a tendency toward immediate gratification is often built in. On the other hand, where the necessities of life are not cause for daily concern, aspects of family life will allow for deferred gratification, and the norms for child rearing will include using formal education as a means of reaching for rewards to be obtained later. The idea of using the school as an avenue for potential advancement in the culture is alien to the people from the lower classes. To them, if school is to be used as an avenue of advancement in any realm, it is toward higher-status employment. Yet their tendencies toward immediate gratification make it difficult for members of these groups to accept the regimen of years of study needed before one obtains certification. Morrison and Ferrante conclude:

> One perspective of the term "disadvantaged" then, is socialization into attitudes, values, and norms which serve to inhibit advancement into the occupational positions which would provide the material rewards desired. . . . We may therefore regard the term "disadvantaged" as synonymous with "culturally different." (4-5)

Because community colleges enroll so many "disadvantaged" and "culturally different" students, the establishment and operation of compensatory programs becomes freighted with overtones of racism. Reading tests are claimed to be culturally biased, and writing tests are said to discriminate unfairly against those whose native language is other than English. Olivas summarizes the issues well, concluding that while community colleges provide opportunities for minorities to enroll, they simultaneously perpetuate inequities.

As long as these colleges admit everyone but maintain certain admissions requirements for different programs, the controversy will continue. Selective admission to any program is as discriminatory as it is justifiable. Regardless of the yardstick applied, the people who are shut out of the programs in which they want to enroll have been discriminated against. Yet with accrediting agencies, state licensing boards, and senior institutions looking on, program directors feel justified in admitting only a select few, particularly if the field of endeavor for which the program prepares people can take only so many graduates or if college facilities allow for only so many matriculants.

Should the colleges restrict admissions to certain programs? The answer to that question relates to the question of whether colleges should teach a level of literacy sufficient to enable students to function within the programs. If some applicants cannot gain admission to a program because their level of literacy is lower than a cutting score, the issue is resolved for them. But if such applicants are admitted to the program, then the program operators must accept responsibility for teaching these students the skills required to succeed. The pattern of allowing all to enter and using the program itself to screen out the unworthy should be abandoned: first, because one cannot at the same time teach and judge; second, because it is too expensive in terms of concern for people to allow sizable numbers to enroll with the expectation that many of them will not complete the course of study.

The pressures for selective admission to various programs have grown in recent years. In the 1950s most colleges screened students into remedial programs if the students' high school grades or entrance test scores suggested they might not be able to succeed in the transfer programs. In the 1960s the pressure to allow anyone to enter a transfer program grew because students demanded access and educators chose to give them the right to fail. The unconscionably high failure rates led to the pendulum swinging back in the 1970s with many institutions building compensatory programs and screening students into them.

The community colleges are not alone; secondary schools in many states have begun competency testing for graduation and are withholding diplomas from those who are, in their terms, functionally illiterate. And many state agencies are no longer willing to fund students who do not make satisfactory progress toward a degree. Accordingly, community colleges are being pushed to give entrance tests and to place students in only those programs for which they are functionally literate.

It is quite possible to teach functional literacy in regular transfer and developmental programs. Most students can succeed if they are provided with tutorial assistance, access to a learning laboratory, special counseling, peer group assistance, and a variety of other aids. The question is how much effort the colleges are willing to put into the extra treatment required by students who enter programs with requirements beyond their current abilities. Given a choice between an admissions screen to keep students out of the programs and the allocation of sizable funds to ensure student success if they are admitted, many institutional managers who are faced with static budgets opt to keep the less well prepared students out of the transfer courses by placing them in remedial courses or segregated compensatory education programs.

Denying students admission to programs of their choice is difficult to justify. It follows from the open-door philosophy of the community college that these students should not be denied. The community colleges have succeeded in opening access to all; if that access is limited to a compensatory program that offers primarily the same type of basic education that failed a student in the lower schools, then that student has been denied access to higher learning. The fact that students who are denied access to the transfer programs are typically denied exposure to humanistic and scientific thought is particularly distressing. Since the colleges cannot afford to operate separate programs, they must teach literacy in all their transfer and occupational courses.

Teaching basic skills to people who failed to learn them in the lower schools is difficult and expensive. Questions of impact on college staff and image pale before the issue of cost. No form of teaching is easier, hence cheaper, than the course for self-directed learners; the teacher-student ratio is limited only by the size of the lecture hall. Nothing—not even education in the higher technologies— is more expensive than the varied media and close monitoring demanded by slow learners. Many college leaders fear publicizing the extent of their compensatory education programs lest their funding be threatened by legislators and members of the public who raise embarrassing questions about paying several times over for the education that was supposed to be provided in the lower schools.

The question of the public's willingness to pay repeatedly for the schools to teach literacy is one of public policy; it cannot be answered by school practitioners alone. It rests on the state of the economy, the power groups in state legislatures, the types of federal funding available, the agency heads in state capitals and federal bureaus—in short, it is beyond the practitioners' control. And no one can predict with assurance how those forces will affect compensatory education in the community colleges.

Those who would impose standards for programs at any level face difficulties stemming from lack of consensus on institutional purpose, antagonism to the idea of group norms, and, in the case of the secondary schools and community colleges, the inability to impose entrance requirements. Selective screening into transfer programs could not be maintained in an earlier era, but it is being tried again because it is easier to screen students out *en bloc* than it is to establish the criteria for functional literacy course by course. Yet unless those criteria are defined, selective admissions will again be unsuccessful. Granted that it takes a special effort to bring students to the point at which they can succeed in the courses and programs of their choice, community colleges must find the funds and the ways to do so lest they be justifiably accused of failing to fulfill their mission.

Since the necessary funds to support all students through the courses of their choice are not likely to be forthcoming, some compromises will have to be made. But these must not take the form of segregated remedial programs; many more balanced measures are available. Miami-Dade Community College, for example, is operating a massive general education, student-advisement system for its thirty-nine thousand students, described by McCabe and by McCabe and Lukenbill. Every matriculant is tested at entry for reading, writing, and mathematical skills and screened into support courses, the general education core, and/or specialized courses. A computerized academic-alert system monitors student progress by checking for course attendance and completions and sends individualized mid-term progress reports to each student. An Advisement and Graduation Information System provides additional data matching all students with their degree aspirations and informing them of their progress. And a Standards of Academic Progress model warns students if they are failing to make satisfactory progress toward completing a program and places them on suspension if they do not reduce the load and take advantage of the special interventions available to them.

In short, Miami-Dade has done more than merely mount a compensatory education program in which deficient students are placed until they are ready to enter the regular courses. It has restructured its entire curriculum by building truly integrated general education courses and requiring them for all students and by maintaining a computerized advisement system that keeps its students apprized of their progress toward completing a program. And all is done within the framework of directives and standards so that the students know exactly what they must do. These sets of institutional aids and expectations may be as close as a college can come to showing that it cares about students, and that concern alone is likely to have some effect on the development of literacy among them.

Some notable efforts at mainstreaming (i.e., allowing students of lower ability to take regular college classes even while they are being assisted supplementally) have also been made. Many of these efforts involve the use of learning laboratories. For example, in the Developmental Studies Program at Penn Valley Community College (Missouri), the Learning Skills Laboratory (LSL) was used as an extension of the math and English classroom, as Ford showed. Students could complete LSL instructional activities, as prescribed by faculty, before taking other courses of their choice or concurrently with those courses. And Sacramento City College (California) initiated a higher education learning package (HELP) to promote the success and retention of students with basic skill deficiencies while mainstreaming them into regular courses. Students who were reading at a sixth-grade level worked with instructors and tutors in small groups and on one-to-one bases, and their progress was measured in terms of established competency criteria (Bohr and Bray).

Several studies done by the City Colleges of Chicago revealed that tracking students into remedial courses had not produced desirable outcomes: student achievement in remedial courses did not result in improved performance in regular college courses; student retention was very low; and enrollment in remedial courses had a highly adverse effect on the student's self-concept (Chausow). The college planners attempted instead to introduce concepts of mastery learning into the regular college courses. Results indicate that in classes using the mastery learning concept, student achievement and retention are not only superior to those attained in remedial program efforts but generally higher than achievement and retention of students in the regular programs and courses taught in nonmastery fashion. Well-planned supportive materials and services can compensate for poor college preparation, and cooperative staff and faculty efforts in improving the learning process can result in more successful college experiences for more college students. Thus remediation does not have to come in the form of segregated remedial courses.

Community colleges have few options. Dropping, failing, or otherwise sending the poorly prepared students away is not one of them. The pool of well-qualified, literate students is too small and the competition too great to allow that luxury. And segregating the students in compensatory programs seems desirable only to the faculty who want classes of self-learners and to the universities that want community colleges to screen out the unworthy.

One available option involves defining exactly the competencies required to enter and succeed in each "academic" course. "College-level," "program proficiency," and "academic standards" are not sufficiently precise. There is too much variation between courses in the same program, indeed between sections of the same course, for these criteria to hold. Standards are too often relative instead of absolute. Screening tests can be employed at the point of entry to each class, but only if precise exit criteria (i.e., specific measurable objectives) are set. This practice would pave the way for faculty accountability.

A second option is to allow all students to enroll in any course but to limit the number of courses that poorly prepared students can take in any term and mandate that those students take advantage of the available support services. Thus such students might take only one course at a time and participate in tutorial and learning laboratory sessions on the basis of three hours for each credit hour attempted. But this pattern must be obligatory; few students use the support services of their own volition (see Friedlander).

The third option is for the colleges to abandon the pretext that they offer freshman and sophomore-level studies. They could enroll high school dropouts, adult basic education students, job seekers, and job upgraders, offering them the services they need outside the "credit hour" structure.

All three options are now in play to some extent. The colleges that are involved in mastery learning and other techniques that rely on precisely specified measures of student progress have built their programs on absolute standards. Those that monitor student progress and insist that students participate in auxiliary instructional efforts have moved toward building the kinds of collegewide instructional effort that are needed to teach poorly prepared students. And those that have erected separate institutes that concentrate exclusively on adult basic education and career-related studies have abandoned collegiate studies de facto. The Urban Skills Institute operated by the City Colleges of Chicago since 1974 makes no pretense of mixing collegiate studies with its basic literacy and career education objectives. There, the idea of "credit hour" is not applied to the time students spend in their studies, nor is it used as a measure of faculty workload. Getting the students' skill level to the point where they can find an entry-level job is the Institute's mission. As Richardson and Leslie noted, the colleges will have to decide whether this type of institute will be tolerated within the framework of the traditional community college.

One more option might be for the colleges to reconcile their relations with the secondary schools from which they broke away. Education at any level depends on proper preparation of the students. The decline in the secondary schools during the 1970s was one of the most notable events of the decade in education. Much of the blame for it can be placed at the colleges' doors. The dearth of communication between college and secondary school staff members, the lack of articulation in curriculum, the failure to share teaching materials except on the basis of a random encounter are all part of the problem. Concerns for social equity replaced a prior concern for admissions standards. And in their haste to expand access, the colleges neglected to assist secondary schools in preparing the people who would be coming to them. In many cases they failed even to recommend the secondary school courses that the students should take.

Whether community colleges pick up the seventeen-year-olds who have left high school early or whether they serve as a bridge between schooling and work for older students, teaching literacy fits within their mission of connecting people with opportunities. They will be involved in compensatory education in one form or another; their career education efforts have already enrolled half of their students. Linking the two may be a natural next step. And if the advocates of the college transfer function want to protect their area of concern, they will have to be more precise about defining the competencies their students need and more vigorous in ensuring that the students use the support services.

Works Cited

American Association of Community and Junior Colleges. *Directory*. Washington, D.C.: AACJC, 1977.

Appel, Victor H., et al. *Impact of Administrative Climate, Instruction, and Counseling on Control Expectancy, Anxiety and Completion Rate of Post-Secondary Educationally Disadvantaged and Minority Vocational/Technical Students. Final Report*. Austin: Texas University, Dept. of Educational Administration, 1977. ED 149 801.

ASCCC Report for Conference on Academic Standards. (MINCO), 1977.

Bishop, Arthur, ed. *The Concern for Writing*. Princeton: Educational Testing Service, 1978.

Bohr, Dorothy H., and Dorothy Bray. *HELP: A Pilot Program for Community College High-Risk Students*. 1979. ED 168 635.

Brawer, Florence B., and Jack Friedlander. *Science and Social Science in the Two-Year College*. Center for the Study of Community Colleges and ERIC Clearinghouse for Junior Colleges, Topical Paper No. 69. July 1979. ED 172 854.

Center for the Study of Community Colleges. *The Humanities in Two-Year Colleges. Trends in Curriculum*. Los Angeles: Center for the Study of Community Colleges and ERIC Clearinghouse for Junior Colleges, 1978.

Chausow, Hymen M. *Remedial Education: A Position Paper*. 1979. ED 170 013.

Ciardi, John. "Give Us This Day Our Daily Surrealism." *Saturday Review*, 12 June 1971, 48.

Clark, Burton R. "The 'Cooling-Out' Function in Higher Education." *American Journal of Sociology* 65(1960):569-76.

Cohen, Arthur M. "Assessing College Students' Ability to Write Compositions." *Research in the Teaching of English* 7(1973):356-71.

———, and Florence B. Brawer. *The Two-Year College Instructor Today*. New York: Praeger, 1977.

———. *The American Community College: An Interpretative Analysis*. San Francisco: Jossey-Bass, 1982.

Conti, Gary J., et al. *New Start. General Education (GED), Job Skills, + Job Placement: A Summary*. 1978. ED 169 983.

Copperman, Paul. *The Literacy Hoax: The Decline of Reading, Writing, and Learning in the Public Schools and What We Can Do about It*. New York: Morrow, 1978.

Cross, K. Patricia. *Toward the Future in Community College Education*. Paper presented at the Conference on Education in the Community College for the Non-Traditional Student, Philadelphia, 31 March 1978. ED 168 626. 1978. ED 159 674.

Ford, Marge L. "Penn Valley Community College Learning Skills Laboratory: A Resource Center for Developmental Education." *Developmental Education in Higher Education. Advanced Institutional Development Program (AIDP) Two-year College Consortium*. 1976. ED 134 272.

Friedlander, Jack. "Should Remediation be Mandatory?" *Community College Review* 9(Spring 1982):51-57.

Howard, James H. *Adult Basic Education Development Center in the Newark Model Cities Area, for the Period Ending December 1, 1971, Final Report*. Newark, N.J.: Essex County Coll., April 1976. ED 133 027.

Johnson, Charles N., et al. *Basic Studies: A Description and Progress Report*. Sept. 1970. ED 044 104.

Ladd, Everett Carll, and Seymour Martin Lipset. *Professors, Unions, and American Higher Education*. Berkeley, Calif.: Carnegie Commission on Higher Education, 1973.

Lyons, Gene. "The Higher Illiteracy." *Harper's*, Sept. 1976, 33-40.

McCabe, Robert H. "Now Is the Time to Reform: The American Community College." *Community and Junior College Journal* 51.8(May 1981):6-10.

———, and Jeffrey D. Lukenbill. *General Education and a Changing Society. General Education Program, Basic Skills Requirements, Standards of Academic Progress at Miami-Dade Community College*. Miami: Miami-Dade Community Coll. 1978. ED 158 812.

Morrison, James L., and Reynolds Ferrante. *Compensatory Education in Two-Year Colleges*. Report No. 21. 1973. ED 078 818.

Olivas, M. A. *The Dilemma of Access: Minorities in Two-Year Colleges*. Washington, D.C.: Howard Univ. Press, 1979.

[Parkman, Francis.] "The Tale of the 'Ripe Scholar.' " *Nation* 9(1869):558-60.

Richardson, Richard C., and L. L. Leslie. *The Impossible Dream? Financing Community College's Evolving Mission*. Washington, D.C.: American Association of Community and Junior Colleges; Los Angeles: ERIC Clearinghouse for Junior Colleges, 1980.

Romoser, Richard C. *Results of Second Assessment Study of Developmental Education Programs in Ohio*. 1978. ED 157 587.

Smith, Michael F. *A Model for Student Development in the Satellite Campus Setting*. 1979. ED 174 293.

Literacy, the Law,
and the Reluctant Learner

Janet K. Carsetti

Survival in a literate society is the goal of Project READ, a national literacy program for troubled youth. Since its inception in 1976, Project READ has worked with more than forty thousand troubled youth from four hundred institutions, alternative schools, and community-based programs in fifty states and the District of Columbia. Close to one thousand teachers and youth workers have participated in teacher-training workshops and more than one quarter of a million paperback books have been distributed to young people across the nation.

The extensive data collected by the project suggest that troubled youth, while clearly possessing the ability to read, will not read:

- until they are provided with highly motivating books,
- until they are taught through motivational techniques,
- until they are given time during the school day to practice reading from self-selected material.

This paper will present data that support these conclusions and explain techniques that have been used successfully to motivate reluctant readers.

In order to survive in a literate society, people need the skills of literacy—skills that allow one to complete a job application, use a telephone book, read newspapers, leases, road signs, labels on prescription medicine, directions on food packages, and more. Literacy is more than the mastery of basic reading and writing skills, however. It also incorporates sensitivity, respect for other people, the confidence to express oneself, self-discipline, and self-appreciation—qualities as basic to independence and productivity in this society as reading and writing. It is not a coincidence that, in addition to being functionally illiterate, young people "in trouble" also—almost characteristically—lack these qualities.

On any given day in 1977 in the United States, forty-six thousand children and youth were imprisoned for acts ranging from misbehavior to murder. As reported by the Law Enforcement Assistance Administration, the average age of all children in custody during 1977 was fifteen years and three months. (This figure does not reflect the number of youth who were referred to private institutions or community-based programs.) In 1978, young people under eighteen years of age accounted for twenty-three percent of all arrests. Boys were arrested three times more frequently than girls, and they were arrested primarily for crimes against property—larceny-theft, burglary, and vandalism. After property crimes, vagrancy and drug abuse were the most frequent causes of arrest for boys. Girls were most commonly arrested for larceny-theft, violation of liquor laws, drug abuse, and running away. Young people under eighteen years old accounted for twenty-one percent of all arrests for violent crimes (murder, rape, robbery, and aggravated assault), and those fifteen years of age and younger accounted for six percent of total arrests for such crimes (Webster).

In 1975, 1,406,077 children and youth were brought before juvenile courts nationwide. Of those, 355,605 were referred by their parents or schools for committing status offenses or "children's crimes," acts for which adults cannot be arrested or held accountable (e.g., "acting out," incorrigibility, promiscuity, and running away) ("Delinquency 1975").

As many as two million young people ran away from home in 1978. Forty-two thousand of them were served by federally supported runaway programs. Reasons for running away vary from family conflict to abuse and neglect. The *National Statistical Survey on Runaways* pointed out that thirty to forty percent of all reported child-abuse cases involved adolescents aged ten to eighteen. Each year, thirty thousand young women under fifteen and another million between fifteen and nineteen become pregnant. Mothers who become pregnant as teenagers are more likely to support their families through public assistance programs and are less likely to find work or receive job preparation or training, a study by the Alan Guttmacher Institute found.

Young people who have passed through the juvenile justice system face employment barriers largely because they have difficulties getting the training and education needed to obtain a job. Although there are no available statistics that suggest a correlation between delinquency and youth unemployment, the Employment and Training Administration records that the unemployment rate for all youth is three to four times greater than for adults.

An estimated two million children do not attend school each year. Poor children with no money to pay for books, fees, and supplies and children with language barriers are those who are least likely to go to school, according to the report *Children out of School in America*. At least one million children and youth are suspended from schools each year for reasons ranging from fighting or having a "bad attitude" to being pregnant or disabled. Almost all school suspensions result from nondangerous offenses. The study *School Suspensions, Are They Helping Children?* reported that truancy accounts for nearly twenty-five percent of all school suspensions nationwide. In New York City in 1976, noted *The City and Its Children*, sixty-three percent of major youthful offenses occurred during school hours.

Impressions, observations, and measurements from the staff at Project READ and participating teachers suggest that these young people have so much trouble because they have been labeled as incorrigible, unmotivated, and beyond control by the courts, the schools, and their families. After repeated exposure to such labels, they begin to live up to them by acting out negative behavior. The prophecy is fulfilled, not only behaviorally but academically, and they fall farther and farther behind in their ability to function in a literate society.

Project READ has tested well over ten thousand youthful offenders, and the results indicate that these young people have limited communication skills. The tested mental ability of these young people is at least three years below their estimated grade level. Similarly, their reading ability is at least three years below their potential and six to seven years below their grade level. When forced to compete with peers of the same age outside the juvenile justice system, they are almost doomed to failure in oral communication and reading and writing activities. Similar results were found in Broder, Peters, and Zimmerman's Creighton University study of youthful offenders with learning disabilities. According to that study, students with learning disabilities in juvenile facilities and students with the same disabilities in public schools differed markedly in their ability to communicate.

One key element in reaching reluctant readers is motivating them, and Project READ's efforts have therefore been directed toward two areas:

- training teachers who work with troubled youth to use motivational techniques;
- distributing free, high-interest paperback books to students in alternative school programs.

Motivational Activities for Reluctant Learners

Many reluctant learners have the ability to learn but choose not to learn. Of the ten thousand young people tested by Project READ, over ninety-nine percent had the ability to read better than their test scores indicated. Of that ninety-nine percent, students were reading anywhere from one to ten years below their estimated potential. While there may be many explanations for the gap between what can be read and what is being read, the primary reason for that gap involves lack of motivation. Until these young people are faced with tasks requiring specific reading skills, such as locating a number in a telephone directory or completing an application, they are often unaware of their need to read.

Focusing on realistic situations that require reading is an essential element in motivating reluctant learners. Such real life materials as telephone books, directions on packages and clothing, road and street signs, and the like have been found to appeal to and motivate such learners.

Since many students in alternative schools are on the verge of dropping out, their learning experiences must be both highly motivating and based on short-term, tangible goals. Teachers in alternative schools experience rapid student turnover with some students remaining for as few as thirty days. Therefore, the techniques and activities designed for these students

- must be tailored to the students' interests,
- must allow for multiple stages of skill development so that students can select activities with which they feel comfortable,
- must be relevant to students' needs and interests.

The pages that follow describe the techniques and activities found most successful in motivating reluctant learners.

Functional Learning Packets

While there is probably no limit to the variety of learning activities that can be developed in packet form, the material used should be as closely related to real-life functions as possible. For example, students about to seek employment are motivated by job application packets. Every subject taught in the school curriculum can be enhanced with learning packets. Cosmetology teachers have found that they can effectively reinforce a curriculum that leads to state licensing by making packets from hair-dye packages, permanent kits, color charts, and beauticians' magazines. Similarly, carpentry teachers have made packets using catalogs of tools, wood, and paints.

Since interest is a primary factor in motivating reluctant readers, teachers should construct packets around sports, music, carpentry, and other fields in which students are already interested. Packets should be as attractive as possible to appeal to students—incorporating, for instance, colorful pictures from magazines. In addition to being attractive, packets should be manageable. The contents should not overwhelm the students, and the directions should be clear and precise and make the purpose of the packet obvious. Directions should tell the students how to respond—by writing their answer, telling a friend, completing a form, comparing prices, locating a city, and so on—and should be no more difficult to read than the material in the packet.

There should be at least two levels of processing required to complete the activities in each packet. For example, writing is usually more difficult than telling, and factual questions are often easier than inferential questions. While there is no set number of activities for each packet, one good problem-solving activity will probably take as long as or longer than three factual questions.

Music as a Motivational Technique

Music has provided countless hours of listening pleasure for nearly all young people, and it is valued especially by troubled youth. In many cases, music—through portable radios, tape players, and phonographs—is the only form of entertainment for these young people.

Since many young people served by Project READ are deficient in communication skills, music activities are used both to motivate and to develop and reinforce listening, reading, and writing skills. Essential to the development of music activities is the students' role in selecting the music to be used, and student decision making can be a tremendous asset to learning. A listening corner may be set up in the classroom with a cassette tape recorder, radio, and a phonograph. It is extremely important that students be encouraged to select songs they know and like. While the teacher may not understand the words, students are likely to be able to recite them verbatim, and listening activities based on such songs are more manageable than those involving unfamiliar songs.

As teachers listen carefully to the words of a song, they will discover patterns. Some songs have a series of rhyming words or many words that begin with the same sound. Some songs lend themselves to categorizing by using words related to food, love, places, people, cities, feelings, colors, or seasons. Teachers may design a music activity to reinforce phoneme-grapheme relationships, syllabication principles, and factual and interpretive listening comprehension skills. The actual activity may be produced in the form of a game or as an activity sheet.

Many songs employ the use of rhymes, and listening for words that sound alike is a good classroom activity. Students who have difficulty in recognizing rhyming patterns may find the task of identifying them easier if teachers provide the word endings in writing. Students can also be prepared for listening activities if song lyrics are written down following the principles of cloze procedure used in reading instruction. The lyrics are written with key words omitted; students then listen for the missing words and complete the sentences.

After listening to a song, students may be engaged in matching activities involving synonyms and antonyms or lists of words and definitions. Discussion of themes found in songs may lead to creative writing, perhaps initiated by asking students to adapt the lyrics to their personal experiences and interests.

Paperback Books and Nonstop Reading

Daniel Fader's program at the Maxey Boys Training School in Michigan in the 1960s demonstrated that, given the opportunity to select their own reading material, young people gained confidence in their ability to read while also improving their reading skills. Based on the success of Fader's program, Project READ began its nationwide paperback book program in 1976. At that time, Project READ began to distribute free paperback books in the juvenile justice system to give thousands of young people the opportunity to practice during the school day the skill in which they were most deficient—reading. The paperback books provide hours of pleasure and stimulate the intellectual and emotional interests of these young people.

To provide time during the school day to practice reading, all participating schools are asked to introduce a nonstop reading period. For a minimum of twenty minutes each day, everyone in the school reads: teachers, students, other school personnel, and any visitors who happen to be present. The philosophy of nonstop reading is based on three principles: students are given a choice of reading what they want to read; they may read at their own pace; no questions are asked of them regarding their choice of reading material or their understanding of what they read. Nonstop reading is designed for practice and pleasure. The various skills related to reading may be taught, but not during nonstop reading periods. Unless students are given free reading time, they associate reading with book reports, quizzes, and other activities they probably dislike.

Before their first nonstop reading period, students have ample time to select any two paperback books of their choice from the shipment sent to their school. When they are ready for a third book they trade in one of the first two. Thus books flow freely among students and in and out of the classrooms. The self-selection process and book ownership encourage even the most reluctant students to read. Students realize that each day everything stops for reading to take place, and they naturally conclude that reading must be important.

To determine which books to distribute, the staff of Project READ compiled a list of 1,200 popular titles. In 1978, this bibliography was reduced to 800 titles containing students' favorites from past years. These lists are based on a simple principle: interest is more important than reading level.

The latest bibliography of some 400 titles is divided into the following interest categories: (1) movies, tv, and theater; (2) science fiction, mysteries, and the supernatural; (3) biographies, people, and cultures; (4) contemporary fiction; (5) contemporary fact (reference, sports, sex, health and personal growth, careers, and puzzles and games). Some of the favorite titles selected by the students were: *Grease, The Hobbit, Jaws, Sarah T., Dressed to Kill, Dawn,* and *The Amityville Horror* from the movie, tv and theater category. From contemporary fact, the following titles were chosen: *Body Building, Everything You Always Wanted to Know about Sex, Our Bodies, Ourselves, UFO, Games Alcoholics Play.* Other top choices were the *Mad Comics* series, *I Can Stop Anytime I Want, 50 Great Horror Stories, The Rights of Young People, Black Is Beautiful,* and *Interview with the Vampire.*

A look at the favorite titles suggests that among these students there is a wide range of reading ability (possibly 10-12 years); an obvious desire to learn; a need to learn more about themselves through others like themselves; and a preference for "known" or popular themes found in movies and tv shows.

A random sample of junior high school students in the District of Columbia public schools participating in Project READ's paperback book program were interviewed by the staff at Project READ. The sample included students who read at, above, or below their average grade level as measured by the Gates-MacGinitie Reading Survey.

When asked whether or not they were reading a book not assigned to them, one hundred percent of the students in the experimental group said "yes," compared to thirty percent of the students in the comparison group. Similarly, students in the experimental group read an average of eight books over the previous six months, while students in the comparison group read an average of fewer than two books during the same time period. It is interesting to note that the same group of students in the experimental group read four times the number of books during the school year than they did during their previous school year.

When asked what they liked best about nonstop reading, students in the experimental group gave the following reasons.

- It gives you time to read.
- No one bothers you.
- The books tell us about our lives.
- It's the only chance we get to read.
- It shows us different kinds of books.
- It helps us understand more.
- It lets us work at our own pace.
- It increases vocabulary.

These statements clearly reflect positive attitudes about reading. Furthermore, when asked what they would like changed about nonstop reading, these students suggested making the time period longer and giving them more than two books each.

Having described some of the motivational techniques used successfully by Project READ, I will now present some of the statistics that depict the gains made by the young people who participated in the program.

Among the institutions served by Project READ, one hundred alternative schools and community-based programs participated from June 1978 through June 1980. All of them provided education on the premises, had a six-month average length of stay, had fewer than three hundred students, and did not have lock-up facilities. These schools and programs, located in thirty-six states and the District of Columbia, serve young people referred to them by the courts, state or local government agencies, public schools, parents, and self-referral. Close to six thousand young people (61% males and 39% females) were served by these programs, and eighty percent of the schools were coeducational. The smallest school population served by Project READ was 3; the largest 275; the average number of students was 61. The student-teacher ratio was eleven to one, significantly lower than that found in public schools, as it well should be, given the diverse and troubled backgrounds of the students. Students remained in the schools and programs eleven months on the average; the range of attendance was from thirty days to three years. About half of the schools were open year-round; the others operated during the regular nine-month school year.

Just over half of these schools had libraries but only a quarter employed librarians. The average number of books per school was 806, about evenly divided between hardback and paperback. Some schools indicated that the only books available were those given to them by Project READ. The range of books per student was from one to 250. A typical school reported having about twenty-eight books per student. Seven of the one hundred schools reported that no magazines were available for student use. Fifty-one schools subscribed to magazines; twenty-one used only donated magazines; and fourteen schools had a combination of subscriptions and donations. Sixty-six subscribed to newspapers, but fifteen relied on donated papers, and twelve did not have newspapers at all.

Given the limited supply of books, magazines, and newspapers available to the young people in these schools, it is not surprising to learn that their attitude toward reading is poor and that their reading levels are far below their potential.

A total of 3,663 young people were pretested by their teachers during the fall of 1978. Of those pretested, sixty-four percent were males and thirty-six percent were females. Their average chronological age was sixteen years. The chronological age for males was fifteen years, ten months (15-10) and the chronological age for females was 16-1. The average mental age was thirteen years, one month (13-1), equivalent to the eighth grade; in other words, the average student tested had the potential to perform in language-related skills at the eighth-grade level. The average mental age for males was 13-2; the average mental age for females was 12-10. The average reading grade level was fifth grade, eighth month (5-8); the mean reading-grade-level score for males was 5-5 and for females 6-5. While the average mental-ability age-equivalent for females was lower than the mean for males, the mean reading grade level for females was one year higher.

Nineteen percent of the total group scored below the fourth-grade level on a reading comprehension test. The consonant, blends, and rhyming sections of the Botel Phonics Test yielded the following results:

Consonants. Out of a possible 18 correct, the total group mean was 16. The male mean was 16 and the female mean was 17.

Consonant Blends. Out of a possible 19 correct, the total group mean was 10; the male mean 10 and the female mean 11.

Rhyming Words. Of a possible 8 correct, the overall mean was 6; the male mean was 6 and the female mean was 7.

On the Piers-Harris Self-Concept Scale, an average score falls between 46 and 60. Any score below 46 indicates a poor or unhealthy self-concept. The total group mean was 52 (male mean = 52; female mean = 50). These data show that, in general, students' self-concepts were acceptable or healthy.

In response to one of the Piers-Harris statements, "I am a good reader," the following responses were obtained:

Total Group	62% yes; 38% no
Males	58% yes; 42% no
Females	70% yes; 30% no

When comparing the responses of males and females to this statement, one should recall that the average reading score for females was higher than the average score for males.

Gains

From the original group of 3,663 Project READ participants, 1,997 remained in the program for the suggested ten-week period. Hence the pre- and post-test data are for the sample of 1,997 young people. The attrition from 3,663 to 1,997 is a result of the normal high turnover of students enrolled in alternative schools and community-based programs. While the average time between pre- and post-testing was five months, some students were post-tested in ten weeks, while others were not post-tested for nine months. The results of post-testing (with alternate forms of the same instrument used in pretesting) for the sample of 1,997 are shown in the accompanying table. To appreciate the gains made in reading by students from pre- to post-testing, it is necessary to look at the history of their performance in reading. On the average, Project READ participants should be at the tenth-grade level. Reading grade equivalents at the time of pretesting, however, were at the sixth-grade level since these students had fallen behind the normal rate of growth in reading development.

The duration of time spent in Project READ activities covered an average of five months, and a reading gain of four months was realized. This gain suggests that Project READ was instrumental in producing changes in reading level commensurate with the actual amount of time passed. It does not suggest, however, that an equivalent rate of growth could be sustained over longer periods of time.

	PRE-TEST RESULTS			POST-TEST RESULTS		
	Total Group	Males	Females	Total Group	Males	Females
Number	1,997	1,340 (67%)	657 (33%)	1,997	1,340 (67%)	657 (33%)
Average Chronological Age	15-5	15-3	15-6	15-10	15-9	16-2
Average Mental Age	13-2	12-11	13-8	13-6	13-3	14-0
Reading Comprehension Grade Level	6-1	5-7	7-0	6-5	6-1	7-4
Self Concept	52.86	52.72	53.19	55.43	55.58	55.07
"I am a good reader" YES	61%	57%	70%	67%	62%	79%
NO	39%	43%	30%	33%	38%	21%

Because many variables were involved between pre- and post-testing, it is necessary to separate those variables to determine which techniques made the most difference.

Teaching Techniques That Make the Greatest Difference

Project READ participants used a number of techniques to motivate reluctant readers. Since most students made gains in reading from pre- to post-testing, it is essential to look at those schools that produced the greatest gains for their students. The range of reading gains and losses for the various schools is quite disparate. The average school showed a gain of four months in reading level. The range of reading gains and losses varied from an increase of thirty months to a decrease of sixteen months. To analyze the effectiveness of the components of Project READ in changing reading behavior, we divided the schools into four groups according to the standard deviation of reading gains:

Group 1: (n = 14) Those schools that showed reading gain scores more than one standard deviation above the mean.

Group 2: (n = 31) Those schools that showed reading gain scores between the mean and one standard deviation above the mean.

Group 3: (n = 31) Those schools that showed reading gain scores between the mean and one standard deviation below the mean.

Group 4: (n = 11) Those schools that showed reading gain scores more than one standard deviation below the mean.

The four groups of schools were then compared according to their use of nonstop reading, functional reading packets, music activities, and creative writing activities.

There were no statistically significant differences between schools using functional reading packets, music activities, and creative writing activities and schools that did not employ any or all of these techniques. The number of students and teachers participating in nonstop reading does not have an effect on reading change. One aspect of nonstop reading, however, made a highly significant difference: the amount of time spent reading.

The amount of time spent in nonstop reading was significantly related to gains in reading comprehension scores. The table below shows the relation between reading gains and the average amount of time spent in nonstop reading for each of the four groups of schools.

Succinctly stated, ten minutes of nonstop reading made the difference in separating the best from the worst, and the difference between reading gains is twenty-six months. Project READ asked all participating schools to read for a minimum of twenty minutes each day, but there was a great range in the amount of time actually devoted to it. Those schools that chose to spend more than

GROUPS OF SCHOOLS

	1	2	3	4
Mean Group Reading Gain in Months	18	8	1	−8
Nonstop Reading Time in Minutes	29	24	23	19

Experimental			Comparison		
7th Grade	Pre	Post	7th Grade	Pre	Post
Vocabulary	4.9	5.4	Vocabulary	5.5	6.2
Comprehension	4.6	5.8	Comprehension	5.3	5.3
Total G.E.	4.7	5.5	Total G.E.	5.4	5.7
8th Grade	Pre	Post	8th Grade	Pre	Post
Vocabulary	6.2	6.7	Vocabulary	5.4	6.1
Comprehension	5.9	7.0	Comprehension	5.5	5.8
Total G.E.	6.1	6.8	Total G.E.	5.4	5.9
9th Grade	Pre	Post	9th Grade	Pre	Post
Vocabulary	6.5	7.1	Vocabulary	5.7	6.2
Comprehension	6.8	7.3	Comprehension	6.0	6.6
Total G.E.	6.6	7.2	Total G.E.	5.8	6.3

twenty minutes reaped the benefits. As a result of these findings, Project READ now advocates a minimum of thirty minutes each day in nonstop reading.

Four public junior high schools in the District of Columbia provided a comparison group. A total of 1,397 students were pretested on the Gates-MacGinitie Reading Survey. The overall average reading level for students in the experimental group was 5-4, while the level for students in the comparison group was 5-2. Students and teachers were also administered a ten-point semantic differential to record their feelings about "reading" and "paperback books." At the time of this writing these data have not been analyzed.

For a six-month period between November and May, students in the experimental group spent thirty minutes a day in nonstop reading. The gains made from pre- to post-testing were significant at the .001 level. The following table indicates those gains.

It is apparent that the overall significant difference in pre- and post-test gains was greatly influenced by the comprehension scores of seventh and eighth graders. Interestingly, these same students responded to an interview question—"What could you do to help a friend read?"—by citing "comprehension type" clues. The comparison group conversely cited "decoding type" clues. Perhaps the need to understand what they were reading during their daily nonstop reading period forced them to apply a system for unlocking meaning.

Preliminary data from Project READ's 1980-81 populations suggest that an even greater number of young people with limited literacy skills are now being turned away from our public schools. In most large cities, at least half of the school age population does not attend school regularly. In New York City, those estimates are as high as seventy-five percent. With more young people on the street, the numbers of youth entering into the juvenile justice system daily are growing more rapidly than ever.

All students can be motivated to learn when they are presented with relevant, interesting tasks and are encouraged to make decisions about how difficult those tasks should be. Regardless of their methodology, all teachers must adopt a philosophy of acceptance: one that teaches to students' strengths, not weaknesses, and one that teaches responsibility to self as well as to others.

Skills necessary for survival in a literate society must be taught as early as nursery school and reinforced continuously through the twelve grades. Schools must provide a wealth of diversified reading material accessible to everyone, placed everywhere in the building and not just in the library. An adequate period of time must be put aside for reading for pleasure during each school day. Everyone should read during that time, and all adults should exemplify good role models for the students by reading with them and to them at every grade level. Above all, the concept of "reading" must become associated with positive feelings and pleasure where success is the goal for everyone.

If we take only one step to alleviate the problem of illiteracy, it should be to increase the availability of reading material. Why is it that even the poorest households have one or more television sets and no books, magazines, or newspapers? Books turn on our minds, while television turns off our senses.

When youngsters are poor and hungry, there are food programs to feed them. When they are disorderly, there are justice programs to incarcerate them. When they want to read, are there books to give them?

Works Cited

Broder, Paul, Geoffrey Peters, and Joel Zimmerman. "The Relationship between Self-Reported Juvenile Delinquency and Learning Disabilities: A Preliminary Look at the Data." Institute for Business, Law and Social Research, Creighton Univ., 1978. Prepared under Grant Numbers 76-NI-99-0133 and 76-JN-99-0022, NIJJDP, LEAA.

Children out of School in America. Cambridge, Mass.: Children's Defense Fund, 1974.

The City and Its Children. New York: Citizens Committee for the Children of New York, 1979.

"Delinquency 1975: United States Estimates of Cases Processed by Courts with Juvenile Jurisdiction." Pittsburgh: National Center for Juvenile Justice, 1979.

Eleven Million Teenagers: What Can Be Done about the Epidemic of Adolescent Pregnancies in the United States? Washington, D.C.: Alan Guttmacher Institute, 1978.

Employment and Training Administration, Office of Youth Programs. Unpublished unemployment statistics, 1979.

Law Enforcement Assistance Administration. *Children in Custody: Advance Report on the 1977 Census of Public Juvenile Facilities*. Washington, D.C.: National Criminal Justice Information and Statistics Service, 1979.

National Statistical Survey on Runaways. Washington, D.C.: Office of Youth Development, 1978.

School Suspensions, Are They Helping Children? Cambridge, Mass: Children's Defense Fund, 1975.

Webster, William H. *Crime in the United States: 1978*. Washington, D.C.: Federal Bureau of Investigation, 1979.

Literacy and Family

Daniel Fader

"Do you think that you're familiar with the sound of your own voice?"

"Well, sure. I know what I sound like."

"And do you think that you know what I sound like? I mean, suppose somebody told you that I had said something and they had taken it down and this was it. Would you believe them?"

I show my student two typewritten paragraphs from a piece of my own writing. He reads them slowly, a slightly puzzled frown narrowing his eyes. He looks up at me from beneath heavy eyebrows drawn together and makes a remarkable reply:

"Yes, and no. It sounds like you all right, but it's better than you talk. I mean, it's better than anybody talks, I think. What it really sounds like is you, the way you talk, but put through some kind of finishing machine so that all the pieces fit together better than when you said them."

He is right with both answers. I know what most writers know about their own successful writing: that it is composed of their auditory vision of their own available voice captured on the page, then revisited by their sense of their own best voice contemplated in tranquillity—a voice unhurried by immediacy and free of inadvertence. In that way I, as a writer, pass from captured vision to contemplative revision, from my voice in my ear to my voice on the page.

"Let me read the two paragraphs to you," I say to him, "and then tell me if you still think that they sound like me, only better." He watches me carefully as I speak. Later he will tell me that he thought he might have offended me, but he is willing to go on. I speak the two paragraphs in a conversational voice, enhancing the illusion of conversation as much as I can by scarcely glancing at the familiar words on the page. But now he does not look at me as I speak; instead, he looks at the rainwater flowing down the glass of the window. When I am finished, we sit briefly in silence.

"More yes," he says, still looking out the window, "but still some no. It's you all right, but it's not exactly you talking although it sounds more like you when you speak it. It's . . . it's just too good for talking."

Now we are ready, he and I, to go on to the more important part (for me) of our conversation. I remind him where we began—with his claim that he knows what he sounds like—and where we have come (to his assertion that my writing

236

sounds like me speaking, only better); then I give him back the following sentence from a paper he had given me two days earlier, and I ask him to read it aloud:

"The persistent economic woes that now plague the United States will not be vanquished, or even substantially curbed, until new currents of thought emerge within the federal government that will force it to commence with the difficult policies required to assuage our present problems."

He reads it to himself first. I can see the small movements of his lips as he practices his own words. He looks up at me, then launches himself into the sentence. The launching is not a success.

"Doesn't sound like me, does it?"

"Not much. Any ideas about why it doesn't?"

He has a few. We talk about the several voices he speaks with and the several other voices he writes with. He speaks of the rare letter he writes, the somewhat rarer successful paper, and the differences between them. One big difference, he observes wryly, is that no one complains about his letters. But even he complains about his papers:

"It's like I was somebody else when I write a paper. Even when I'm pretty sure about what I want to say, most of the time I don't feel as though I've found the right words to say it with."

"Do you often feel as though you're writing with somebody else's words? That the ones you've found don't belong to you?" I realize with dismay that I am trying to put thoughts in his mind and words in his mouth. And again, they will not be his own.

"Well, maybe. Something like that, I guess. What I really feel, it's somebody else writing and *he's* writing somebody else's words."

As best I could, I recorded the foregoing conversation as it recurred in my memory in the minutes immediately following the actual exchange. The young man who spoke with me was then a senior in economics and philosophy who was taking a professional writing seminar with me because he was only too well aware of the chasm between his good training and better mind on the one side and his poor writing on the other. He had prevailed upon me for a place in the class—in spite of the fact that it was advertised as a seminar for competent writers who wanted to improve their writing, with admission by portfolio and interview—because he was so obviously quick-minded, serious, and distressed about the quality of his writing. As he had every right to be, for the passage quoted from his paper was a fair example of his writing, and he was committed to preparing for a career in the scholarship of international law.

At a late evening meeting in Santa Barbara, California, in 1967, Carl Rogers, psychologist and author, challenged a group of consultants to the U.S. Office of Education to explain to him why one of the persons among them, generally unknown to the rest (who were generally well known to each other), had seemed to guide and sometimes to dominate the daylong discussion of an exceptionally divisive question. He answered his own query by observing that the person was, for him at least, so apparently in visual command of her own voice that her words had a closer and more illuminating connection to their meaning than he was accustomed to expect or experience from anyone's spoken voice. It was, he said, as though she were seeing what she said before she said it, adjusting her words to the needs of meaning and audience, then releasing them only when she was satisfied with their condition.

Later in a private conversation, he said that one of his rarest personal or professional experiences was to hear a voice both individual and exact. Had I noticed, he asked, that the woman spoke in sentences?

I have begun my paper with reference to these two events because they seem to me to be closely connected with each other although separated by almost fourteen years in time and because they are closely related to the subject of this volume. Each illustrates what I believe to be a different aspect of the same problem, the single most significant problem of literacy in the decade of the eighties. Call it the unfamiliar personal voice; call it the blunted tool of written language; call it the decline of eloquence; call it the discomfort of students and teachers alike (not to mention virtually all other occasional writers who are neither students nor teachers) in anticipation of the act of writing and in con-templation of the language it produces; call it the English Composition Board at the University of Michigan.

Call it what we will, it is as much the able students embarrassed by reading their own sentences aloud as it is the less able student embarrassed by their inability to write anything acceptable even to themselves. By whatever name, it is a control of language so rare in the most pervasively educated large nation in human history that a great psychologist should draw special attention to its presence. It is a control so rare that several hundred colleges and universities in North America have or will soon have agencies like the English Composition Board, whose purpose is to guarantee the competence in written English of students who have no problems of interference from a dialect or another language, have been in school almost all their lives since they were five years old, and have little reason to know that they already possess a reliable means and measure-ment of effective expression. That instrument is the voice in which they think they speak, the voice they know as their own although it is a voice heard by no one but themselves.

I believe that each writer possesses three voices, the third being a metaphor for the mute eloquence of written language chosen and adjusted to reflect ex-perience of words primarily seen but sometimes heard, then arranged according to the writer's selective rhetoric. This voice is the only one shaped by the requirements of permanence, for the other two are the voices of audible discourse and both are ephemeral although the second may be recreated at will.

The first voice is our instrument of speech—capable of enormous variety, subject to every influence of unpredictable demand. Left ephemeral, it is likely to succeed at all appropriate tasks; given the permanence of script, it suffers from inadvertence and indirection when not altered by translation.

If the first voice speaks for us, the second speaks to us: It is the bridge between language spoken and language written, the voice that enables the writer when the writer is experienced and comfortable enough to heed it. Unlike the first voice, it cannot be heard by anyone except the speaker, although it is no less real than the first voice, which it both precedes and improves upon. This is the voice that speakers know as their own.

This is also the voice often unrecognized by those who emphasize the differences between spoken and written discourse—those differences being indisputably many and significant—when in fact the likeness is very great between the language we hear ourselves speaking (not the language we actually speak) and the language we write. This likeness, I believe, is the key to competent writing. The person familiar with the voice in his or her ear is the person prepared to take his or her own best counsel as writer.

I have said that this second voice both precedes and improves upon the voice used for speaking. The paradox is only apparent, for it is this voice-in-place (accumulated by practice, shaped by intention) that refuses admission to infelicity even as it reshapes the spoken voice for its owner's ear. It is to this voice-in-place and not to the spoken voice that writers refer when they claim that what they have written "doesn't sound like me." It is to this voice-in-place that teachers of writing must send their students, and editors refer their clients, if students and clients alike are to possess a standard for competent writing more available and more reliable than the transitory judgment of others.

In a quarter-century of teaching reading and writing by any name—whether seventh-grade English or graduate Shakespeare—I have never had a student who didn't recognize the discrepancy, where such a discrepancy existed, between the quality of his or her spoken and written voices. That my philosophy and economics student should have been acute enough to identify the difference between my spoken and written voices is testimony to the strength of his intellect; that he should have written the sentence he read aloud—he who by his own testimony was in school for his seventeenth consecutive year, spoke only standard middle-class English, and had always been a good student—is testimony to the disorder of a social era whose language practices in both the nuclear and extended families are still largely unrecognized for their destructive influence upon the teaching of literacy in the schools.

Psychotherapists of almost every training and persuasion accept the thesis that children at five years of age are emotionally formed—excepting the influence of trauma—for the rest of their lives. Most long-term therapeutic approaches, and even many short-term ones, aim in part toward inducing or provoking a clearer understanding of those years; but if few therapists ignore the preschool years, they are disregarded by most teachers, school administrators, and writers or publishers of materials for the teaching of literacy in the early grades. If this disregard were only at their own peril, it would be destructive enough; unfortunately, it is even more perilous to children and to the society that depends upon them for its future.

What is the source of this peril? It arises from the heroically persistent

belief, property of home and school alike, that children coming to school for
the first time in 1981 are in all fundamental and important ways like children
who came to school in 1951. (Yes, of course the world is different and so are
children; but, after all, children are children and what is thirty years when
compared with the thousand generations of recent development that precede it?)
What is thirty years when we count them against the evolution of the human
form? Nothing, or little more. But what are those years when we measure them
in the scale of the child's growth within a family whose familial time, whether
shared between parent and child or among parents and children, has been dominated during the last three decades by a source of language and image other
than conversation, radio, or the printed page?

When measured in that scale and against that question, when compared to
any equal and preceding period of time, the past thirty years have seen a change
so profound in the lives of children that those children must now be regarded
by their teachers as a species different in kind from the species that inhabited
North American classrooms in the first half of the twentieth century. One dimension of that change is defined in the same tale told by two teachers unknown
to each other, separated by the length and width of a continent, yet teaching
similar children with like materials and making the same discovery.

One teaches in Belle Glade, Florida, a nurturing environment for alligators,
sugar cane, and the children of migrant laborers who work the cane; the other
teaches in Valdez, Alaska, where the Alaskan pipeline disgorges itself into oil
tankers at our northernmost ice-free port. Both responded to the fashionable
nostalgia of the late seventies by purchasing tapes of radio programs remembered
with joy from their youth: *The Green Hornet, The Lone Ranger, The Shadow,
Inner Sanctum*. Let the woman who teaches in Belle Glade tell her story:

> I looked forward to sharing something with my students that really
> belonged to me. For the hour before dinner, every day from Monday through
> Friday, my sister and I would lie in our beds with the radio equidistant
> between us—measured equidistant, that is—and listen to two consecutive
> thirty-minute programs. It was incomparably the best hour of the day;
> nothing could ever be better. I couldn't wait to play tapes of those programs
> for my kids in the ninth grade, and I decided to begin on the Monday after
> the Saturday I bought them, to begin with *The Lone Ranger*, who had
> always been my absolute favorite. And I did.
>
> That night, that Monday night after that endless day in school, I
> went home and took off my shoes and put up my feet and cried. My
> childhood is irretrievable, lost and never to be found by children again. I
> played *The Lone Ranger* tape, I played it twice, and then I played it again.
> I've got so many nice, I mean *really nice,* people in my class. Migrant
> workers' kids are the nicest kids in the world. Living so close together the
> way they do, in temporary housing or cars and trucks on the road, they
> really know how to be careful and kind. The poor kids, they wanted so

much to please me, they wanted so much to like the tape for my sake, but they just didn't *see* anything. I mean, they didn't *see* the Lone Ranger, they didn't *see* the Great Horse Silver. . . . They had never had any practice in making their own images, and I wasn't smart enough to understand what the problem was. I know I hurt their feelings, but they just broke my heart.

Can we truly believe that these students of hers are the same children, more or less with variations allowed, who came to school in 1951, because thirty years is not such a long time after all? Can children who have watched ten thousand hours of television by the time they leave the first grade and twice that number by the time they enter the twelfth grade, can those children who have spent more of their time before they enter school in watching television than in any other activity except sleeping—can they be essentially the same children, in their preparation for and predisposition toward acts of literacy, as those who preceded them to our classrooms only thirty years ago? They are not, they cannot be, and yet in the most significant possible way we treat them as though they were.

What is that way? It is treatment based on the dual, disastrous assumptions that the child who enters school at the beginning of the eighties has come from a family that models the functions of literacy and provides reinforcement for the individual voice. These two assumptions are no less mistaken than they are pernicious, for they lead to perfect misunderstanding of elements in the child's education as various as class size, peer grouping, and silence in the classroom.

Take these two assumptions as they apply to the matter of class size. So far as can be determined from figures published during the past three decades, average class size in American elementary and secondary schools has grown about thirty and forty percent respectively during that period. This means that the number of children in elementary classrooms has increased from twenty-two to twenty-nine while it has swelled from twenty-five to thirty-five in secondary schools. The reason is not far to seek. Even as the population of school-age children was increasing, so were the demands of teachers for better pay. School boards, understanding the budgetary implications of these demands and contemplating the community horror of parents having to attend to their children while teachers struck for their rights, made the linked discoveries that teachers had to be paid more but that more of them did not have to be hired. And thus class size grew in the same proportion as teachers' salaries. Who was to say that it shouldn't?

Parents and teachers, of course, both of whom should have known that this growth was inimical to the best interests of students, teachers, and parents alike. In a society of stable communicative forms, that is, in a world where most formal knowledge is communicated between adults and through adults to children by means of methods and models essentially unchanged across generations—in such a world, class size will matter more in the dimension of physical properties (can all students be seated, see, and be seen?) than in the skills of educational preparation (can all students learn to read and write?). But where communicative forms have been as unstable as they have been in American society for the past thirty years, class size becomes critical to the teaching of literate skills because the family can no longer be depended upon to predispose the child to those forms of communication known as reading and writing, forms that demand skills that must be taught by the schools before they can teach anything else. With indisposed children in large classes, teachers come to know themselves in terms of the same frustration and failure that characterize their students.

Teachers who understood that their students were coming from homes where the telephone was replacing the personal letter in communication beyond the home and the television set replacing personal conversation within the home—not to mention books, magazines, and newspapers—would not have allowed the size of their classes to grow by thirty or forty percent because they would have known that precisely the opposite movement was necessary. They would have known that the decline and disappearance of models for literacy in the home would demand a kind of learning and teaching in the schools that could only be accomplished in smaller rather than larger classes.

When evaluating the child's preparation at home for acquiring functional literacy in school, we cannot afford to confine our observations to the presence or absence of models for reading and writing. Many well-intentioned parents believe that they have provided significant modeling for their children when they have read to them in their early years. Parents are likely to be right in this belief if what they desire is children who will become parents who read to their children. But they are almost certainly wrong if they believe that they have provided in the home the pattern most likely to encourage their children to become readers themselves. For that pattern is the model of adults reading in front of children, as well as to them.

It is just this model that is generally unavailable to children who live in the average North American home, where a television set is turned on for more than six hours a day (unless the home has preschool children; in that case, the set will be turned on for more than eight hours a day). For a child in such a home, the influential sight of an adult reading is as rare an experience as that of the attention to one another's voices that was one of the chief characteristics of family life before being replaced by attention to the many voices of television. So far as I can determine from extensive, unscientific inquiry, most of my students and colleagues who write in a voice recognizable as their own—a number significant in impact if insignificant in size—have come from homes where reading was modeled for them and where conversation was an honored form of attention.

If we do not believe in miraculous intervention—in a divinity that values our reading and conversation so highly that it will soon intervene in human affairs to remove the fact and memory of television from our lives—then we have only four choices. We can ignore the profound change that television has made in human communication in the past three decades. We can work to abolish television. We can try to convince parents that they should admit less television into their family life, while instead they read in front of their children and speak with them frequently as well as attentively. We can restructure schools and classrooms to extend the family beyond its shrunken bounds so that activities critical to the functions of literacy that once occurred in the nuclear family at home can now take place in the extended family at school.

Since I believe that ignoring the profound influence of television on the spoken and written voices of children has been in significant part responsible for the decline in American literacy and the dilemma of teachers in American schools—how to convey a belief in the values and functions of literacy to children not predisposed to that belief?—I cannot embrace the option of ignorance. Since I believe in neither divine intervention nor miraculous event, I cannot participate in an attempt to abolish television. But I can work to educate parents in the salutary effects on their children of television reduced while conversation and exemplary reading are increased. And I can restructure my classroom, perhaps even my school, to include and reinforce the attentive and modeling functions of the extended family.

Those who were teachers and those who were taught in one-room schools seem to be nearly unanimous in their memory and evaluation of one aspect of that experience. They recall with pleasure the feeling of well-being that arose from their sense of attendedness, from their knowledge that they could not be lost, because no corner or cranny existed that was secret or remote enough to remove them from the unremitting attention of their peers, who were expected by their teachers to attend to their peers.

The distinctive educational phenomenon of the one-room school, in the memory of its inhabitants, was the responsibility of child for child and older child for younger children in schools where fifty to sixty students in six to eight grades with a single teacher was neither unusual nor remarkable. It is this phenomenon, extraordinary now if unremarked then, that I believe we must recreate in our classrooms if we are to have any hope of countering and reversing the movement of society away from the attended speech and practiced literacy of the nuclear family. We must create the extended family of peer grouping in American classrooms so that we and our students can profit from its unique benefits of attention and example. Any lesser effort, any lesser objective can only result in the unpracticed and ineffective literacy which now plagues our society.

Since the autumn of 1970 I have employed some form of peer grouping in almost all the classes I have taught that have not been too large to fit into the mode of recitation and discussion. This size is determined not so much by the number of students in the class—I find that seventy-five students can function well as a class taught in that manner—as by the number of three-person groups I can form and help to profitable internal relationships. Because this number seems improbable to me when it exceeds fifteen, I limit my work in peer grouping to classes of forty-five or fewer. Although that is my outside limit, I have noted that my students and I seem to find the most useful relationship with one another when the class is divided into no more than twelve groups of three persons each.

By "useful relationships" I mean the multiple, attended opportunities for speaking, writing, and reading that are implicit in effective peer grouping but generally unavailable in classes composed solely of individuals where the teacher alone must be audience, resource, and guide. Deliberate ordering of the two serial groups in the preceding sentence places "speaking" and "audience" first because they are meant to indicate the value that my students and I place upon the various functions of attending peers.

Although I will inevitably judge my students' performances in terms of the quality of their writing in a course where writing is their primary means of conveying both information and wisdom, I know that I cannot myself put them in touch with voices that will carry them from speaking to writing. But if I cannot, their peers can. My first formal instruction to the group is that I will accept nothing from any of its members that the author cannot comfortably read aloud to me. Therefore, the members' initial responsibility is to know one another's several voices well enough to recognize them not only by their presence but also by their absence in a written mode.

How shall they come to know one another's voices in ways that will make their judgments both reasonable and valid? The first step is unprescriptive: Put three people in a group that must produce cooperative effort and they will talk to each other to establish territory and identity. Prescribe the second step— discussion of and complete agreement about the nature of an assigned task— and three people who are students are well on their way to knowing the best of two other voices in addition to their own. This first prescribed step, that they must have complete agreement about the definition and requirements of the assignment, can be supported by the teacher with the unvarying practice of making the assignment on a single occasion only.

Although I will repeat any assignment as often as I have unfrivolous requests to do so and I will in extremity even paraphrase it from the written form in my possession, I will never repeat it on any occasion other than the first class meeting for which it is scheduled. When asked for later clarification or for repetition by persons absent on the day of assignment, I always refer supplicants to their own groups. My purpose is that they should learn and confirm their new dependence upon one another's voices and memories rather than reconfirm their old dependence upon me. Furthermore, in a characteristic and profitable usage of peer grouping, when I receive a paper written in an inhuman voice, I do not hold the author solely responsible. One of my requirements of the group is that each member must read his or her paper aloud to an audience formed by his or her two peers; when I receive the paper, their approval of its voice is implicit in its form and explicit in the signatures of the partners that follow its final paragraph.

From this practice have grown some of my students' most profound observations about the nature of the personal style in language as it is manifest in the relationship between spoken and written forms. When teachers and scholars chide me for encouraging a confusion between language in the mouth and language on the page, I defend myself by repeating words like those of my philosophy and economics student with which I introduced this paper: "What it really sounds like is you, the way you talk, but put through some kind of finishing machine so that all the pieces fit together better than when you said them." The paired recognitions of that observation are available to a growing number of students as they are required to hear and to identify their own voices and those of their peers.

One of the most significant functions of the family attentive to the voices of its individual members, in addition to provision of a responsive audience that confirms the importance of those voices by providing opportunity for their practice and affirmation of their impact, is the unambiguous identification of that audience. When this function cannot be dependably supplied in the nuclear family, then it must be supplied by the extended family in the classroom.

Perhaps the problem most difficult to resolve for all writers after the problem of voice—and especially for student writers—is the identity of their audience. Although this problem is ultimately one of performance for students, it is originally one of understanding for teachers and students alike. Which is to say that teachers do not understand how much the fulfillment of their writing assignments depends upon their specification of audience, and students do not understand how much the quality of their writing depends upon that specification.

For students most writing assignments made in school suffer from the great defect of unspecified audience. At no other time in their personal or vocational lives will students have to guess the identity of their audience. Because vocational writing is always so audience-specific, one could expect that it would not generally suffer from the defects in aiming that so often cripple its subcategory of academic prose. The fact that vocational writing does suffer from precisely those same defects—legal and medical writing being at least the defective equal in this respect of scholarly writing in the humanities, for example—is testimony to the permanent and often incurable damage perpetrated by school writing done for no audience known to the writer.

Two actions can remedy this defect: Teachers can describe an exact and familiar audience for their every assignment, in that way removing themselves as readers and hearers so essentially unknowable that students retreat into the protective distance of third persons and passive voices, or teachers can diminish the importance of their inscrutable selves by providing the primary audience for students in their own eminently knowable peers. "Your first audience is the two other members of your group," I tell my students, "and your sole purpose is to clarify *their* understanding. Their clarity will be your accomplishment and my satisfaction."

If verifying individual voices and defining audiences were the only virtues of peer grouping, they would be virtues enough to justify its use in the teaching of writing. But this version of the extended family in the classroom has a third capacity to support its members which addresses one of the problems that has interested rhetoricians and distracted writers for more than two thousand years. The problem has long been named "invention" or, more recently, "discovery"; the unique capacity in peer groups for its solution lies in the attention of three minds rather than one to the expansion of a topic or the growth of an argument.

What has always been wrong with the "places" of invention in classical rhetoric has been their inorganic nature. Whether defined and taught by Greek rhetoricians in Antioch in the fourth century or by English schoolmasters in Stratford in the sixteenth, the result of their use by Greek or English schoolchildren was as mechanical and uninspired as the formulaic paragraph or three-paragraph theme written by their contemporary American counterparts. Although we are now too wise to teach invention by formula, we are still not conspicuously successful in teaching writers at any level to discover the further implications of their material. Whether we are in relationship of teacher or editor to the writer, invention remains the most difficult aspect of the writer's work—and ours.

This difficulty can be substantially diminished by the intimate knowledge of one another's habits and patterns of thought that members of peer groups develop as they speak, write, and read together. They often attain in their work with each other the optimum accomplishments that all editors seek in their work with their clients: improvement and amplification that are not only acceptable but also useful to the writer because they are consistent with his or her own style and processes of thought.

As part of instructing each peer group in the extent and limitations of its responsibilities to its individual members, I make a careful difference between suggestion and demand. I ask them to recall the occasions when information was of little use to them because they could not integrate it into their point of view or style of learning. I ask them to apply this generalization to the specific instances in their lives or the lives of friends when information or even wisdom offered was rejected because of the mode or style of offering. Then I draw its lesson for group thinking and writing: If you want to help your partner to expand a thought, develop an argument, or improve a statement, you can be sure your suggestions and improvements will receive their best reception and therefore have their most useful effects if you try to match them to that partner's mode of thought or style of writing. Furthermore, your partner must have real room for demurral and at least apparent room for ignorance. Your responsibility in the group is never satisfied merely by being right. You must also be able to be helpful, not only in the immediate instance but also in the long-term effect of your assistance, or you and your partner will both lose one more of the rare opportunities to give and receive acceptable, profitable aid.

The intent of this advice to my students is essentially the same as the intent of the analyses and arguments in this paper: to advocate the extension of certain familial functions, now infrequently found in the family at home, into a form of family in the classroom. This extended family, sometimes called peer grouping, has its primary function in the attention to each individual's voice that members of the group are able to give. The purpose of this attention is to invest the individual voice not only with identity but also with significance for its owner; in so doing, the peer group may accomplish in school what the nuclear family no longer accomplishes in the home.

Literacy for the Eighties:
An Alternative to Losing

William E. Coles, Jr.

> If we concentrate our attention on trying to solve a problem of geometry,
> and if at the end of an hour we are no nearer to doing so than at the beginning,
> we have nevertheless been making progress each minute of that hour in
> another more mysterious dimension. Without our knowing or feeling it, this
> apparently barren effort has brought more light into the soul. The result will
> one day . . . very likely be felt in some department of the intelligence in
> no way connected with mathematics. Perhaps he who made the unsuccessful
> effort will one day be able to grasp the beauty of a line of Racine more
> vividly on account of it. . . . Every time that a human being succeeds in
> making an effort of attention with the sole idea of increasing his grasp of
> truth, he acquires a greater aptitude for grasping it, even if his effort produces
> no visible fruit. An Eskimo story explains the origin of light as follows: "In
> the eternal darkness, the crow, unable to find any food, longed for light,
> and the earth was illumined." If there is a real desire, if the thing desired
> is really light, the desire for light produces it. There is a real desire when
> there is an effort of attention.
>
> —SIMONE WEIL (45-46)

> The question "Who am I?" obsesses the mind and all human activity provides
> answers, ever changing, uncertain, risky. Grammatically, it would seem that
> "I" am a user of prepositions. "I" see something as above or below, to the
> left or to the right, before or after, but the thing itself ever eludes me. And
> "I" myself turn out to be a maker of patterns, of orders, a constructor of
> worlds.
>
> —THEODORE BAIRD

Most of the people who come out here don't see it my way and that's OK by
me. They just don't come out here to handicap horse races, that's all. They're
not serious and they know it. I wouldn't call them losers. Plenty of guys come
out here who are serious and are still losers, but most of the people here come
out here just for fun and that's OK by me. You want to go to the track a couple
of nights a season, have dinner, bring the kids, watch the horses run, fine. I can

understand that. Bet on the names or the numbers, show bet the favorite, gamble a little, the way you'd do with a wheel in Las Vegas. Fine. It used to bother me the way they never even look at a program really, or the field either, the way they never *see* anything, and it still bothers me when they think what I do is bet a system. But OK. They're just not out here to handicap and they're straight on that. They're not serious and they're straight on that too. It's one of the first things you want to get straight about coming out here because. . . .

. . . One of the first things you want to get straight about teaching writing is the vital importance of the question of what you're going to make the whole thing mean, for your students as writers, for yourself as a teacher of writing— what you're going to make it mean and how you're going to keep that central. Against what sea of troubles do you see yourself taking arms as a teacher? In the name of what do you fight? And if there is no sea of troubles for you, no fight to fight, why bother? Why not just sell shoes?

I mean what are you going to make the whole thing mean specifically too, as an idea rather than as some easily labeled ideal: Well, I want my students to be Good Citizens, or Wise Consumers, or whatever. And by how you're going to keep the idea central, I mean how day by day, with what sorts of materials and writing activities, moving from what kind of here to what kind of there, are you going to put your students in the position of seeing what good writing is good for and in what senses it can be said to be worth someone's while to work at—particularly when you know it's not something most people are going to enjoy doing very much, or do very much of, or ever become very good at? And now, right now at the beginning of your teaching career, is as good a time as any to see why, however you go about addressing this question, the answer to it is not one you can simply take for granted or be supplied with in any form that is likely to do you much good. It's important that you get clear. . . .

. . . It's important that *you* get clear on what the whole thing means not just for the sake of the other addicts you're going to be working with, but for your sake. If *you're* not clear on what getting clean is all about, you can't work with them, and if you don't work with them you're going back to drink and drugs, you're going back to die. That's the way it is with addiction. So you start there, with addiction, with what it means to be hooked—and with trying to understand how that's the last thing in the world an addict understands, which is one of the primary reasons we become addicted to begin with. And that we stay that way. What did you and I know when we finally asked for help? All I knew when I came to this program was that I hurt and that I didn't want to hurt anymore. I didn't come here to change my life or to save my soul. I came to save my ass. If I thought about it at all I'd have said that the problem was drink or that the problem was drugs. What I didn't begin to see was how drugs and booze are the solution to problems for people like us and that that was the problem. The real problem was I didn't know how to do life. I didn't know how to live. And I didn't know I didn't know that and that that was the root of things, because I'd found something that made me think I could live without my having to go through the pain of learning how to do it and of needing other people to be able to continue to do it. It's not just the chemicals that hook us. It's the promises they make. You'll be all right. You can do it alone. It's going to be all right. That's why it takes us so damned long to get here. Everybody else, and years before we do, can see what the stuff does *to* us, but nobody else sees what it does *for* us. What it does for us. Christ, if I'd known what liquor would do for me, I'd have had a shot on the way to kindergarten. It made me dead to life, sure. It made living dead to life too. But at the same time it made both of us into something I couldn't live, or do what I called live, any other way. That's why I could get clean, or could seem to, but I could never stay that way. You're an addict when you're somebody who cannot not use death to live life, sooner or later. No wonder addiction is the only disease the primary symptom of which is the conviction that you don't have a disease. You've got to understand this in order to. . . .

. . . You've got to understand the importance of creating a meaning for the activity of writing for your students in the context of what can be said to have happened to the teaching of writing in the United States—I mean what can be said to have happened historically or at least by the pattern I have made of what I would call history in order to locate myself with what I believe to be worth doing as a teacher.

In a world, that is, in a culture or a society, where the meaning of writing is in some sense a given, where teachers can behave as though they believed that their students believed what they believe—that good writing is necessary to, say, godliness (as it was for Emerson in 1836), or to moral rectitude (as it was for Adam Sherman Hill and Genung in the 1890s), or to good manners (as it was in the 1920s and 1930s), or to success (as it was in other than a last-ditch way for all of us not more than forty years ago)—then teachers can offer the activity of writing to everybody as that which it can be taken for granted has importance to everybody as a somebody. In such a world substantive knowledge *about* writing—the terminologies with which the activity is described and all that they imply about how the activity is to be taught and learned—all this can be understood by everyone as a vital inheritance, as the organic link of the individual with a living tradition, as a legacy, a kind of trust fund of the spirit, rather than the deadweight accumulation of a thousand thousand rag and bone shops of as many foul hearts. In such a world there is no divorce, in other words, between substantive knowledge *about* the activity of writing and the activity of writing itself, no divorce between substantive knowledge and the agreed upon importance of such knowledge, the shared understanding of why it matters. With such a cultural frame for things, to focus on the relationship of the writing and its intended audience is as natural as it is effective.

In a world where the meaning of writing is *not* a given, however, in a world such as the world we're living in, where nothing can be taken for granted in our classrooms about what it means to write a sentence in English, this meaning must be in some sense created. When it is not, when in such a world the focus remains fixed on the relationship of writing to its audience without being widened to include the relationship of a writer to that writing, the activity becomes ever increasingly an exercise. This is what I think happened with the teaching of writing through the forties, the fifties, the sixties, bottoming out finally in the seventies in the phenomenon known as the literacy crisis—the direct as well as the indirect result of teachers of writing not realizing that what could once be counted on as the vital knowledge of a living tradition had petrified into a dead metaphor for a world that no longer existed. Clung to more and more desperately by teachers, however (as though an inherited tradition would do for us as a profession what there would then be no need for us to do for ourselves), this knowledge became more and more internally elaborated, more and more systematized, dogmatized, theologized, at the same time that it grew less and less in touch with anything outside itself. With anything or with anybody. Writing in fact became a mechanical action rather than an activity, that anybody could be taught to teach to anybody or that anybody could learn from anybody, but within which nobody, teacher or student, could find himself or herself as a somebody. Hence the literacy crisis, the inevitable consequence of teachers of writing refusing to take into account how at the level of teaching and learning it is the frame for meaningful knowledge about writing, what the activity is offered in the name of, that makes both that knowledge and the activity of writing substantive for students. It is neither the knowledge nor the activity all by itself. Seen this way, the literacy crisis is the result less of a failure of knowledge *about* writing than a failure of imagination *with* what knowledge we already had. It is the consequence, in Henry Adams' metaphor, of our remaining a nineteenth-century profession trying to operate in a twentieth-century world—but with no sense of our need for a different spool on which to wind history. Not to understand this. . . .

. . . Not to understand what handicapping is all about is to have nothing to hang on to yourself with out here. And unless you're out here just to screw around, and are clear about that, without something to hang on to yourself with, you're not just going to lose, you're going to be a loser. You don't want to kid yourself about that either, that not being a loser is just a matter of being careful or being serious. Like I say, there are plenty of guys come out here that are serious, real serious. But they're losers. They're not handicappers. The big score. Money. That's what they're after, and they take it seriously all right. They're here night after night, with six, ten different trifectas boxed in every lousy $2,500 claimer. Race after race. They got systems, see, and that's what they bet. They bet systems, not races. They don't even *see* the horses anymore. They got pocket calculators to read the program. Slide rules. Honest to God. When they win it's all them. When they lose they got a bad drive, or the horse is a plug, or the fix was in. They don't *see* anything anymore. All they believe in is luck or some kind of magic they call science. They believe in it but they don't trust it, so they don't even know that's all they believe in, like those screwballs with the Zodiac. That's not handicapping. They never worked out, or maybe they don't even care anymore, that the track is set up to make money on people who are out here to make money that way, particularly when they win races they haven't figured out. There's nothing can make you a loser faster than that—take it from me, I've been there.

All you got to do is win once on some crazy long shot, forty to one, with your last five bucks at the end of a bad night where everything you do right comes out wrong. It happens that way sometimes, and so you say what the hell, and you start to look for some gimmick like a month-old speed fraction or bloodlines, but you're really looking only at the odds on the tote board, not at the field, not at the program—and by God, in he comes, by a couple of lengths maybe, in a suck-along race, and something happens to you. Something happens way down deep, way down past what you know, where you start to think that maybe there isn't anything *to* know. You start to think that maybe what you know, because it's never good enough, isn't any good at all. Maybe luck is all there is. Maybe magic is all there is. And you're hooked, Mister, and that's what a loser is, somebody hooked that way. Split up and hooked just that way. You become a loser not because you never win, sometimes you do, and not because you don't win over the long haul, maybe nobody does that, not big anyway. You're a loser because of how you see things. You lose when you don't have to lose, and you always end up losing more than you have to, and you quit learning from when you lose. You spoil everything for yourself. You let the track make you crazy. So part of what handicapping is about is self-protection. It's a way of hanging on to yourself out here, a way to keep from going crazy. It's a way of knowing where you are when. . . .

. . . Part of the way you know where you are as a teacher of writing, then, is to know where you're not, where none of us are, not any more. For better or worse, that is, it's no longer possible for us to be very effective as teachers by defining writing or the benefits of it in traditional terms only. It's no longer possible for us to get very far by offering writing to our students as a predominantly mechanical activity the importance of which we assert only with the half-truths of predominantly negative arguments: if you *don't* write well then you will not be thought nicely mannered or well rounded or decently educated. If you *don't* write well then you will not be successful, you will not obtain a high-paying job, etc. etc. For it is no more difficult to see how people could fail to care very much about writing conceived of primarily as a set of conventions or rules to be mastered than it is to see why they might have trouble believing that such mastery is a necessary condition for survival or even success, let alone an indicant of knowledge, intelligence, or character. Not just on *your* say-so, thank you very much. Not any more. Besides, to whatever extent such assertions were ever reasons for anybody's learning to write, they are still more an explanation of how an ability to write is valuable than they are an explanation of why the ability should be valued in the first place. Only in a very limited way do they suggest that there can be something in the activity of writing for the *writer,* for the writer as student, let alone for the writer as anything other than a student.

So OK, if we're not where we're not as teachers of writing, then where are we? Or more to the point, where am I? Where am I and what do I do?

I guess I start with why I value writing in the first place. I value it for myself as a uniquely powerful instrument for learning, as a special way of thinking and coming to know. I value it as a form of language using, language using understood as the primary means by which all of us run order through chaos, thereby giving ourselves the identities we have. Looking at writing from this point of view gives me a way of seeing the ability to compose in sentences as an ability to conceptualize, to build structures, to draw inferences, to develop implications, to generalize intelligently—in short, to make connections, to work out relationships—between this idea and that idea, words and other words, sentences and other sentences, language and experience. And from this point of view also I have a chance of offering writing to students as an activity of language using that can enable them to become better composers, better conceptualizers, better thinkers in whatever other languages they may work with: mathematical formulas, chemical equations, pigments, gestures, speech. Thus I have a way of offering writing as an avenue to a special kind of power, the only power I know that is uncorrupting and that for my money it therefore makes any sense to have: the power to choose with awareness, to change and adapt consciously, and in this sense to be able to have a share in determining one's own destiny. And I have a way of suggesting that this power is available not just to those students who *become* writers, whatever we may mean by that, but even to those who are willing to do no more than work at it, to work at imagining what they could do if they were writers. I value writing in the first place because power-lessness is an invitation to victimization. . . .

. . . Addicts, you got to understand, are victims of themselves, and that's why they're losers, just the way you and I were. You can't be an addict and be anything else. I made up a world to live in with booze and pills at the center of it, a world where everything supported everything else. I could even diagnose myself. Hell man, I'd been diagnosed, upside down and back nine ways to Sunday. I was a paranoid neurotic with schizophrenic symptoms subject to attacks of anxiety, acute depression, feelings of alienation and despair. Why a guy like that would just have to have something to get through a day, wouldn't he? Some antidepressants, or mood elevators with antiseptic-sounding names like Meloril or Thorazine? Or I had my California Kung Fu group therapy talk. My trouble was I needed Positive Reinforcement and Support. My trouble was that I engaged in Suicide Ideation. I was Uncomfortable with my Feelings. I had a Negative Self-Image. It was a goddam circle is what it was, a circle of talk, bad talk. The wrong names. That's what I was really addicted to. Sure everything propped up everything else in the world I'd made. The only trouble was I couldn't live there. And if nothing could get to me, I couldn't get out of where I was to anything else. I was Genesis 1.1 but without any power. The King Kong–sized monkey on my back was both the only thing that made things bearable and my Cross-Eyed Bear, is how I saw it. I was damned, I said of myself. I was doomed.

Talk about your one-way ticket on a midnight carousel. And I had no way to get off, no way to stop, and there sure as hell was no brass ring. There was nobody anywhere in the world, not so far as I was concerned, that knew my name. Including me. Especially me.

I mean that's how I saw it before I did what you did too. I asked for help, just the way you did. And they came to see me, just like I went to see you. Jesus, I'll never forget that. You know what they said when I told them I was damned? They asked me what made me think I was that important. I went through my diagnosis number and you know what they did? They laughed. That's not what your trouble is, they said. You know what your trouble is? Your trouble is the same as ours. We lived it, same as you. The real trouble is that you're a self-centered, arrogant sonofabitch who never once, not for one minute, ever gave one thought to anybody but himself. There is no King Kong that's separate from you, Mister, not until you make the separation, and you can't begin to make the separation until you realize how you're one and the same. What's on your back is your own self-pity, your own dishonesty. King Kong isn't drugs. He's got your face and your name and address. It's yourself you're going to have to deal with, but not just with yourself anymore. Your're going to need us just the way we need you. That's how things are going to be different. You're not going to be fighting alone any more. If you work with us you won't be able to give King Kong his old names anymore because we got that bastard's number. I didn't understand much of all that, of course. Christ, I was sick. But I heard them. They broke the circle. And that was the start. . . .

. . . Seeing the activity of writing as involving the development of the kind of power that can be an alternative to losing is what allows me to restore an Emersonian frame to teaching and learning it. Good writing, good use, using language well, literacy: this for Emerson, and he says it again and again, was intimately a matter of character, involved a vital and dynamic connection of the human with the divine. Hence, as he says in *Nature,* "a man's power to connect his thought with its proper symbol, and so to utter it, depends on the simplicity of his character, that is, upon his love of truth and his desire to communicate it without loss." Further, this power "is at once a commanding certificate that he who employs it is a man in alliance with truth and God."

It is an equation with which his audience seems to have had no trouble.

And writing that was not so good, the disheveled use of language, what was that a certificate of; with what, by implication, would an inept user of language have to be in alliance?

Neither the speaker nor his audience, apparently, had any trouble here either.

But of course for us, with our students, there's going to be a hatful; we're going to have to write the equations differently. I do not mean that we must find a new way of defining and specifying illiteracy for our students as a form of Emersonian ungodliness, but I do think we have got to find a way of designating illiteracy both literally and as a metaphor with terminologies that can have for our students an equivalent significance and the same kind of transforming force. We have got to find a way of defining and specifying what illiteracy is and is about in terms that matter and to do this in as many different ways as we can. I am talking about the need to imagine illiteracy as Paulo Freire saw it, as an instrument of oppression. I am talking about seeing what we would call the "un-right" use of language—in the sort of political context someone like George Orwell gives it. I mean discussing clichés as Hannah Arendt describes their role in marching Jews to gas chambers. I mean seeing the problem of sentence subordination as a problem with how to put the world together. I mean making use of the whole ragged reticule of English teacher concerns such as vocabulary, syntax, even punctuation, in the sort of frame that Richard Mitchell provides for them in his ironic contemplation of the social consequences that could attend someone's knowing how to use language well:

> Just think what happens in the mind of the person who knows the difference between restrictive and nonrestrictive clauses. Anyone who understands that distinction is on the brink of seeing the difference between simple fact and elaborative detail and may well begin to make judgments about the logic of such relationships. He may start bothering his head about the difference between things essential and things accidental, a disorder that often leads to the discovery of tautologies. Furthermore, anyone who sees the difference between restrictive and nonrestrictive clauses is likely to understand *why* modifiers should be close to the things they modify and thus begin to develop a sense of the way in which ideas grow from one another. From that, it's not a long way to detecting non sequiturs and unstated premises and even false analogies. . . .
>
> A fluent command of English cannot exist as an isolated skill, a clever stunt. A person who speaks and writes his native tongue clearly and precisely does so because of many other abilities, and those other abilities themselves grow stronger through the fluent manipulation of language. The simple matter of being logical is a function of language. A million high school graduates capable of fluent English would be a million Americans capable of logical thought. What would we do with them, especially if they were black? You think *they're* going to buy those lottery tickets and lamps in the shape of Porky Pig? You think they're going to hang out on the corners and provide employment for everybody from the local social worker to the justices of the Supreme Court? (154, 159-60)

I'm talking about the necessity of making students aware of the un-right use of language as easy and as addictive—bad language as forty-to-one-shot horse. Bad language as a standing invitation to your own beheading, as the real toad that swallows every imaginary garden. Bad language as the ticket down the river that you sell yourself. Bad language as prison argot, the mumble of the slave corrals. . . .

. . . Don't get me wrong. When I say you got to bet a race and not a system, I don't mean you can come out here and do it all by feel or something—not any more than knowing what a loser is will keep you from turning into a loser, or than it makes you a winner. You'd better know what you're doing when you come out here. You *got* to know what Andrew Beyer says about speed fractions. You *got* to know how Chapin figures the horse least likely to lose. You *got* to know what Ainslee says about pace rating, even if you think he's wrong. Because you got to know how to *study* a performance record. You got to know how to read a program, because you got to know how to use it to tell you what's going on out there.

See, it's like this. There are rules. You got to know the rules because you got to know when they won't work, when to break them. You got to have a way of making sense of things out there, but things don't always make the same kind of sense. Early money on a horse, for instance. Sometimes it's stable money, smart money, and sometimes it isn't. It depends on the horse, the race, the conditions. Lots of things. Or, say, you see a horse bolted his last race. That means he's out of shape, right? Not necessarily. Not if you know how to read a performance record. Not if you know how to use it to see what you watch. So you got to pay attention to what's going on, but you got to know how not to pay attention to certain things too, things that don't mean what they look like they mean, things that aren't going to matter the way they're supposed to matter.

At least the way you figure it. You can never know for sure, and right along with knowing the rules you got to know that and remember that. You can never know for sure and neither can anybody else. The best handicappers in the world make maybe twenty percent of their bets. And that's the best in the world. They don't make a lot of money, but they come out ahead. And that's what handicapping is about, coming out ahead in the long run. It's not a way to win races. It's how not to be a loser. You can beat a race, but you can't beat the races. You ever hear that? Really, it's the other way around. Anybody can get beat by a race. Anybody. But if you can't *beat* the track you can stay with it; you can make expenses anyway; you can stay in the game. And, like I say, you've got to remember that because you're going to need it.

You can come out here every Friday, for instance, the way I do, for four or five weeks, and if you're playing right you play maybe no more than eight or ten races. That's two a night, maybe three, on a ten-race card. You stay out of all the garbage stuff in between. Let's say you bet every one of those ten races just the way you know you should have, for just as much money as you figured they were worth. And you got ten losses in a row. I had that once, ten in a row. Then here's the eleventh race. You know you ought to be in it solid. And the board has two favorites against you. You better have rules to get you where you are then, but when you're there you're going to need more than somebody else's rules to do what you ought to do. It's then you need something you can believe in, because without that. . . .

. . . Defining illiteracy as a form of powerlessness for our students, and showing in what ways powerlessness is an invitation to victimization, will not be enough of course. Indeed, without providing students with some vision of the transformation that can attend the attempt to become more responsible to oneself as a user of language, it is worse than unprincipled to encourage them to see the inability to use language well as a kind of addiction, addiction as a kind of despair. Addicts are not better off simply for seeing themselves as addicts. The Good Samaritan left money with the innkeeper not to make sure that the injured man would be comfortable but to prevent the possibility—it was so stipulated by law—that the man would be sold into slavery for being unable to pay the innkeeper's bill. And by "vision of transformation" I'm talking about providing students with something more than a description of the kind of miracle that seems to happen only to other people. Augustine, Helen Keller, Richard Rodriguez, Viktor Frankl. What's wanted is a way of making clear to students the availability of such seeming miracles to them, presenting transformations in terms that help students see that they can have a share in. Take the revisions of these three student sentences, for example:

> My mother used to love my father, but she left him when he became an alcoholic and wouldn't admit it.
> My mother loves my father; she had to leave him because he's an alcoholic who can't admit it.

> My high school math teacher was tough but fair.
> My high school math teacher was tough and fair.

> There were four main causes for the War between the States.
> What are seen as the four main causes for the Civil War seems to depend on the point of view of the historian.

None of these sentences in either its first or its revised form is immediately arresting. There is even a point of view from which the sentences as a group could be said to scrape the edge of banality. And because it could be done accurately, I suppose it would be possible to imagine one were doing the sentences justice by describing the changes in them with no more than English teacher terminology: as a matter of altered punctuation, supplied connectives, changes in tense, differences in vocabulary, and so on. But from another point of view— and no one has to suppose any more here than that the sentences can have contexts—from another point of view what can be said to have "happened" in each revision is something that cannot be described completely without some reference to the reviser, at least as we imagine him or her. From this point of view, the revisers of those sentences, in changing how they have put the world together, have changed their relationship not just to the world but to themselves— and not just to themselves as writers but to themselves as more than writers. In the sense that life is, as John Gardner puts it, "all conjunctions, one damn thing after another, cows *and* wars *and* chewing gum *and* mountains," the revisers of those sentences are no longer life's victims. In the sense that art, what Gardner calls "the best, most important art—is all subordination: guilt *because of* sin *because of* pain" (6), the revisers of those sentences have become artists. No longer, at any rate, is the world that which simply happens to them. They have begun to happen to the world.

It is a change, so far as I am concerned, no less momentous in its implications than the "deliverance" that Walker Percy argues attended Helen Keller's famous learning experience at the water pump with her teacher Ann Sullivan. Before the event at the pump, Helen Keller had been using words for some time, but she had been using them as what Percy calls "signals" rather than "symbols":

> When her teacher, Miss Sullivan, spelled out *water, mug, drink* in her hand, she "understood": she responded by drinking water, going to water, fetching the mug, etc.—that is to say, she interpreted the word in a signal context and *did* something. What Miss Sullivan could not make her understand was that the word water was not a command to *do* something with water, but *meant,* denoted water. Then at last and in a sudden flash of insight, Helen understood that the gesture in her hand *meant* the water. It was an experience of tremendous excitement. Having learned that this "is" water, what she had to know immediately was *what everything else was*! (quoted in Coles 82)

So it is that the mind is awakened, that a being becomes human. From an understanding of language as signal only, and in consequence of herself as responsible only to adapt to signals of various kinds, Helen Keller moves to the seeing of language as symbol and in consequence to the seeing of herself as a maker of meaning, someone who through the power of symbolization has gained what Percy calls "possession" of the world. And something analogous to this awakening, this "deliverance," this thrust from victimization to freedom, I would argue, is implicit in the direction being taken by the revisers of those three sentences—an implicitness that were it made explicit would enable the writers of those sentences to come into "possession" of themselves as being more than just the writers of those sentences. . . .

. . . The biggest problem I had with getting clean, and you can count on this being the hump anybody you work with is going to have to get over too, the biggest problem I had was one of belief. I don't mean just believing it was going to be possible for me to get clean to begin with, particularly the way they told me I was going to have to work at it, which made absolutely no sense. I mean beyond that. Suppose it did work. That's what I had trouble with. Suppose I could stay clean. I couldn't fully believe there was any way it was going to be worth it. I couldn't see what was supposed to *make* it worth it, not as a way of life. All they told me was that everything was going to look different. Nobody promised me a new car, or a steady job, or that I'd get my family back. In fact they said that didn't matter. None of it. Nobody promised me I wouldn't feel afraid any more ever either. And I thank God that nobody promised me any of that psychiatrist crap about getting myself back for myself, which I didn't want anyway. In fact that's exactly what I used the booze and pills to get away from. They just told me that things were going to be different. And it came up that very first day.

The same guy that told me about King Kong told me something else. He told me I was going to have to learn how to believe in something bigger than I was, more than I was. That's just how he put it too, "you'll have to learn how to." But of course I didn't get it. I figured he was a Christer or something, a candy-ass, and I got nasty. Not too nasty, understand; you know how sick you feel, but quiet scared nasty. "Tell me," I said, "how do you pray to a God you don't believe in?" I'll never forget the way he handled that. "Son," he said, "I think if I were you I'd just pray anyway." And then he said something else. "Look," he said, "nobody in the Program you'll be in asks you to *believe* anything that way. All we ask is that you act as though you wanted to, as though getting well could have something in it for you. You don't even have to act as though you *did* believe it. Just act as though you wanted to." And then he said, "You do that, and I'll guarantee you something. I absolutely guarantee you that if you stay clean *our* way, everything in your life will get better."

It was crap to me then, of course, even what I understood. He didn't convince me of a thing. But you know what I couldn't get away from? I couldn't get away from how sick I knew I was and from knowing he'd been there too and from seeing he wasn't there any more. I mean the way he talked about his own life I knew he'd been there. And he'd been clean for ten years. He told me that right off and I could see it. So I didn't believe what he told me, but I did believe that he believed it, and that's what I hung on to. I wanted what he had. I wanted to be me the way he was him. That's why I did what he told me to do. And it was only through that, through doing what he told me to do, that I found out what he meant.

All those things they told me to do, none of which had anything to do with anything, like writing out a moral inventory of myself—can you imagine me doing that?—and asking for help in the morning, from a Power Greater than Myself they called it, and even if I didn't believe in it—talk about craziness— and attending meetings, and working with new people, and trying to straighten out my past, not one bit of which ever made any sense to me, not one bit of which ever felt natural to do, except that all those things, doing those things I mean, somehow they gave me a way of living life that gave me a life to have. In the Program we fight a mystery with a mystery, they told me. And by God things got better. Not perfect, understand, but they got better, and in a totally different way from the way I thought they would. I was becoming somebody new. I never did get my family back, as you know. I still feel afraid a lot. But it's OK in a way it never was. What the guy couldn't tell me that first day, see, was that the me that getting clean was going to be worth it to wasn't here yet. Understand, all the rest of me is still here too. I'm not *brand* new. I'm going to be an addict till the day I die, right along with all the things that make me one. Nothing changes that. But I've got a me I never had before. I'm not what I was.

. . . Offering what the activity of writing involves in the name of what it is about and for can enable a teacher of writing to invite students to participate in an activity with meaning—whatever forms of discourse we may ask our students to experiment with, whatever conventions we may expect them to master. Very simply, we have a better chance of getting better sentences from our students when they have some understanding of what composing a sentence can be a matter of, and of what it can mean for someone to compose them, than when they don't. It's in this sense that Richard Lanham suggests writing can be seen as an "act of socialization" plus; and, he says,

> it is by repeated acts of such socialization that we become sociable beings, that we grow up. Thus, the act of writing models the presentation of self in society, constitutes a rehearsal for social reality. It is not simply a question of a pre-existent self making its message known to a pre-existent society. It is not, initially, a question of message at all. Writing is a way to clarify, strengthen, and energize the self, to render individuality rich, full, and social. This does not mean writing that flows, as Terry Southern immortally put it, "right out of the old guts onto the goddam paper." Just the opposite. Only by taking the position of the reader toward one's own prose, putting a reader's pressure on it, can the self be made to grow. Writing should enhance and expand the self, allow it to try out new possibilities, tentative selves.
>
> The moral ingredient in writing, then, works first not on the morality of the message but on the nature of the sender, on the complexity of the self. "Why bother?" To invigorate and enrich your selfhood, to increase, in the most literal sense, your self-consciousness. Writing, properly pursued, does not make you better. It makes you more alive. This is why our growing illiteracy ought to distress us. It tells us something, something alarming, about the impoverishment of our selves. We say that we fear written communication will break down. Unlikely. And if it does we can always, as we do anyway, pick up the phone. Something more fundamental is at stake, the selfhood and sociability of the communicators. We are back to the basic peculiarity of *writing*—it is *premeditated* utterance, and in that premeditation lives its first if not its only value. "Why bother?" "To find out who I really am." It is not only what we think that we discover in writing, but what we are and can be. (105-06)

And such a frame for the teaching of writing is as necessary for teachers or at least for me as a teacher, as it is for students. I thought for a long time that I was unique in being as good a teacher as I know I am and in being as unsuccessful in teaching writing as I know myself to be. Few of my students learn what I think they ought to have learned; few of them come as far as I begin every course supposing they can and will and end every course knowing that they have not. And it's only in a limited sense that the particular achievements of particular people help very much, for there are many, many more particular people who, for a variety of reasons, not all of them bad by any means, simply turn off to writing or, worse, choose to have no choice with it, find the price of freedom, involving as it always does the sacrifice of one's immediate sense of one's own well-being, just too damned high to pay.

But I do not believe that I am as unique as I once thought I was in concluding that no teacher of writing teaches writing very well. I do not believe that I am alone in having worked out that for this reason—my primary obligation as a teacher is to preserve myself from what I would call the besetting sin of the profession: unacknowledged self-contempt, that form of existential despair the precise quality of which, as Kierkegaard noted, is that it ceases after a time to be experienced as despair. The junkie's nightmare and the junkie's dream. I no longer believe that I am alone as a teacher in knowing that I've got the temptations of my own kind of addiction to deal with. And it's a lot more than fragments, in the form of the newest logarithmic, clinically validated, heuristical, ultimate-problem-solving-quick-fix of a system, that I want to shore against that kind of ruin, I can tell you. A deliberate belief is what Conrad's Marlow calls it, when techniques and even principles won't do. A deliberate belief. . . .

. . . Because finally, see, handicapping as something you can believe in, as a way for yourself, is all you've got to put against all of this out here, to stay in the game. And I mean all of it too, the color, the noise, the money going every which way, the hustlers, the touts, the creeps and the losers, the odds changing on the tote board every fifteen seconds, the whole goddam mess out here. You've got to have a place for yourself see, some place to come from, somewhere to stand in the middle of all this action. You've got to have something to hang on to.

But you know, I'll tell you something. When you got that, everything changes out here. Everything. You *see* everything out here different. It's not a place where just anything can happen anymore; it's a place where things are possible. Every race is new then, the first and last time in the history of the world. It'll never be again, not in the history of the world. You watch the bets go up on the board, odds up, odds down, everything changing every fifteen seconds. By God, it's *like* the history of the world, the dinosaurs out there eighty to one, here's the cave man, ten to one at first, then he's out of the cave at eight to five, then he's even money, and then it's the race, bottom-line time, and in two minutes it's all over. But you got a place in that, a chance to be with the final flick of the board when it's all over: win, place, and show, and you count your money. It can be wonderful that way, wonderful, because win or lose, when you do it right—well, it's all a question of how you feel on the way home I guess, and that's what keeps me coming out here. I don't mean to say I don't get bad nights and feel lousy. I do. I act like a loser sometimes too and I feel even lousier about that. But when I pay the right kind of attention, and figure things out the best I can, and don't sucker myself into races I shouldn't be in or into wrong bets, too much or too little, when I keep my goddamed ego out of the way—well, it's like nothing else in the world. I'm alive on the way home then—not a big gambler or the guy who beat the system, because I don't even have to win to feel what I can feel sometimes. I mean I'm me alive. I'm just me but I'm somebody. I can see what kind of night it is. I'm glad to be going home. And even if I don't feel like it right then, I know I'll want to come back. . . .

. . . What I do for my students, I'm saying, I do for myself, and vice versa. Taking arms against a sea of troubles, as you will recall from the metaphor in context, is more than a complicated way of describing a simple conflict. Can it be that there are troubles that are ended, rather than defeated or resolved, by the action of certain kinds of opposition only? To judge from how I can feel sometimes on the way home at night, I just guess I'd say that there can be. At any rate, in dealing as a teacher of writing with writing not as a way to be a winner, or even as a way to win, but as an alternative to losing, I obligate myself to make alive for my students what can keep me alive as me, and alive in the face of the fact that my students may never *become* writers, not any more than every addict gets clean, or than the horse has to win.

Works Cited

Coles, Robert. *Walker Percy: An American Search*. Boston: Little, Brown, 1978.
Gardner, John. *On Moral Fiction*. New York: Basic Books; Harper and Row, 1981.
Lanham, Richard A. *Revising Prose*. New York: Charles Scribner, 1979.
Mitchell, Richard. *Less Than Words Can Say*. Boston: Little, Brown, 1979.
Weil, Simone. "Reflections on the Right Use of School Studies with a View to the Love of God." In *The Simone Weil Reader*. Ed. George A. Panichas. New York: McKay, 1977.

Appendix

The English Composition Board at the University of Michigan

Barbra S. Morris

In the early 1970s President Robben Fleming delivered a state of the university address in which he expressed deep concern about increasing numbers of reports that students were having difficulty reading and writing well enough to master the content of their courses. Soon thereafter, a graduation requirements commission was convened to investigate whether revision of the existing undergraduate curriculum was needed to address new educational needs of students. The commission conducted hearings throughout 1973-74 and concluded its year-long review with recommendations for reforms in the curriculum. In its final report, the commission recommended that a committee be established to investigate student literacy and devise appropriate ways to extend and integrate the teaching of writing throughout the College of Literature, Science, and the Arts (LSA), the largest undergraduate college (with an enrollment of 15,000) in the university. To that end, six faculty members from different disciplines in LSA were named in 1976 to the English Composition Board (ECB).

The ECB began work by consulting LSA faculty members to determine the types of writing they expected from students in their courses. While faculty members agreed that young adults in higher education were by no means illiterate, they indicated that students' reading and writing habits were not adequate for the demands of college-level study, particularly for modes of inquiry and exposition that involve argumentative, persuasive, or speculative writing. Describing their students as "unpracticed writers," faculty recognized that the curriculum had become increasingly sophisticated and that students needed additional instruction in the modes of literacy it demanded.

Before the ECB was established, most undergraduates were obliged to take the one-term composition course offered by the English department; about one fifth were exempted (automatic exemptions were granted to students who had completed introductory composition elsewhere, earned Advanced Placement credit in high school, or achieved an SAT verbal score of 700 or above). LSA faculty suggested that even if introductory composition courses were made more effective, instruction of two other kinds still would be necessary. Many students arriving at the university needed more practice in writing than any single semester

265

course could provide; these students would benefit from special attention to their writing. In addition, faculty saw in all students a need for instruction in appropriate styles of argumentation and exposition that characterize different disciplines. In light of discussions with many faculty members, the ECB formulated a plan that would improve instruction in writing by recognizing the various levels of writing ability among entering students and by spreading the responsibility for instruction in writing throughout the college.

By January 1978, the ECB had completed the design of a collegiate writing program and presented its plan to the faculty, who overwhelmingly endorsed it at a well-attended meeting. The program contains five parts: assessment, tutorial, introductory composition, writing workshop, and junior-senior writing courses.

According to the new plan, entering students—regardless of their past course credits or their scores on other tests—are required to compose an impromptu essay on an assigned topic before enrolling in classes. In 1978 ECB faculty evaluated approximately 3,900 essays written by LSA undergraduates; in subsequent years that number has increased (4,701 students were tested in 1981) as other colleges in the university have chosen to participate in the assessment. The writing samples determine students' placement into one of three entry levels of the writing program: tutorial, introductory composition, or exemption from introductory composition. Whatever their placement, students may also be required to visit the ECB's writing workshop for further instruction; and whatever their skill, students are encouraged to visit the writing workshop as often as they like for special help with particular writing tasks.

With three levels of placement possible at entrance to the college, students receive from the outset the type of instruction most appropriate to their needs. About twelve percent of entering students are exempted; nearly ten percent need tutorial instruction; the others enroll in one of several introductory composition courses, all of which have been revised to place greater emphasis on the variety of writing skills demanded by college-level work. In the tutorials, taught by the ECB in seven-week units, students profit from individual attention to their writing. At the end of each unit, students write another impromptu essay, on an assigned topic, that is evaluated by at least two ECB instructors (who are not their teachers). Once again, the writing samples determine whether they must continue into a second seven-week tutorial, go on to introductory composition in the next semester, or be exempted from introductory composition. Introductory composition remains the responsibility of the English department, though now supported by the ECB through training of teachers and development of instructional materials.

Once undergraduates complete lower-division writing requirements, they must all fulfill the college's upper-level writing requirement: a writing course in the junior or senior year, preferably in the student's major field of study. Assisted by the ECB, most departments have designed junior-senior-level writing courses to offer students extensive practice in the forms of inquiry and expression characteristic of the discipline. The kinds of writing vary considerably in upper-level writing courses; mathematics, art history, chemistry, and political science, for example, have their own specialized vocabularies, symbol systems, and preferred rhetorical modes. In spite of the substantial differences in the content of these courses, however, instructors of all junior-senior writing courses benefit from ECB faculty seminars on topics relevant to the teaching of composition. These weekly seminars concentrate on such issues as the design of writing assignments, stages in the composing process, and the revision and rewriting of texts.

Writing required in upper-level courses is divided typically between formal attention to finished essays and less formal production of journal entries, which give students practice in using writing to promote their own thinking and learning. The value of such practice is emphasized by Jack W. Meiland, director of the university's honors program, who observed in his recent book *College Thinking* that students can discover nothing "more practical than learning to think, read, and write" (5).

In the 1981-82 academic year, more than 150 junior-senior writing courses were available in twenty-nine different disciplines, each one supervised by tenured faculty in the departments offering them. Robbins Burling, an anthropology professor whose commitment to teaching writing long predated the formation of the ECB, maintains that writing is best thought of as a craft that continues to evolve throughout a writer's lifetime. In his view, the new writing requirements at Michigan have already had positive effects on students' beliefs about writing. Students, he observes,

> have begun to think seriously, and in productive ways, about the craft of writing. I would like to feel that they can continue to work at their writing in the years to come, that they will have learned that there is lots of work but no mystery to good writing. No one learns to write in a single term. If we can help students begin to understand how they can work toward learning to write, that is probably enough.

The writing program at Michigan has affected the college in at least two important ways. First, the writing requirements help transmit to students the beliefs of faculty and of employers that literacy is a significant and evolving skill. Second, writing instruction in all disciplines helps students master the special varieties of reading and writing actually employed in the fields that engage their interests.

The writing program at Michigan has captured the imaginations of teachers both in the college and elsewhere, and it demonstrates a powerful idea: that full faculty commitment to the teaching of writing can persuade students to write as well as they can in all their courses. It is through such diverse practice that the craft of writing is understood and ultimately mastered.

Works Cited

Burling, Robbins. "An Upper-Class Writing Course." Unpublished English Composition
   Board paper, Dec. 1978.
Meiland, Jack W. *College Thinking: How to Get the Best out of College*. New York:
   New American Library, 1981.

Biographies of the Authors

Richard W. Bailey is professor of English and director of research for the English Composition Board at the University of Michigan. Among his teaching and research interests are composition and the social and regional dialects of American English; he is coeditor of *English as a World Language*.

A. L. Becker is professor of linguistics and of anthropology at the University of Michigan. With Kenneth L. Pike and Richard Young, he is the author of *Rhetoric: Discovery and Change*. In addition to his continuing interests in English and in linguistic theory, he has done extensive field research in Indonesia and has written about the music and drama of the Javanese people.

Florence B. Brawer, research educationist at UCLA, is concerned with faculty and student development and with personality assessment. She is the author of *New Perspectives on Personality Development in College Students*, and coauthor of *Confronting Identity, The Two-Year College Instructor Today*, and *The American Community College: An Interpretative Analysis*.

Janet K. Carsetti is the founder and director of Project READ, a national literacy program for young people in trouble with the law. Her teaching of literacy involves motivational activities that derive from popular music and high-interest paperback books.

Arthur M. Cohen is professor of higher education at UCLA and director of the ERIC Clearinghouse for Junior Colleges. His books include *Dateline '79, Objectives for College Courses*, and as coauthor *Confronting Identity, The Two-Year College Instructor Today*, and *The American Community College: An Interpretative Analysis*.

William E. Coles, Jr., is professor of English and former director of composition at the University of Pittsburgh. Author of *Composing, Composing II*, and *The Plural I*, he has devoted his professional energies to the training of composition teachers and the design of programs for the teaching of writing.

Frank J. D'Angelo is professor of English at Arizona State University and a former chair of the Conference on College Composition and Communication. His primary areas of interest are rhetoric and composition, and he is the author of *A Conceptual Theory of Rhetoric* and *Process and Thought in Composition*.

269

Edwin J. Delattre has been president of St. John's College, Annapolis, Maryland, and Santa Fe, New Mexico, since 1980. His graduate study was devoted to ethics, epistemology, and American philosophy. As director of the National Humanities Faculty, he worked as a faculty colleague with some 180 school districts and independent schools.

Daniel Fader is professor of English and former chair of the English Composition Board at the University of Michigan. Developmental literacy and the rhetoric of revision are his primary areas of teaching and research. He is the author of *Hooked on Books* and *The Naked Children*.

Robben W. Fleming recently retired from the presidency of the Corporation for Public Broadcasting. He was president of the University of Michigan from 1968 to 1979 and chancellor of the University of Wisconsin at Madison from 1964 to 1967. While serving as an administrator, he was also a professor of law at the University of Illinois, the University of Wisconsin, and the University of Michigan.

Robin Melanie Fosheim received her B.A. in philosophy from the University of Michigan and has been employed as a research assistant with the English Composition Board since 1979.

Dixie Goswami is serving as a consultant to the American Institutes for Research and is teaching in the Writing Program at the Bread Loaf School of English. The winner of a Mina Shaughnessy Fellowship, she is writing a book on research in composition. With Lee Odell, she has completed a three-year study—funded by the National Institute for Education—of writing in nonacademic settings.

Barbra S. Morris is associate chair of the English Composition Board. Her graduate work centered on the relationship between the media and language learning in schools. In 1982, she produced an animated film about composition titled *Write Write*.

Lee Odell is professor of language, literature, and communications at Rensselaer Polytechnic Institute. His primary areas of interest are evaluation, writing across the curriculum, and writing in nonacademic settings. He is a trustee of the NCTE Research Foundation and is coeditor of *Evaluating Writing* and *Research on Composing*.

Sarah Goddard Power, a regent of the University of Michigan since 1974, served in 1980-81 as deputy assistant secretary for human rights and social affairs in the U.S. Department of State and was twice delegate to general conferences of UNESCO. She has been active in organizations aimed at improving the status of women and represented the U.S. at the World Conference for the UN Decade for Women.

Doris Quick is chair of the English department at Burnt Hills (New York) Senior High School and is coordinator of inservice programs for the Capital District Writing Project. She is a vice-president of the New York State English Council and is a member of the National Advisory Panel, which advises the New York State Education department on its statewide program for assessing students' competence as writers.

Janice C. Redish is director of the Document Design Center at the American Institutes for Research in Washington, D.C. Her research is devoted to explaining why legal and bureaucratic documents are difficult for lay people to read and use, and she has worked with writers in many government agencies to help them improve their writing skills. She is coauthor of the forthcoming textbook, *Writing in the Professions*.

Jay L. Robinson is professor of English, former chair of the department of English Language and Literature, and acting chair of the English Composition Board at the University of Michigan. Among his teaching and research interests are variation in English, discourse, and composition. He is coeditor of *Varieties of Present-Day English* and coauthor of a text series in language for junior high school students.

Gavriel Salomon is professor of educational psychology and communication at Hebrew University, Jerusalem. His research has been devoted to the study of cognitive effects of the symbolic forms inherent in visual media. He is the author of *Interaction of Media, Cognition and Learning,* and *Communication and Education: An Interactional Approach.*

Paul A. Strassmann is vice president of strategic planning for the Information Products Group, Xerox Corporation. Before assuming that position, he was director of administration and information systems for the corporation and general manager of its Information Services Division. In that capacity he managed data center operations, telecommunications networks, administrative services, management consulting services, and software development.

Deborah Tannen is an assistant professor of linguistics at Georgetown University, where she teaches in the sociolinguistics program and conducts research on textual analysis and cross-cultural communication. She is editor of *Spoken and Written Language: Beyond Orality and Literacy.*

Ralph W. Tyler is director emeritus of the Center for Advanced Study in the Behavioral Sciences. His teaching and research have focused on curriculum development and educational evaluation. He was university examiner in the University of Chicago and responsible for the development of comprehensive examinations. Among his publications is *Appraising and Recording Student Progress*.

Paul B. Weisz is manager of the Central Research Division of the Mobil Research and Development Corporation. His career has taken him from physics and electronics to chemical and energy technology as a scientist, inventor, writer, and manager.

James Boyd White is professor in the Law School, the College, and the Committee on the Ancient Mediterranean World at the University of Chicago. He has a special interest in the nature of legal thought and expression and is the author of *The Legal Imagination* and coauthor of *Constitutional Criminal Procedure*.